Professor Neil Forsberg, an aging and out-of-shape professor- a man inclined to enjoy reading The Economist and the New Yorker on his couch- is invited by friends to climb Mt. Kilimanjaro in Tanzania. Without a great deal of physical nor mental preparation he undertakes the effort but immediately confronts a far more demanding effort than he had anticipated. He quickly learns that Kilimanjaro is not a trivial hike but is one of the "Seven Summits" - the Seven highest peaks on the Seven Continents. The book details Professor Forsberg's first encounter with Africa and the challenges he faces in attempting his climb. He develops unique mental strategies - managing to escape the confines of his own "self" and to metaphorically join the more agile and accommodating ravens populating the Kilimanjaro flank. While elevated from his corporeal existence, revelations come to him that Forsberg could not have conceived of prior. Indeed, the loss of the familiar comforting elements of Forsberg's life, his couches, cause him to reach out and explore other spiritual supports – dimensions having more relevance to life than what contemporary Western existence provides. Forsberg distills the experience meaningfully into a cogent and useful philosophy – a philosophy that transcends the strictures of the more organized religions that bind so many.

Included also are vivid descriptions of Kilimanjaro's magic- and Kilimanjaro's stars.

Aside from this spiritual journey, Professor Forsberg makes observations on the exotic bird and plant life that support him on the climb and, equally important, the descent. He describes the environmental impact of climate change on the Kilimanjaro ecosystem - the imminent loss of its glaciers, flora and fauna.

This book will inspire anyone with quests for outdoor adventure, to climb mountains and to search for enlightenment that only nature and deeper thought can provide.

Readers' Reviews

"It hooked my sister Donna like a steelhead"- GM- Bend, Oregon

"What an amazing man you are. Wow. Finished the book. I've read non-stop all day. You've written about it in such a descriptive, honest and compelling way that I could almost feel your pain, and your exuberance. Kudos on completing that arduous hike and for re-telling. I feel
I've learned a lot about you in the reading. RESPECT." TB- Philomath, Oregon

"Wow, your writing is impressive and your saga is a compelling one – it would be a page turner under any circumstances but knowing you personally makes it all the more riveting!" GFB- Corvallis, Oregon

"I finished the book... I loved it; in fact, I couldn't put it down. It had all elements ... riveting, soaring, down-to-earth, funny, touching, poetic, spiritual. What an adventure! I am sure you are changed forever. Thanks so much for telling me about it. I am lending it to some friends next. Incidentally I think your conclusion as to the meaning of life is "brilliant"... really. Also some elements brought personal experiences to mind. My son John had a close call on Mt. Hood two years ago and he lost two dear friends who climbed Aconcagua 8 years ago. All of this made your book extra meaningful....thanks again!" HC- Corvallis, Oregon.

"Neil! You've been lying around all day! Get off the couch, go outside and do something!" Azizah, Corvallis, OR

Climbing Kilimanjaro

Avoiding the Metaphorical Couch

A Novel by: Neil Elliott Forsberg

Dedication

This narrative is dedicated to my family who were often *with* me in my thoughts during my climb and who would have been proud to either have climbed it themselves or in knowing I undertook the challenge. On your behalf I hope that I have distilled the effort into something useful.

Table of Contents

Kilimanjaro, (Corey, 2016)

I hiked up a mountain in a marvelous place
That most people may not think of
But to the people who personally peaked it,
Part of them will stay put forever

And I left with such relief

I left wanting air conditioning and free feet
Wanting a warm shower and fresh food
Too bad I spent a day on an airplane
But who's to blame but myself

And I walked around in pain

I walked around trying my best not to complain
But it's hard when you've spent days up there
In the thin air and the messy hair
Snacks and memories being shared

And I was asked how I fared

I was asked if I was over-prepared
Asked if I would go back and repeat
I told them the job was complete
I already made it to the peak and....

Well. I would go back in a heart beat

I would go back and walk through the scree
I would go right back to the start
And walk through snow and through dark
Kili is the hardest thing I've done thus far

But I would go back if, for nothing else, the stars

Prologue

As a young man, I'd known of "Kilimanjaro". I knew it rested somewhere upon the enigmatic African continent but I had understood few of its particulars, its physical structure and exact location, the sounds of its rivers, its smells, its birds, its climate and its mythology. Some of what I had understood of Kilimanjaro derived from Hemmingway's fictional "Snows of Kilimanjaro", a novel I had read forty years prior. My copy had endured quietly, tucked away amongst my yellowing paperback collection on my intermittently-dusted shelves. With my periodic rediscovery of its brittle pages I would be briefly reminded of the mountain but did little to investigate it further. Commensurate with my meager understanding of the mountain I would have been hard-pressed to inform others regarding much of any detail of it: what country it lay in, what its notable features were or any of its lore. Had I been asked I would have incorrectly informed others Kilimanjaro dwelled within "Kenya". And yes the view of Kilimanjaro is said to be better from Kenya, from the North, even though no physical aspect of the mountain resides there. Kilimanjaro resides wholly within Tanzania, a country formerly part of the more exotically-named Tanganyika. Despite my limited understanding of Kilimanjaro its name had always resonated in me as an intriguing and worthwhile destination.

I possess a substantial desire to travel and experience new realities before becoming too infirmed, too incapable of physical adventure. Important to me is the conviction, at very least, I needed to plant my feet meaningfully on all seven continents. Only two continents remained to be trodden upon in early-2017; Australia and Africa. Although I had planted my feet upon on the blackened tarmac of the Cairo airport during a late-night transit from Istanbul to Bangkok years ago, I prohibited myself from including that brief stopover in Africa among my tally of travel-related feats.

Accordingly, when an unexpected entreaty from Richard Thacker roused me from a damp Oregon reverie in early-2017 asking whether I might be inclined to join him and a clutch of other optimists on a climb of the storied peak, I promptly agreed: this without seriously evaluating what the climb might entail. The climb seemed to fit with what I knew I must undertake: to be adventurous, to experience romantic destinations, to see all I could see and to continually challenge myself. With little thought I made the commitment to join Richard and his colleagues the same day. This tale is the story of that attempt; an effort made in late-October, 2017.

Chapter One
The Preparation

Richard Thacker and I had both worked as faculty in the College of Agriculture and Fisheries at Sultan Qaboos University in the Sultanate of Oman from 1998-2000 and, at the time, had suffered from the capriciousness of a power struggle we both had unwittingly fallen into. Our relationship, lubricated with Bombay Sapphire, was thereby forged in that sweltering and unpredictable desert kingdom. Emerging somewhat victorious we had maintained infrequent contact over the ensuing two decades.

The planned ascent of Kilimanjaro was organized by an adventure tour company located in the UK: "Kandoo Adventures". But I never troubled myself with seriously investigating "Kandoo" on-line. I was instead preoccupied with the vestiges of a consulting arrangement, the golden handcuffs I was informed, arising from the sale of my agricultural R+D company in late-2012. Had I made effort to investigate Kandoo's literature I might have become alarmed upon discovering Kandoo's readily-apparent tagline: "The High Altitude Specialists". Other hikes Kandoo coordinated included Everest Base Camp in Nepal (EBC: 5,365 meters AMSL) and Aconcagua in Argentina (6,964 meters AMSL). For the non-mountain climbing of my readers "AMSL" is an abbreviation for "above mean sea level". Kilimanjaro's summit lay between these two hikes at 5,900 meters AMSL.

The uppermost of my prior peregrinations had been logged within the "Upper Mustang" in northern Nepal in early-2017. There I had hiked with my daughter and different troupe of friends. The "Upper Mustang" had not been a climb however it required traverse of several moderately-high passes to reach the penultimate destination of Lo Manthang with the highest traverse near 4,268 meters AMSL. Kilimanjaro's glistening Uhuru peak rested yet 1.5 km higher. Had I known of Kilimanjaro's elevation prior I might have appropriately developed some apprehension. I also might have worried had I read any of the Kilimanjaro trekkers' narratives; narratives abundantly and menacingly accessible on-line. I understand it is a cliché to assert this but sometimes "ignorance confers bliss". Knowing little of the climb beforehand allowed me to glibly inform friends and family of my intent, to bask in their surprise and adulation and at the same time to project confidence in my untested abilities. After all, had I not just trekked in Nepal? Had I not hiked Machu Picchu (2,439 meters AMSL)? Had I not recently and successfully managed to hike Torres del Paine (2,900 meters AMSL) in Patagonia; albeit with periodic ingestion of expired opioids prescribed for a root canal?

Preparing for a hike involves the physical preparation of one's body *and* the acquisition and assembly of the appropriate clothing and equipment. The former requires several months of effort (if done correctly) and the latter requires a concise list: a list of everything imaginable one might need. And foremost on the list are the hiking boots. So important are the boots that Kandoo recommended we wear them on our flights. Whereas all other equipment could be re-purchased in Tanzania hiking boots could not be purchased and then broken-in if they were found missing in baggage claim upon arrival.

To undertake each of these hikes, I had relied upon the same hiking boots; a sturdy pair of leather Vasques my daughter Amelia had given me for Christmas a few year's prior: a sweet and considerate gift. I don't think I am unique in asserting multiple hikes in a pair of boots creates a relationship with them; something akin to an affair. I found myself on more than one occasion sitting with them, examining them and carefully discerning their wear, the chips of Vibram torn from their soles, the soiled creases in the leather where the strain has been the greatest, the accumulation of grime and the changing contour of the sole; from flat to concave. I understood I could draw satisfaction from knowing these boots had been indispensable elements of robust adventures. They had carried me across foam-shrouded rivers, up and down mountains, across snow and ice and I had stood in them when I found and saw amazing things when I challenged myself the most. My children were with me when I experienced much of this. Yes, the boots had become part of my family of equipment. Certainly I came to care for and depend upon my other equipment: my light-weight tent, my orange inflatable mat, my backpack and my felt-covered pillow that considerately provided a comfortable indent for my head. But I never cultivated the depth of relationship with these items I cultivated with my boots.

In the months prior to departure, I received nearly two dozen e-mails from Rachael Bode the UK-based Kandoo representative who coordinated all aspects of the anticipated effort. Her recommendations included everything we needed to pack, limits on the weight of our kit, hotel reservations, information on travel and evacuation insurance, expected Kilimanjaro weather and anything else she believed was essential to adequately prepare for the climb. Such was the volume of her emails I overlooked an important e-mail; one detailing a need to bring prescription medication for altitude sickness.

Of the equipment we were expected to bring with us a few items caught my attention. For example, "pee bottles" were suggested so one would not need to extricate one's self from one's cozy sleeping bag and warm tent during the night to visit either the "toilet tent" or Kilimanjaro's famed "long drop toilets". "Brilliant!" I thought. Earlier in the year I had tired of peeing outside of my tent in the middle of the night in remote Nepal and subsequently repurposed one of one my three Neoprene water bottles for this purpose. I didn't disclose this "innovation" to anyone on our Nepalese trek lest they consider me a little peculiar. However, discovering a "pee bottle recommendation" among the official Kandoo equipment list mitigated those feelings. Indeed, I had been innovative!

The list also included recommendations for a broad spectrum of clothing; clothing to protect us in temperatures ranging from warm and humid (at the base) to arctic (at the summit). Temperatures were expected to range from 27-29 °C at the rainforest base to -10 °C at the summit. Heavy winds at the summit could reduce effective temperatures to well below -18 °C.

I began assembling the recommended kit two weeks prior to departure and to the consternation of my wife to obsessively pile it up in categories in our living room. Seeing it accumulate gave me pleasure but challenged her anxieties for cleanliness. With my check-list, I could then know what was left to find or buy. "Amazon" made the necessity of buying equipment much easier than it otherwise could have been. Included in my Amazon purchases were replacement covers for my camera lenses (a regular need), silk sock liners, red "Danish" woolen hiking socks, long-legged hiking underwear (to prevent "chafing" between my thighs; a common problem), a light-weight wide-angle lens with requisite polarizing filter, an east-African bird identification book and memory sticks.

I harbored reservations about bringing a heavy SLR camera up the mountain and was especially apprehensive of my 500 mm telephoto lens. It's only utility might relate to photos of Kilimanjaro's birds. All of my gear needed to fit within a 15 kg weight limit and that lens alone weighed 2 kg. Ultimately I left the telephoto behind bringing instead a versatile 55-300 mm telephoto lens (albeit with a less accommodating F-stop) and a light-weight 10-20 mm wide angle. The agreement between Kandoo and its customers was trekkers would individually hike with a "day pack" (for which there was no weight limit) and porters would cart up to 15 kg of whatever else was not contained within the day pack.

The use of porters to climb Kilimanjaro might appear to constitute "cheating"; like having someone else take an exam for you. Having been raised by depression-era parents whose own family farms had succeeded without assistance of any "helpers" I believed "If one intends to climb a mountain shouldn't one be fully capable of carrying all one needs to accomplish this task one's self?" But then none of my parents' families had done much mountain climbing. Further, there weren't mountains to climb in Saskatchewan, Canada!

Once on the mountain it did not take long to understand I could not have attempted the climb without support of porters. In fact, no one undertook Kilimanjaro without porters and guides. Certainly, others *must* have climbed this mountain unaided. But, from what I saw no one was attempting to do so on the days I was on the mountain. Further, the Tanzanian Government has recently forbidden climbs independent of local guides and porters; an economic issue and a safety issue. Similarly, in Nepal we had also used local porters.

Like an early Christmas the sundry items ordered from Amazon began to accumulate at the lower gate of my driveway a week prior to departure. What I forgot to purchase on Amazon I purchased at a local outdoor adventures store; a store where one typically pays a premium: where an elastic band of fabric used as a "buff", a piece of fabric worth no more than 25-cents, sells for $27.99. That specific expense was somehow compensated for by the design; a design I was later told made me appear as a "grizzled old hippie" and a "Harley Davidson owner". On Kilimanjaro, I learned to take comments to those effect as compliments.

A few months prior to departure, I began looking into flights from Portland, Oregon to Tanzania. The capital of Tanzania is Dar es Salaam and I therefore expected my flight of discovery would necessarily pass through the capital. In August, 1998, the American Embassy in Dar es Salaam had been bombed by Al-Qaeda at the direction of Osama bin Laden and I therefore harbored vague concern about spending any time there. However, I located one flight, originating in San Francisco, on Turkish Airlines "direct to Istanbul" then followed with a direct connection to Moshi! This obviated the need to fly through Dar es Salaam completely. Total time *en* route would be only 24 hours. "Perfect" I thought.

The discovery Kilimanjaro was accessible from Moshi, a city in Tanzania, itself, was a revelation. So was the discovery of how far south Tanzania *was* in Africa; well below the equator: below Ethiopia, Kenya and Somalia. Added to this was the discovery my Wells Fargo Visa card was in fact an airline card! I had never known this and I was pleased to discover nearly one million miles of unused airline credit languishing on the account- the result of several years of travel for business!

Flush with airline miles, I squandered a significant number them on a one-way Business Class ticket from Portland, Oregon to San Francisco and which then followed the above-described itinerary. It felt like a windfall! "A 'free' business-class ticket!" Via e-mail, I provided my arrival time (1 AM) to Rachael at Kandoo Adventures with the expectation someone would meet my flight and transport me to the benignly-named "Bristol Cottages" in downtown Moshi. I expected to arrive at my Moshi hotel by 2AM. It seemed more than incongruous I could coordinate travel to so remote a destination and feel confident the plans would come to fruition.

The day prior to departure I began arranging and packing my two bags; my daypack for "valuables" (e.g., camera equipment and passports) and my black North Face duffle bag. Soon it became abundantly clear my need to pack clothing for both warm and arctic weather and all types of weather between, both wet and dry, translated into my having purchased far too much gear. Shirts, pants and socks were then winnowed-down to the minimum. I resolved to wear underwear for two days before changing, socks for two days, to hike with a spare number of shirts and to limit myself to two pair of hiking pants. My outerwear however could not be pared-down. I owned a good set of rain wear; GoreTex jacket and pants. This set had cost me $700 but I had never tested its reliability. In addition, I included thermal long underwear, a fleece jacket, a red Patagonia down vest and a parka replete with faux wolverine fur the National Geographic organization had provided me when my son and I had visited Antarctica prior. I was fond of the National Geographic jacket because its lining was imprinted with the names of the crew members who had manned "The Endurance" during Ernest Shackleton's ill-fated but heroic attempt to reach Antarctica in 1914-16. In addition I included two pair of gloves (one set thermal and one set optimistically touted as "rain-proof"), hats, first aid kit, travelling pharmacy, empty water (and pee) bottles, journal, bird identification book, passports (Canadian and US), trail mix, fig bars, fruit-flavored electrolyte powders (a new innovation for this trip), polarizing sunglasses, two packages of pre-moistened baby wipes (heavy but necessary), inflatable mattress and pillow and an extra pair of light-weight shoes to wear in camp at night. Compressible items were compacted into 1-gallon plastic Ziploc bags then sealed to enable the most-dense packing possible. In the end, I was proud of my selection of support items, my organization and of the density of my packing. As was my habit my kit came together only a few hours prior to departure.

I did not experience a great deal of trepidation prior to departure. And not to beat a dead horse but had I read relevant literature concerning the climb prior to departure I *would* have experienced some. Instead other challenges were diverting my attentions from the upcoming effort. The departure date (October 18, 2017) simply came closer and closer and when the day arrived I loaded my gear into a car, hugged my forgiving wife goodbye, drove to my Vancouver, WA condo, parked my car and requested an Uber to the Portland International Airport. There, I tentatively checked my North Face bag in for the duration of the flight (PDX to Moshi). Foremost on my mind was the worry "What are the chances this critical bag will successfully transit with me through San Francisco and Istanbul airports all the way to Tanzania?" Dismissing these concerns I boarded a 3 PM United Airlines shuttle down to San Francisco and dozed-off intermittently en route.

Prior to departure I had harbored an unreasonable uncertainty of traveling to "Africa". But I know this apprehension was wholly ill-founded. A lifetime of being on the receiving end of "less than flattering" news concerning poverty, political dysfunction, intractable diseases ("guinea worm" and "Ebola"), genocide (Rwanda), apartheid (South Africa) and other disagreeable facts had inculcated into me a wariness concerning the entire continent. Left out of that equation however were the people; people with whom I had had very little direct experience. "What would the people be *like*?" I worried economic disparity and my European skin might engender hostility toward me. "Will I be safe?" These insecurities had thus far kept me from Africa; the continent of human origins; the continent whose physical and biological characteristics and climate had forged human evolution.

Kilimanjaro! It came out of one's mouth like a magical incantation - syllables rising and falling gently and reinforcing one another. "Kilimanjaro!" Mellifluous without question. One could imagine - with the proper flourish its recitation might vanquish one's foe or cause solid bars of gold to appear in front of one's self. One could conceivably name a child "Kilimanjaro!"; or a novel! Was there really such a place and could one discover one's self at the base of so intoxicating a challenge by simply purchasing an airline ticket - a ticket that cost nothing?

Chapter Two
En Route - Unexpected Complications

San Francisco airport can be a challenge to navigate especially when one is switching from a domestic flight to an international flight. Most international flights depart from the "international terminal", an exquisitely-designed terminal existing remotely from its dour domestic cousins. An unaccustomed flyer traverses the international terminal via labyrinthine passageways which ultimately deliver one into a second TSA screening area - a TSA screening area seeming to be deliberately understaffed. If one is running late as I have often been in the past waiting in line at this second TSA insult can be an agonizing wait - especially an insult knowing restaurants lying on the other side charge $10 (plus tax and tip) for a beer. Fifteen dollars for a pint of beer! Damn I used to pay 50 cents for a beer back in Winnipeg in the 1970's! And those were Canadian cents; worth only 3/4th of their American counterparts.

Today- crowds were light and I found once I had cleared TSA three hours separated me from my departure on Turkish Airlines. I relaxed in the spacious terminal and people-watched - a favorite pastime of mine in airports and forewent the beer. Quickly bored I texted friends and family about my circumstances.

The Turkish Airline flight departed from the furthermost collection of gates in the international terminal. These were located one level below the main international departure area - a region of the terminal I had not experienced prior. Once situated and with my anxiety beginning to lessen somewhat I began to savor the thought of an international adventure. Unlike passengers departing for the less-exotic destinations (Japanese, Chinese, Filipino) upstairs the passengers waiting for this flight derived from a spectrum of less frequently-encountered cultures - the Mediterranean, Middle-East,

Pakistan, India and Africa. It was as if this aspect of international departures was somehow intentionally hidden in this airport.

The Turks milled about - lesser-statured men dressed in pressed gray polyester pants and white shirts, fashionable yet inexpensive faux Pierre Cardin belts, ties, sports jackets and polished black loafers- often with tassels. Dark hair combed back with a Brylcream-like sheen. Turkish women - well-coiffed and trendy - some accommodating a nondescript hijab. Darker skin tones. In fact, in *this* waiting lounge I felt I had already departed the United States. Oregon and my family already seemed far away. I was in limbo - wedged betwixt my snug Oregon life and the truly unknown.

Because I was flying on Turkish Airlines I had little expectation for punctuality. Certainly there would be some, as my mother would say, "schmozzle" to hold the plane up for at least an hour. Yes I was unfairly expecting some type of snafu to accompany the departure process. Yet to my chagrin boarding operations proceeded efficiently. The pell mell of passengers lined-up cordially and boarded politely. I encountered no riots on the sky-bridge nor live chickens running to and fro amongst the aisles. Hubbly-bubblies were forbidden as were the more conventional styles of smoking. Uncooperative whirling dervishes were no where to be seen on the aircraft. I silently chastised myself for my silly, some might say tactless, stereotyping. I briefly understood myself then to be no more sophisticated than the incompetent moron who serves as our current "president".

I was assigned to Seat 1B, an aisle seat in the front row of the plane - not my first choice. All traffic to and from the washroom and galley thereby shuffled by my seat for the duration of the 13-hour flight. Being in the aisle with no seatback in front of me to block others' views of me I was left exposed. Certainly I had not paid for this flight but I was missing the privacy and anonymity I was used to when I previously had had the fortune to fly "Business". Indeed, this was a "Larry David way of thinking."

The non-stop flight to Istanbul was notable in two respects. First, the flight was substantially longer than I was anticipating. Thirteen hours no matter which class one is *in* requires patience and distraction - perhaps an ability to sleep when one is not used to sleeping. Second, the food was more than excellent. Three white-clad chefs, *these* were the dervishes in fact, swirled amongst us entertaining us with their sophisticated Mediterranean demeanor, their effusive smiles and excellent cuisine. Each chef was in his late-twenties through mid-thirties and each projected a captivating glint in his eyes. These handsome and energetic men served both an evening meal and later a substantial breakfast as we approached a darkened Istanbul.

The aircraft was a modern Airbus - a luxurious and an indisputably quiet machine. The ceiling lighting was subdued and alternated unhurriedly from soft pink to gentle blue; azure, perhaps. Service was impeccable and when I wasn't eating sleep came easily. I intermittently dozed and woke throughout the flight and from time to time rose to exercise my legs. In doing so I bantered with the female flight attendants who when they were not serving food nor drink gathered convivially in the galley. I felt welcomed as part of the crew - welcomed in a way one would not be welcomed on a North American airline. I used the same "lavatory" the pilots periodically used. Yes, at the front of the aircraft one becomes vicariously part of the mechanical and operational aspects of the flight and is not relegated to the corrals intended to house the unwashed classes aft. Family of sorts.

To pass the time I considered whether I could land this sophisticated aircraft should both pilots unexpectedly expire. In my mind I reviewed the steps I would need to take to aviate, navigate and communicate - how I might leap from my seat as the only spare pilot on board and offer my services. I convinced myself the plane would be in good hands - I'd somehow manage to land safely and I'd be welcomed on the Ataturk tarmac as a hero. My control of the ailerons, elevator and horizontal stabilizer would be impeccable. When I banked into Istanbul, I would soar as an eagle would across the city's wide expanse West of the Bosphorus. Passengers on the port side would marvel at the city lights below. I especially anticipated my interviews with Anderson Cooper! Sully Sullenberger would call me and we would go for dinner together and share our stories of devil-may-care bravery. I'd write a book and maybe it would be turned into a movie Clint Eastwood would offer to direct.

In such a manner I was able to pass another thirty minutes before being lulled again into restorative sleep.

En route I periodically consulted the flight map displayed on the wall in front of my seat and noted we followed a route over the North Atlantic and then down across the UK, Europe and into Turkey. Fascinating the shortest distance between SFO and IST deviated so much from the obvious latitudinal heading!

A notable aspect of the flight caught me off guard: it was, in fact, the expected snafu. Because of head winds (not a late departure) the flight arrived ninety minutes late thereby forcing me to miss my connecting flight to Moshi and to necessarily spend the night in Istanbul! Our late arrival only became clear to me a few minutes prior to landing because as we arrived into Istanbul I was unsure of the local time.

As we taxied toward the Ataturk Istanbul terminal I naively queried a familiar flight attendant if I might "make" my connection. Somewhat defensively she informed me I would need to "check with a gate agent" in the terminal.

We reached our arrival gate at 6:30 PM Istanbul time - the identical time my Turkish Airlines Moshi flight was set to depart. I yearned the connecting flight to Moshi might be similarly delayed. That flight is going to Moshi, Tanzania, how could it *not* be delayed I mused. Or maybe there could be additional flights to Moshi on

Turkish Airlines later this evening. I might still get there! Well - as wise people oft opine "if wishes were horses, beggars would ride".

Disgorged into Ataturk airport I was reminded airports function well when flights arrive and depart on time. Arrival and departure gates are typically nearby one another with opportunities for meals conveniently located nearby. However, whenever there is a glitch (as I had unfortunately been unwittingly thrust into) one immediately finds one's self deposited into a no-man's-land of uncertainty and angst - a land lacking signage or any other form of guidance that might efficiently guide one through a process that might deposit one's self into overnight accommodations with a new boarding pass and perhaps some optimism in hand. My memories of previous bad airport experiences raised their ugly heads. I immediately checked my watch and surrendered to the three hours of confusion, line-waiting, frustration and uncertainty I was more than likely condemned to endure. I let out a quiet sigh and my head tilted perceptibly sideways. Other passengers from my late-arriving flight scattered willy-nilly, unconcerned with my dismay. There seemed no pattern to the directions they followed. It was every man for himself.

I rambled alone and forlornly through a cavernous Ataturk Airport following other disenfranchised passengers some of whom seemed to know more than me about where they were going and when my survival strategy failed I queried a lone uniformed individual who languished improbably to the side of the terminal as an official of the Turkish Airlines. In good English I was directed toward "Gate 24" - refreshingly not so far away. There a short line had collected at a service desk. Reassuringly a large logo for "Turkish Airlines" hung over this service desk and this naturally communicated to me some confidence I might resolve my issues easily at this precise location. I was reasonably convinced I had made a good first effort. I was fifth in line. Not a great deal of time had passed since my arrival - perhaps 15 minutes.

The habit of forming a queue is not always well-practiced in other countries. While patiently waiting for my turn at the service desk others of uncertain nationality demonstrated no reticence to cut the line to ask questions or to beg for accelerated service. I successfully held my cool and worked to become the "observer" - the person with no stake in the outcome of the scene I had found myself to be cast in. The fly on the wall. This allowed me to come to enjoy the professionalism of the women behind the Turkish Airlines service desk because without betraying their insights they somehow understood who was cutting in line and would thereby steadfastly ignore eye and ear contact with the transgressors. I derived some pleasure from the situation - a Turkish version of schadenfreude.

After a further fifteen-minute wait my turn to make inquiry at the service desk presented itself. There, uncomfortably situated between two vociferous and indignant queue jumpers, I was informed the next flight available to Moshi perhaps not unexpectedly would depart "24 hours hence!" Apparently only one flight departed from Istanbul to Moshi each day! Resigned I accepted the news and scanned the airport for possible signs of solace – perhaps a flight to Moshi on a different airline? Couches to sleep on? Perchance to dream?

Our conversation then turned to a discussion of a possible hotel for the night. The Turkish Airlines service agent asked for my passport and I showed her my US passport to which she responded "Do you have another passport?" Because I was traveling as a chameleon I admitted to possessing a Canadian passport. The desk agent smiled and replied she could not provide an overnight hotel to a US citizen but could if I derived from Canada.

I carried a second passport because I had been born in Canada and had spent my first twenty-four years in Canada before moving to the US for a graduate program in California. Both Canada and the US permit dual citizenship although the US does not recognize second citizenships. Since the 2016 US election I had begun to travel more frequently on the Canadian passport as a result of the ignominy sometimes associated with "being an American".

With my precious hotel voucher and confirmed next-day boarding pass in hand, I was directed to "the hotel desk down the hallway, to the left, to the left again, down one flight, through immigration, then outside of baggage claim and then to the right". Hell! I thought. What are the chances of finding this fucking 'hotel desk'? Although complicated, I was committed to give these directions a heroic effort and perhaps with luck might find myself resting in a pleasant hotel room within the hour. It was 7:15 PM. Forty-five minutes had elapsed since arrival. I still felt I was doing well! Ahead of the game.

Finding a well-lit and cavernous immigration hall one floor down I lined-up 100-people deep and waited twenty minutes to reach an immigration agent. There a youthful male agent behind a glass partition gave cursory examination to my Canadian passport and then pointed toward its obvious deficiency - the absence of a Turkish tourist visa. I had somehow believed a hotel voucher and boarding pass for a flight the next day might obviate this requirement. This seemed especially appropriate given the national airline had caused me such inconvenience. The unsmiling and unsympathetic immigration agent instead directed me toward a visa desk behind me possibly 30-40 meters away. Yes, I would need a visa to enter Turkey even though I was staying only overnight as a result of a missed Turkish Airlines flight! It was your fault, not mine, I wanted to say. The glass partition separating me from the immigration agent prevented me from reaching forth and wringing his neck.

Becoming increasingly grumpy I made my way to the visa desk and encountered a machine into which visa seekers were required to manually enter all of their personal data (name, date of birth, citizenship, passport number, home address) and have their passport scanned with the expected subsequent release of a paper-printed visa with one's photo - all for $60. Try as I might I could not compel the infernal visa machine to function - this despite having entered nearly a thesis-like volume of data into it. In exasperation I approached a nearby visa desk manned by a group of three highly-disinterested immigration agents - two men and one woman. Not only did these three people betray no interest in handling my visa request but when they eventually did they charged me an even higher price ($70) for my one-night Turkish entry visa. Once acquired I re-entered the now-refreshed immigration line and this time was granted access to Turkey for my single glorious, albeit further-abbreviated, evening.

Later I determined I should have been more grateful for the ease and cost with which I obtained my Turkish visa. While Canadians were allowed entry into Turkey for a fee, Americans lacking visas were denied entry because of a diplomatic spat between the USA and Turkey. A cleric (Fethullah Gulen) thought responsible in part for last year's attempted coup in Turkey resided in Pennsylvania! Of all places! Understandably the Government of Turkey wanted him extradited to Turkey and the US had refused. Further an American pastor was being detained in Turkey for alleged support of the same coup attempt. This as one might anticipate had spiraled into both countries amongst other things denying tourist visas to the others' citizens. I estimated this was the reason for my being told I could not be granted a hotel voucher as an American. Had I traveled only via a US passport I would likely have slept in the airport. God Save the Queen!

By this point nothing at either the Turkish Airlines desk nor in immigration had been communicated to me regarding the fate of my North Face duffle bag and even though I knew it should automatically be forwarded to Moshi on the next evening's flight I was concerned it might have been mistakenly off-loaded and placed onto a carousel in Istanbul instead. Hence I thought it important to search all dozen of the Istanbul airport carousels to ensure my bag had not been off-loaded. With some finesse and direction from baggage porters I yhen located the "hotel desk" outdoors at the distal terminus of the airport!

"Distal" would be an understatement. This was as distal and as nondescript an "office" as one could design - possibly pre-meditated to minimize the numbers of actual hotels needed to be dispensed at the expense of Turkish Airlines. When not in use it could have served as a broom closet - albeit a broom closet affixed with a window through which one could speak with an impertinent and uninformative woman who sat stiffly inside! I waited in another line, 5-6 people deep (20 more minutes) before reaching the window and presented my now-favored Canadian passport, my next day's boarding pass and my hotel voucher. All were taken from me by the taciturn attendant, a mildly-worrying development, and I was told to wait adjacent to the "hotel office" around the corner. Doing so and rounding the corner I became more dispirited when I discovered dozens of other similarly-afflicted souls waiting for their hotel assignments. Two hours since arrival had elapsed.

Thirty minutes later and with no apparent progress in hotel assignments having been made my spirits sagged further. How long might this take? One hour? Three hours? All night? It was 9 PM! No one communicated any information to any of the stranded passengers who languished morosely beside me. None whom had arrived prior to me had been beckoned for transit to their hotels! Other equally unfortunate newly-arriving passengers were still in line - waiting to possess their own assignments and the line was longer than when I had first encountered it. As a result, I was unwilling to line up for a second time and query the desk attendant. I wandered briefly and located a panel display of hotel advertisements with telephones used to call hotels directly. Should I perhaps just acquiesce and access a taxi to one of these airport hotels and pay for the night myself? I would have done so had I not harbored uncertainties concerning where these hotels were situated in relation to the airport. I didn't want to be shuttled-off into Central Istanbul on a 1-hour taxi run. Further none of the other afflicted passengers were resorting to this option. Hence I concluded finding my own hotel might be a mistake.

Resigned, I returned to the same chair in the waiting area whereupon the Turkish Airlines hotel assignment lady who had taken my passport and visa exited her broom closet and called out the names of several other passengers! “Progress!” I thought. Although I was not called within this first group, it seemed to me there might be some light laying at the end of this long and otherwise dark tunnel. More than an hour had passed since I had arrived at this desk.

Within another thirty minutes and two-three groups later I was summoned by name (“Nail”) to follow the desk attendant and was led to a taxi along with one other woman- a Hungarian lady who had been travelling to San Francisco to visit a daughter who was attending UC Berkeley. What an interconnected world! Together following a ten- to fifteen-minute ride we were delivered to a modern 4-star hotel - well-appointed and more than adequate for the evening. The foyer as is the nature of such hotels rose four-stories in glass. Marble waterfalls and comfortable seating areas graced the entrance. English-proficient Turkish women attended the check-in desks and processed me quickly while proffering warm smiles. These attributes in part made up for the degradations I had so far endured. From an ascending elevator I bid my Hungarian traveling companion adieu and retreated to the familiar comforts of my hotel cocoon - three and a half hours of waiting in lines, hand-wringing and eye-rolling having elapsed before decamping here. I sent a quick e-mail to Rachel Bode with Kandoo Adventures to inform her of my delayed arrival and was then quickly and gratefully asleep between two freshly-starched linen sheets.

Had I been remotely energetic the next morning I could have risen early and taken a taxi to see some of the more intriguing aspects of Istanbul - an atmospheric restaurant on the Bosporus, the museums, the Emerald Dagger, the Blue Mosque, Takin Square. However, memories of my last visit to Istanbul where I was trapped inside a dance bar and had had to kick the entrance doors down in order escape a ludicrous $800 bar bill suggested to me I should exercise some discretion. Instead I lounged in my hotel room until noon then meandered to the airport via the hotel shuttle. As I had been wearing the same clothes for over twenty-four hours I was eager to buy at least one new shirt. This secured I located an over-crowded Business Class lounge and scarfed-down some day-old food in the cafeteria-like atmosphere.

Turkish Airlines flight THY571 left at 7:30 PM - six hours to Moshi! On the arrivals screen I noted tonight's flight from San Francisco like yesterday's would be arriving ninety minutes late. In my mind I reviewed the actions all the late arriving non-American passengers would be following actions identical to mine. I thought too of the Americans who would be condemned to sleep in the airport overnight. Twenty-four hours had just evaporated.

Chapter Three
Into Africa

Once airborne I monitored the video display tracing an improbable flight path - across the Mediterranean and above the North coast of Egypt then across Sudan (and near the newly-christened "South Sudan"), Ethiopia, Kenya and, finally, Tanzania - crossing the equator. My seat mate was a young woman who worked for The World Bank. Her presence in Business Class at NGO expense, convinced me The World Bank and likely similar organizations such as the UN take very good care of their employees - certainly better than my former university.

I was eleven time zones away from Oregon and was finding it increasingly difficult to believe in so short a period of time I had managed to come so far into a territory I had no familiarity with. It dawned on me I had sponsored a child at an orphanage in Gondar, Ethiopia. His name is Abebaw and he was twelve years-old. His mother had died and his father was in jail for murder. Why had I not even considered the possibility of visiting with him or telling him I was in the vicinity prior to this trip? Such was my inability to completely fathom the concept of entering this part of the world. I hadn't even connected those two elements of my life - now they coalesced. Abebaw, a boy with whom I had corresponded and for whom I bore some responsibility a few km beneath me!

We came in low over the Tanzanian escarpment and from my window seat I struggled to discern some features of the terrain - even though it was almost completely dark. Terra incognita! All I could distinguish were individual widely-spaced lights - dim ones-scattered across the darkened and flat terrain in an uneven pattern. No evidence of a city or of roads were present. Tanzania was initially presenting as remote, unpopulated and a little disheveled.

We accomplished a safe landing at Moshi and the plane, instead of exiting onto an adjacent taxiway, completed a 180-degree turn and then back-taxied down the runway toward the terminal - this, a hallmark of a small airport. Passengers disembarked and approached the terminal but before entering and still on the tarmac each was required to present his/her boarding pass to a security officer. Why? I had no idea.

I was 99% confident I had left my boarding pass in my seat back pocket but rather than turn back and re-enter the plane to locate it I feigned a thorough search of my pockets. Because I was one of the first to exit the airliner a long line accumulated behind me as I "searched" all of my pockets for my boarding pass....to "no avail". And after a few minutes with passengers becoming increasing agitated behind me the youthful Tanzanian guard waved me into the terminal. At least I was not placed on the return flight to Istanbul!

Upon entering the Moshi airport facility, actions of other passengers made it immediately obvious I needed to again complete an application for a visa and pay a visa fee. A short line had already formed at a narrow wicket by the few passengers who had completed their paperwork. As I approached the window to pay the application fee a prominent notice caught my eye:

> ***"CHANGES OF THE VISA FEE FOR THE AMERICAN PASSPORT HOLDERS- With effects*** **(sic)** ***from September 20, 2007, the Visa fee for the AMERICAN PASSPORT HOLDERS travelled*** **(sic)** ***to Tanzania shall be US$ 100.00 (US$ One Hundred Only). The new visa fee shall apply for single, double & multiple entries. It should be understood that these changes are for the American passport holders only and not for any other nationality."***

The visa for all other nationalities cost $50. Learning this I immediately fished-out my Canadian passport- the fortunate chameleon I am. But the differential in price for a Tanzanian visa made me wonder: What happened between the US and Tanzania in

2007 that would have caused Tanzania to double the cost of visas for US citizens only? It followed by nine years the bombing of the US Embassy in Dar es Salaam. Maybe it had something to do with the growing Islamism of the time. Maybe it was just reciprocity. Whatever the underlying cause I had already benefitted twice on this trip from having in my possession a Canadian passport and felt a mild pride. Some might refer to this as "smugness"; a smugness I recall began to develop in early-November, 2016.

Within this immigration area I was presented with my first appreciation of Tanzania and its people. This airport was in fact a marginal facility attended as expected by a dozen or so uniformed customs officers. These officers moved slowly and projected a laisse-faire image very much unlike the menacing CBP officers and their dogs one encounters upon entering the US. But to give these people some credit understand it was the middle of the night!

Further, I had anticipated I might encounter some anxiety upon first exposure to Tanzania however nothing of the sort materialized. I felt safe. No threatening or angry stares were directed toward me. Everyone was just doing their jobs as they would have in any other, or my, country.

My next concerns were two-fold - I needed to first locate my duffle bag and then find the driver who would ferry me to the hotel in Moshi. My driver would have arrived for last night's flight. But, would he have learned about my missed connection and come for me again tonight? It was already near 1:30 AM. All baggage seemed to have been off-loaded during the lengthy immigration process and placed on the floor adjacent to the conveyor belt in a dimly-lit, yawning baggage claim area. And despite being one of the first off the plane and through immigration I could not locate my bag anywhere. Other passengers were actively collecting their bags and exiting past a sleeping guard and I began to covet their good luck. Their bags had arrived! I briefly considered my naiveté in imagining I could check-in a bag in distant Portland, fly half-way around the world, miss a connecting flight in Istanbul and then still harbor any glimmer of hope I might be reunited so efficiently with my bag. I asked a Tanzanian attendant; Have all the bags been removed from the plane? He seemed to indicate they had but I was not completely satisfied with the conviction of his response. Disappointed, I decided to re-examine the remaining bags and address the apparent loss of all of my expedition gear the next day in Moshi. The Kandoo Website had indicated "in the event of a bag loss (which was apparently a particularly common occurrence for those arriving from Nairobi), much of the needed equipment could be purchased or rented in Moshi". At least I had worn my precious hiking boots, as directed, on the flight.

To my surprise I stumbled across my duffle bag laying on the floor in a highly conspicuous location - a location I would have walked by and scanned at least twice prior. Sure the bag was black and nondescript and the arrivals hall was dark however I had apparently convinced myself the bag could not possibly have arrived and as a result my eyes had refused to register it when they came upon it prior. One sees what they expect to see I suppose. I had tricked myself into believing my bag could only have been lost. But no there it was!

Relieved I clutched the bag reassuringly to my chest and walked to the sleeping guard - his feet propped on a table and his body slumped sideways. He rested beside an X-ray machine with its attendant conveyor belt. Collectively they guarded a darkened hallway leading immediately outside. I surmised all bags needed to be run through the scanner prior to entering Tanzania. However, visitors in front of me walked by him paying neither him nor the scanner any heed. I did the same half-expecting some recrimination from him - a recrimination that never arrived. And from there, I tentatively stepped into the warm, sweet-smelling, dimly-lit night of Tanzania! Indeed, *this* was Africa!

A dozen or so Tanzanian drivers all with names of prospective passengers displayed on pieces of ragged cardboard squares surrounded the exit and within a minute I recognized my name! It was 2 AM and Moshi was expected to be an hour's drive (35 km) away. The driver took my duffle bag and we traversed broken pavement and chunks of concrete, passed torn chain-link fences under poorly-lit, leafless acacia trees toward a battered white van. I entered the passenger seat on the left hand side and tried to make small conversation with the driver as we began to lurch toward the city. My anxiety level rose slightly. I was with a stranger in a remote location with no recourse but to trust him. It was just the two of us on an unlit Tanzanian highway. Two guys. How were we so different?

The driver (Charles) was 39 years old apparently had three children and seemed quite talkative given the time of night. I quickly became at ease with him as he betrayed no malevolent intent. The land appeared desolate and from what I could divine at this time of night seemed devoid of any greenery or of animate life. We traversed small towns with houses and storefronts constructed of painted cinderblock and illuminated by yellow incandescent filaments - the road being narrow and quite rough. Yards appeared to consist of well-trodden dried mud. Tethered goats and cattle slept on the earth adjacent to their owners' homes.

En route we passed two police road checks where we were required to stop and where policemen came to the driver's right-side window and shone flashlights both at me and into the rear of the van. While this was accomplished other officers stood two meters away with automatic rifles positioned downward across their chests. This was somewhat unnerving and Charles explained to me the reason for this was we were traveling on a road serving as the main conduit that connected Kenya to Tanzania. The weapon-clad officers were checking vehicles for contraband - transport of untaxed goods. Even with this information I found the road blocks unsettling.

As we made our way toward Moshi Charles adopted the unusual and mildly-alarming habit of repeatedly flashing his high beams on and off repeatedly - even though no other cars were approaching (or coming from behind us). It was as if he was using his headlights to ward off something I could not see- ghosts perhaps? Maybe he was night blind - Vitamin A-deficient. There was no obvious purpose served by Charles' actions and it served to increase my wariness. His actions made no sense. Was he searching for cattle on the road? I should have asked.

We passed the off-road exit to "Machame Gate," the turn-off where we would commence our hike in two- to three-days time. We passed a seminary, the "French Rose Rest House" and a raucous, two-story, cinder block night club just on the outskirts of Moshi. Music was still blasting- audible from the road, walls reverberating and dozens of battered cars lounged helter-skelter outside on an uneven, gravel parking lot - even at this very late hour. Knowing Richard should have arrived from Glasgow into Moshi twenty hours ago and knowing he was known to enjoy his nightlife I imagined he was possibly quaffing an ale or two inside. Hence, I did not believe it would be completely unreasonable to request the driver to pull over. However, discretion again prevailed. It was getting late.

Speed bumps cropped up frequently, unpredictably and for no obvious reason along the entire trip. Because the van lacked suspension we needed to slow down for each bump to 5-10 kph. Their presence, besides the police checks, largely accounted for the hour it took to travel 35 km.

At 2:45 AM we reached the oddly-named "Bristol Cottages" contained within a small enclave of twisted and dimly-lit streets near downtown Moshi. An ominous metal gate blocked entry and my driver rousted Amari the ancient night watchman to open the creaky gate. I tipped the driver $20 - a generous amount I believe and let Amari carry my two bags up to my third floor room. Even though it appeared Amari could not speak English I tried to make him understand I had no money to tip him. The smallest bill I had was US$20 - too extravagant a tip for what he had done for me. Further I had not yet acquired any local currency. Using English and sign language I informed Amari I would get money soon and be able to tip him later. Without equivocation Amari seemed to comprehend my intent and left me in my tiled and clean hotel room alone with a bed surrounded with mosquito netting. By 3 AM I was in bed and soon fast asleep. What a difference thirty hours can make in one's life!

Chapter Four
Discovery of Moshi, Friends and a Local Beer

My first night's sleep in Moshi had re-oriented my internal clock and I woke near 7 AM - having stirred only once during the night. The window to my room had been left slightly ajar - a soft breeze entered and caused the sheer floor-length curtains to billow softly- in and out, in and out- as if respiring. Their movement was both mesmerizing and calming. I could possibly have watched them for an hour and let my mind enter a reverie however their movements were accompanied by an exotic cacophony of unfamiliar yet compelling sounds- thumping bass music, car horns, unfamiliar bird song. Indeed, there was a new world needing to be explored!

Approaching the window to the South, I parted the near weightless curtains and imbibed the sunlit and chaotic street scene below! Yellow morning sun filtered through profuse yet dusty greenery - the copious wax of each leaf delineated by its contrasting buttery venous network. Wild tangles of electric wires connected blackened, uneven power poles. Moshi's residents ambled familiarly along rubbish-strewn, sooty streets. Street hawkers rested among all manner of goods on sidewalks - used shoes, sunglasses, woven baskets. Dented cars and trucks accelerated, shifted gears noisily and raised their horns. Middle-aged women, dressed in bright fluttering greens, blues and yellows, navigated calmly across the raucous thoroughfare; carefully balancing brimming woven baskets upon their heads - their necks elegantly straight, their eyes vigilant, their children in tow. Elderly men rested in small groups along aging white-washed cinderblock walls, collections of broken cement and sidewalks seemingly accepting of their modest circumstance. Their sandals hung only half on their feet. Hymns filtered across the street from a churchyard - a Sunday morning ritual in a faraway Moshi as it elevated its day.

The panorama reminded me of my arrival in the middle of the night into New Delhi in 1980 via a runway lit by individual fires in oil pots - oil pots individually tended by crouching dhoti-clad men. There I woke to a comparable scene and experienced the same sense of being an interloper. These were daily rhythms and pulses of life preceding my arrival. They were certain to continue well past my departure - my consequence to this world and millions of other worlds irrelevant. What *meaning* could be possibly ascribed to my brief observation of it?

Contemplating the opposing window toward the North I was presented with a view into the hotel's eighty meter-square courtyard - an oasis of relative calm amid the hectic city. The courtyard was filled with tall tropical trees many of which stretched higher than the three story elevation of the hotel - nary any sunlight filtered to the hotel grounds. The firmament of the courtyard presented a mixture of blackened and well-packed oily earth, cement and small, well-trimmed olivine bushes. A few employees milled about - unaware they were being observed.

A short distance down the corridor, just past an imposing tree I encountered an unobstructed view toward the North. And there it stood! Kilimanjaro! Unexpected and magnificent - lying above a haphazard and disorganized Moshi skyline. Its storied snow-capped peak was clearly delineated against a deep blue sky! Alone and unobtrusive. Quiet and gentle. Natural. As if I knew this mountain and it knew me. I had known it for millennia. It sat in harmony with its surroundings as if the landscape could not have existed without it. How many eyes have gazed toward it and thought the same thoughts as me?

Kilimanjaro dwarfs itself! As the world's largest free-standing mountain and the world's largest volcano, the reaches of its base are massive (some 40 km) and this width thereby diminishes its 5,900 meter peak.

Kilimanjaro or "Kili" in the local parlance rises above the surrounding plain of Tanzania- it's width eight-fold greater than its height. The word "kili" denotes "snow" in Swahili (or other of the many local languages). Not apparent from my distance were the multiple climatic zones of the mountain - progressing from a cultivated and populated zone at its base and then upward through a tropical rain forest, heather and moorland, highland (alpine) desert and finally an arctic summit. I later discovered each person's description of Kilimanjaro's varied climactic zones differs from the specific terms enumerated here.

This unexpected sighting of Kilimanjaro was a jolt. I adjusted my head slightly and considered its peak - barely comprehending we would attempt to reach the lonely dome in the not too distant future. How do we fit into this picture?

I returned to my room then showered, dressed and ventured downstairs via the hotel's expansive cement corridors and stairways. The clunky, concrete architecture indicated, at least to my untrained eye, the hotel was constructed in the 1960's - a time when it appeared to also have been last painted - fading yellow and, in corners, grimy - but otherwise clean. Fire- and smoke-blackened wooden carvings lined both the spacious corridors and stairwells generating a new and distinct sense of an "Eastern Africa" within me just as Balinese carvings, batik clothing and the smell of durian engender a feeling of "Southeast Asia" in me. Each carving was vaguely humanoid - a style I had collected from Asia and the kind my wife will not tolerate near her because she retains an animist belief - menacing dark figurines function as repositories for "black spirits".

A profuse collection of birds hidden amongst impenetrable shrubbery and the twisted centuries-old trees ululated their unfamiliar morning songs. Perhaps one was a rare Scarlet-tufted Malachite Sunbird - a bird whose name and appearance had immediately become the focus of my interest when I had considered details of Kilimanjaro's avian life prior to departure.

Insects, perhaps cicadae, vibrated - their shrill sounds collectively rising and falling as I cautiously made my way to an apparent breakfast nook contained within the hotel courtyard. Hotel staff busied themselves quietly here and there - a coverall-clad gardener meticulously trimmed a 20 cm hedge beside a sidewalk - absorbed in his thoughts. The leaves he was trimming were only one cm in length. Each was cut precisely. Indeed, his work was a meditation.

A stocky, middle-aged maid, dressed in starched white, deep in her thoughts burdened an unsteady cart with fresh linens and towels. Adolescent kitchen staff readied food for the morning buffet - their metal food containers jangling and clattering. Animated Swahili conversations resonated from the walls surrounding the court yard. All paid me no heed. No, I was not part of this world. These people had encountered people like me, people of no consequence, numerous times. I was alien and transient in their vibrant and densely scented world.

Will this world too be lost to 'progress'?

Two plucky visitors, a youthful European couple, hovered over the breakfast offerings while an older European woman privately consumed a page-worn novel at the edge of the breakfast space. These people too paid no attention to my presence. I remained invisible. Leaves, burdened by accumulating humidity, drooped further.

Not yet sufficiently emboldened to assert any aspect of my presence I remained silent as I gathered a collection of food for my first meal - cold toast with jam, scrambled eggs, a questionable near-white sausage and coffee. A container of milk had been provided to whiten the coffee yet I was concerned - Is milk production adequately sanitary in this country? I reasoned the temperature of the coffee would destroy pathogens and whitened my coffee with some trepidation. Sustenance in hand, I retreated to a free table - a table equidistant from the young couple and the older lady and there I entered into a reverie. How strange *this is* and yet how familiar!

Laughter again emanated from the young Tanzanian workers who inhabited the adjacent kitchen. As they came and went our eyes occasionally met - a sense of interest arose between us but their almond eyes were then quickly averted. My arms were sticking to the wooden table whenever I tried to lift them to accomplish any small task - a mixture of the oils of my skin and yesterday's spilled juices and jellies.

No sooner was I seated when the lady who had been reading her novel approached me and inquired "Are you Neil?". Awakened and lifted abruptly into the scene I quickly acknowledged her and realized this person must be Trish, the former girlfriend of Richard Thacker. She and Richard had planned the hike as a couple a few months earlier but to Richard's chagrin she had "dumped him" a month or so prior. Despite this considerable setback they had elected to continue with their travel plans including the sharing of a small tent even though neither retained any romantic interest in the other. Fortunately, I was to learn, what romantic interest may have existed between them had not been replaced with animus.

Yes, I'm Neil! I announced, feeling some relief with the newly-presented opportunity to speak. I had been isolated from conversation for nearly two days - and as a consequence had retreated fully into my thoughts. Thereby extracted I immediately asked Trish to join my table whereupon we engaged in a full hour of delightful conversation.

Trish taught Biology in a private Glasgow high school and her profession had caused her to meet with Richard at a Biology conference nearby. I learned Trish was 62 - a year younger than me but I immediately sensed she did not appear to be in sufficient shape for a strenuous climb on the world's tallest volcano and Africa's tallest mountain. She admitted she did not regularly exercise nor did she prepare athletically for the climb. She presented like me as carrying a few more kg than one might otherwise desire. Still she also presented as a kind and reliable person - just the sort one would *want* to climb with- the one who might take a maternal interest in others. Aside we determined we both had professional highly-driven daughters who were attorneys-daughters who nevertheless struggled occasionally with self-doubt. This commonality aided us in finding further common ground. Of course we both knew Richard - a "good bloke" and a "bit of a character". His continued absence from the breakfast table provided additional freedom for insightful conversation about him. Trish again made clear to me Richard and she were "no longer a couple" but they had made the decision to travel together despite this awkward development. Their hike would involve the sharing of rooms and tents throughout the journey - a bit of discomfiture and humor to follow along with us.

I knew Trish and Richard had arrived a day earlier and did not need to face a time zone challenge as radical as the one I was handling. Hence I was curious about Richard's continuing absence. Trish simply informed me "Richard is still sleeping". But an hour later when it reached near 9AM I began to surmise Richard's absence might in fact be attributed to a pint or two of exuberance the night prior - perhaps at the aforementioned nightclub. We nodded knowingly at each other when the discussion again turned to Richard's absence. Sometimes what is *not* said speaks louder volumes than what *is* said.

When Richard finally *did* arrive for breakfast near 10 AM I made no comment on his late arrival but instead committed my thoughts to memory for this record. "Good morning Professor!" an energetic Richard shouted toward me in his distinguished English accent. Indeed, his booming voice emanated in strong juxtaposition to the otherwise calm the courtyard had enjoyed prior. The young couple twisted their heads to understand the disturbance.

Richard, fully bald, entered the kitchen area wearing a set of exaggeratedly baggy, khaki cargo shorts and close-fitting thin T-shirt, his teeth gleaming, wide smile, radiant brown eyes - the picture of a friend welcoming another long-unseen friend. Good morning Richard! I shouted as I leapt from my sticky wooden chair and ran enthusiastically toward him.

If only we might experience the satisfaction of meeting a dear old friend daily.

We collided in a collegial embrace, slapped each others' backs then walked still clutching each other around each others' shoulders to my breakfast table. While I had known Richard since 1998 as a Professor at Sultan Qaboos University (SQU) I had seen him only twice since then - once in 2004 in Largs, Scotland (his then and current home) and the other only two-months prior during a reunion trip to Muscat, Oman. And as friends are wont to do we easily picked-up our conversation from where we had left off. Richard had not changed. Nor had I. Trish remained a robust and pleasant counterpoint to our conversation - the two of them fortunately betraying no animosity nor evidence of a recent separation.

Richard was hired as an Entomologist at SQU and I as a Nutritionist. Richard had arrived with his wife at the time (Cynthia) and daughter (Fiona) whereas I was with my wife (Azizah) and two children (Amelia and Johan). Richard and Cynthia while in Oman conceived one more child (Dylan) and after returning to Scotland in 2000 gave birth to twins (George and Duncan). While in Oman, Richard and I developed a friendship around a common pastime - SCUBA diving - and typically found ourselves diving along the Omani Coast twice each month. Together, we completed the PADI Rescue Diver course and fantasized about remaining in Oman and perhaps opening our own diving center. In a university populated by abaya-clad Omani women who communicated with men only via their sensuous eyes, exposed ankles and perfumes we had both similarly thirsted after the same bikini-clad Swedish girl named Ulrika who often attended our dive boat wearing only the briefest of bikinis - her bronze skin still a strong memory for me. And after each dive we would retreat to an adjacent bar in the marina, sometimes accompanied by the slender, bronze and nearly-naked Ulrika, order a hamburger and fries and I'd announce a toast to our good fortune by stating sagely - You know Richard, it just doesn't get any better than this! Time passed and life had retreated seventeen years. It was time to toast to our friendship again - this time with coffee.

Breakfast passed at a leisurely pace after which the three of us decided to exit our sanctuary onto the adjacent street for some sight-seeing. Our peregrinations revealed largely what I had earlier noted from my third-story hotel room window except we were thrust directly into the maelstrom - amongst Tanzanians living their ordinary lives, amongst uniform-clad school children running and laughing, amongst brightly-clothed women, amongst traffic, amongst wide blindingly-white smiles, amongst dust kicked-up by the cars, amongst an extensive networks of power lines clinging to over-laden and blackened power poles, crossing roads and dodging traffic, amongst street sellers who glanced in our direction with no evidence of anger or hostility behind eyes - some curiosity, some indifference. Although residents of Moshi generally paid little attention to us, several attractive younger men, some presenting dreadlocks retained in large, woven Rasta-style hats did take interest and admonished us to visit their curiosity/art shops. In each case, their sales pitch involved their somewhat unconvincing assertions their shop served as a "charity". If we purchased souvenirs "the proceeds would benefit children or a community" of some sort. These charismatic salesmen followed us for a few minutes but we felt no recriminations when each time Richard politely affirmed we would visit each later. I felt protected within our small group but will admit I would have felt less so had I been alone. Change had come so quickly.

Even though we explored the unfamiliar street scene of Moshi for several hours we covered very little ground - perhaps only four square city blocks. Each street we investigated within this small area contained unexpected adventures - a cozy park where locals hung-out, where young couples cautiously held hands, gazed into each others' eyes and held quiet conversations - out of sight of prying parents' eyes, and where we could have had we wished ordered food at one of several questionable food stalls, a liquor store, where Richard and I optimistically made plans for what spirits we might ferry to the summit, a blindingly white mosque where several twelve year-old boys took an interest in us and told us about the religious classes they attended, hiking supply stories, art stores, restaurants and a central bus station - crowded with colorfully-clad street vendors (orange, yellow, blue, rust and green-all billowing), dust- and mud-clad windowless buses, taxis lurching hither-and-thither- a vibrant clot of humanity. Sporadically we encountered other fair-skinned aspiring climbers who were similarly engaged in their own adventures. We generally avoided their eyes as they avoided ours, not wanting to taint our sense of adventure with their scent of ordinariness.

Notable purchases included wristbands inscribed with the Swahili term "pole pole" ([pronounced "polay polay"]; meaning - "slowly slowly"). We later discovered the importance of this saying - the reliable mantra our climbing guides would use to provide succor to us throughout the forthcoming arduous climb. "Pole Pole"- a Tanzanian approach to life. Take it easy. Don't rush through life. Stop and smell the roses.

Richard's enthusiasm for novelty, for exploration and for interaction with strangers, was remarkable. Whereas I was cautious Richard exhibited no such reticence and struck-up conversations with a broad spectrum of Moshi residents irrespective of their age, gender or apparent social position. I admired him for all of this and attributed it in part to his recent experience in administration of a University of Western Scotland degree program in Ghana. He had "Africa experience" - Trish and I did not. I trusted Richard and therefore followed his lead.

Hungry, we located a nondescript restaurant on a side-street. We attempted to sit in the more palatable aspect of this enterprise, an area commanding an elevated view of the adjacent dusty street and stucco architecture but were turned away when it was determined Richard needed to smoke. Smoking was apparently not permitted in the more-upscale section of this rather dilapidated restaurant. Instead we were relegated to an internal darkened grotto where Richard's cigarette smoke was certain to foul others' lungs. We ordered both beer and hamburgers reasoning "The hamburgers would be cooked and therefore should be safe".

Note to the Reader: *I recognize I entered "Africa" with a wariness described as "unsophisticated" or "American". I was apprehensive as anyone should be when traveling. However, much of my wariness was not justified. I am embarrassed by this attitude and hope others may be emboldened to more openly embrace other cultures as a result of this narrative.*

Food safety issues were at the front of my mind. In February of the same year I had trekked through the Upper Mustang in Nepal with an assemblage including three physicians. Unremittingly, each meticulously considered the source and preparation of all food on offer and openly and frequently voiced their perceptions of its safety. That had caused me to forgo fresh locally-grown vegetables and most uncooked agricultural products for the three-week entirety of the hike. I had been required to get vaccinated for Japanese encephalitis, typhoid, hepatitis and rabies and to consume, despite one of the physician's admonitions, a potentially hallucinogenic malarial medication (mefloquine). For this trip, burned-out by excessive caution, I forewent consultation of the US

State Department's Website for its country-specific vaccination recommendations. My naïve expectation was the diseases I was protected from by the vast array of injections I submitted to earlier in the year might protect me here as well.

AIDS was prevalent locally and so was teen pregnancy. I had learned teen girls in local schools were forced to submit urine samples periodically during school times to prove they weren't pregnant. And, if they were found to be pregnant they were expelled from school. Girls were given sex education including instructions on "not exchanging sex for kind acts from men". Girls at time of their monthly periods often missed school for lack of funds to purchase sanitary products. These are typical of the travails of girls in all underdeveloped countries. In many countries it's often not easy to be a woman.

Chilled bottles of "Kilimanjaro" beer arrived in reassuringly large 500 ml bottles- a beer we would repeatedly order whenever opportunity presented itself. And while not a memorable beer the novelty and cache of a beer named "Kilimanjaro" more than made up for its mediocre taste. It was an admirable light lager - appropriate to the warm and dusty weather of Moshi. While imbibing, two strapping 12-13 year-old Tanzanian boys sat at the adjacent table and engaged us with their eyes and body language. I joined them briefly and entertained them with some banter and ultimately a request for a photo. Their meal was simple - large, boiled pasta noodles with ketchup - lots of energy but not much more.

Three beers later our increasingly-energetic group discharged itself noisily onto the adjacent sooty street and made its way to a "charity shop" run by one of the young, Rastafarian men who had marginally convinced us of his passion for helping others. The sun was lowering in the sky and the muted evening light was substituting my feeling for the city into one of melancholy. That feeling motived me to buy a few souvenirs. Somehow the two blackened wooden totems I purchased found their way home to Oregon undamaged some four weeks later. However as expected they were not permitted to inhabit the main living quarters of our home and instead banished by my dear wife to a remote corner of an upstairs bedroom - a bedroom where they could inflict minimal harm.

Remaining members of our hiking group were scheduled to arrive from the UK and from Zambia at the Bristol Cottages later in the evening. Hence, a decision was reached we should await their arrival in the hotel bar where most importantly the familiar Kilimanjaro beer was abundantly available and quickly delivered. So situated we chatted vociferously and ignored the malevolent spirits contained within the meter-high, carved and blackened wooden deities that surrounded us.

Dinner time arrived and our food arrived coincident with our anticipated UK-based hiking companions. These included Richard Arthur (Rich), a chiropodist (foot doctor) and long-time friend of Richard's from London, Rich's cousins Natascha and Alex, and Natascha's friends Debbie and Angie - one new guy and four new women! We were a group of eight. Another friend of Natascha's, Gillian, was scheduled to arrive from Zambia later in the evening.

By this time, perhaps near 5 or 6 PM, Richard, Trish and I had had more than enough beer to drink however the arrival of the newer members of our climbing party necessitated orders of even more Kilimanjaro. I had planned to head up to bed early however I convinced myself that staying-up and partying with the near complete hiking group would aid my adjustment to the full eleven-hour difference in time zones I was facing. I had only been "in country" for sixteen hours and I knew one needed to force one's self to acclimate to the change in time if one wished to make a smooth transition to so remote a destination. This was essentially an oblique way of justifying further excessive consumption of beer.

Many contained within our newly-assembled group were strangers - meeting for the first time. I was the only member of the group who had flown in from North America and I knew only Richard. Richard only knew Trish and his friend Rich who had invited him. Rich of course knew his cousins (Natascha and Alex) but not the other women (all of whom were friends of Natascha). Natascha of course knew her friends (Debbie, Angie, and Gillian), her sister (Alex) and cousin (Rich) but she did not know Richard, Trish or me. Hence what I am able to recall of this evening largely consisted of each of us getting to know each other and coming to understand names and connections which had brought us to this improbable location. How quickly strangers can come together and enjoy each others' company! They only need a common animating purpose - including Kilimanjaro beer.

The Kilimanjaro ascent had been conceived by Gillian, the woman who had yet to arrive from Zambia. Gillian had wished to accomplish something significant for her 50th birthday and asked Natascha if she might wish to climb "Kili". Natascha had agreed, made contact with Kandoo and had invited her sister (Alex), friends (Debbie and Angie) and cousin (Rich). Rich then invited his friend of 41-years (Richard) who subsequently invited me and his girlfriend (at the time) Trish. When Richard arrived with his former girlfriend he had no idea the remainder of the group (besides his friend Rich) would consist entirely of women. Nor did I. Three men and six women! It was a haphazardly-assembled group but from the first night we became determined to make a "go" of it. Why not? Even though none of us were mountaineers. Even though Kilimanjaro was a reasonably-challenging destination for those mountaineers who strive to conquer the "Seven Summits" - the seven tallest peaks on the seven continents.

Richard and Rich were both 54 years-old and I judged both to be in reasonably good physical condition. Rich had recently run half-marathons and Richard had at least posted photographs on Facebook, complete with contestant number appended to his chest, of his participation in shorter races in Scotland. I was older by nine years and definitely the least fit of the men. Was my age going to be an impediment? I was privately worried. On the other hand, I didn't smoke. Richard smoked and showed some evidence of a smoker's hack. Might tobacco render Richard and I onto an equal footing?

Richard and Rich informed me also of their durable friendship not only on this evening but periodically throughout the hike. This long relationship implied they had known each other since 1976; from ages of twelve or thirteen years old and this reminded me of my own long-lasting connections with those I went to high school with until 1971 - a duration of even longer. The two Richards admitted to me of attending a school at which the Queen Mother arrived to plant a tree in the schoolyard. The entire school was naturally roused to observe the Queen Mother ceremonially planting the aforementioned but unfortunately doomed tree. As boys are inclined to do Richard, Rich and others returned later to chop the tree down! I will admit my friends and I at similar ages engaged in comparable injudicious acts - acts bonding us to this day. Boys are the same everywhere!

Today these antics would be cause for criminal prosecutions and juvenile court. Then, even though kids would not brag about their exploits their disruptive behaviors were somewhat tolerated. I'm pleased I grew up in a more tolerant age - otherwise my friends and I may have experienced gaps in our lives as free men.

As earlier stated Trisha was 62 and, like me, did not present an athlete's aesthete. Natascha and Alex, sisters, perhaps in their late-30's and early-40's seemed fully capable although certainly not marathoners nor mountain climbers. In making this assessment it was difficult to fathom the extent to which Alex's frequent use of her "vape" might sabotage her attempt. Of these two sisters I initially distinguished Natascha by her long blonde hair and Alex by her short red bob. Dense clouds of smoke billowed from Alex' mouth regularly and I found this practice contrary to her otherwise calm and steady demeanor. Debbie, possibly in her later-30's, was clearly athletic - presenting a toned, muscular and compact body and an olivine freckled complexion I would later understand derived from a father who originated from a mysterious island off the coast of South Africa. Remaining was Angie Foy - a calm and eminently lovable woman whom I believe was in her mid-40's, a friend of Natascha's, a smoker and an obvious non-marathoner/mountain climber as well. Her plan was to quit smoking at the bottom of "Kili" (*i.e.,* just prior to the climb)- a decision adding to her challenges.

As for me I had made moderate efforts to prepare for the climb. I had walked the "circle" near my house wearing my coveted Vasque hiking boots - a distance of five km, several times before departure. And I had begun the practice of working-out a month or two prior. However, my preparation fell far short of what I should have undertaken. In terms of being in shape I was probably at 20-25% of my peak shape and was 9-10 kg above an ideal body weight of 80 kg. Like Trish, I too did not present an "athlete's aesthete". But such was the polite nature of our increasingly cohesive group no one dwelled on this obvious deficiency with me. Also I was the old man of the group at age 63 and closing-in quickly on 64. I didn't feel *that* old as no one ever does. I had attempted to disguise this aspect of my presence by dying my hair 2 months prior (supposedly to a more vivacious "gun metal gray with aqua tips") - however gun metal color, if it ever could have been described as such, had long since washed-out and my hair was unfortunately Trumpian orange. The only individual who commented somewhat disparagingly on my unfortunate hair was "Innocent", the charismatic Tanzanian concierge of our next hotel. His comment "Here's Papa" while patting my orange hair at breakfast was comprehended but politely ignored by all of my new hiking colleagues.

By 8 PM I had had more than enough Kilimanjaro to drink and somehow managed to locate my room and its familiar king-sized, mosquito net-protected bed. The route to my room again passed the dozens of evil wooden figurines lining the stairwells and hallways. Their malevolence did not concern me as I do not believe in the supernatural.

I will attribute my early departure for bed to many things: to discretion, to age-acquired wisdom and the time difference between Tanzania and Oregon - not to my age.

My departure left the remaining seven less than seasoned and somewhat inebriated hikers in the hotel bar. Gillian arrived later in the evening, possibly near 11 PM (3 hours later) and it is my understanding all seven remained in the bar, had consumed beer until then and had managed to welcome her noisily upon her arrival. Fortunately, I wasn't there. Their boisterousness did not wake me even though I was only two floors above.

By the time I slept I was hopeful I had established myself within this group as a person capable of the climb and who would be reliable. Naturally I had worried about this. Coming from the US and hiking with a group of Europeans I worried I might come across as tainted by the politics of the day. To compensate, at every chance I emphasized my Canadian-ness and my genuine loathing of Donald Trump.

Chapter Five
On First Learning the Details

Now we knew one another better and congregated congenially at breakfast tables the next morning - a group of "older" hikers (aged 39-63) among two or three other hiking groups consisting of people in their twenties. This disparity in age did not alarm us although it probably should have. Optimists all - no one had discussed any of the challenges we might potentially (or obviously) face in scaling a 5,900+ meter volcano with an arctic summit - a climb we would begin in just 28 hours. No one questioned our individual and collective abilities. We were all in Tanzania to "just do it" as the Nike ad admonishes.

The climb remained an abstraction. Instead our banter meandered onto all topics outside of the physical efforts we would be calling upon in short order the amazing pancakes on offer, the art in the hallways, the blackened carvings. Had any of us climbed so significant a mountain as Kilimanjaro in our lifetimes the topic of the imminent undertaking may have come up. However, none of us had.

T-shirts were for sale in the hallway outside of the hotel restaurant. The one appealing to me and which was ultimately squirreled in my bag represented an advertisement for Kilimanjaro Beer. On the back was printed "If you can't climb it, drink it" surrounding an image of a Kilimanjaro beer bottle. I wanted to achieve both! Already, I had accomplished the easier of the two. Further, the accomplishment could be argued to have been completed with élan. I was ready for the more difficult of the two.

As earlier stated Gillian had arrived the night prior for the ostensible purpose of undertaking something meaningful to commemorate her 50th birthday. Gillian was an exuberant, slight, freckle-faced and serious woman who had lived and worked in

Zambia for two decades - most recently as a commercial airline pilot. She appeared to be in excellent physical condition, perhaps second only in our assemblage to Debbie. Her life was interesting - she had married in the UK at a very young age and a few years later while visiting a friend in Zambia took the radical decision to jettison her husband and to move to Zambia. Would it be we were all so bold. One thing led to another. Gillian obtained a pilot's license, a ranch and a new husband and lives a remarkably exotic life in a country most people in the West might shun - a country Donald Trump would consider a "shithole". Her stories of rafting the Class 6 rapids on the Zambizi River and of encountering all manner of wild animals in their watering holes along the river captivated me. She had led and was living a more adventurous life than most could contemplate. Indeed, an inspiring woman.

At 1 PM our newly-minted group boarded a shuttle bus and embarked for our next residence, the "Stella Rose" - a hotel located closer to "Machame Gate"- the embarkation point of the climb. Amari, the frail night porter who had carried my gear up two flights of stairs two evenings prior, understood I would be leaving and was downstairs near the check-out kiosk casually waiting for me. He introduced himself to me again as "Amari" expecting I would recall my promise of a tip. I had acquired Tanzanian money and gave him a $5-equivalent tip for carrying my bags. Using my customary "10-fold multiplier" to establish the "value" of monies spent in developing countries, I calculated this was equivalent to a $50 tip in the US. His satisfaction convinced me this calculation pertained to East Africa as well as to Cambodia and Indonesia.

The Stella Rose was an odd hotel. It was a philanthropic enterprise established by a US-based group which used income from the hotel, its restaurant and bar and from sales of locally-produced batik to support an adjacent school. Several of the American donors were concomitantly staying at the hotel and provided these details to me. These were couples in their 60's or early-70's who dressed well and, as is typical of Americans, accommodated more than a few extra pounds around their waists. This excessive weight was disguised by XXL short-sleeve safari print shirts and Size 40 khaki cargo shorts. Because these philanthropists were of similar vintage to me, they were impressed by my determination to scale the mountain fully. Wisely *their* plans for *their* stays in Tanzania were for day hikes limited to the plebian lower elevations of Kilimanjaro. Naturally I took their praise and admiration with as much humility as I could muster.

"Innocent" the lithe and smooth-talking native shirt-clad hotel manager, closet Rastafarian and ubiquitous "close friend" quickly assigned me to Room 110. I lugged my gear one floor up and discovered I had been assigned a magnificent corner room with views not only of Kilimanjaro to the North but of the rolling Arusha plains to the West. The room was well-lit by large windows and made comfortable by an enormous bed and walls camouflaged with fresh yellow paint. I put the air-conditioner to immediate use - the air being inoffensively muggy, fragrant and dense.

We were informed a group meeting would be held at 5PM in the conference room - one hour hence. In the intervening time we were encouraged to re-pack our belongings - when we departed for Machame Gate tomorrow our duffle bags were to weigh no more than 15 kg. The balance of our gear could be either carried in our smaller day packs or left in stray boxes in the hotel's storage room. We were instructed to leave room within our 15 kg allotment for the inclusion of a robust (-30 °C-rated) sleeping bag should we decide to rent one from Kandoo. These weighed 2.5 kg. Consumed by lethargy, I decided to undertake this sorting challenge later in the evening.

At 5PM our incongruent group congregated jovially around a long wooden conference table in a narrow conference room adjoining the hotel foyer. An evening sun filtered in - filling the room with a comforting warm yellow light. Our Lead Guide (Freddy) arrived, introduced himself and presented a well-organized summary of the anticipated effort. One full wall of the conference room comprised a mural of Kilimanjaro with its various climbing routes indicated. In this manner, for perhaps the first time, we came to understand what we had elected to undertake. We learned there were many different approaches to summit. The Machame route we were to follow was a 1-week climb and descent (5-days up, 2 days down) - a route that afforded the "highest probability of success". And while success rates claimed by Kandoo in its Web materials, by its representatives in person and by other companies appeared to be somewhat contrived, we were given to understand Kandoo had a 90-95% success rate in getting climbers safely up and down without mishap, grave illness or death. Still my gut knew these statistics were likely not accurately nor regularly tallied. One could claim any success rate and who would be there to substantiate the claim? Further, what penalties could possibly exist for inflating one's company's success rate? No, at best I began to understand some might not complete the climb but I remained reasonably confident I would not be one of the weaklings who might not succeed. Upon returning from Kilimanjaro to North America a month later I found a more detailed government-sponsored study online reporting a 61.3% overall success rate. This lower rate likely reflected success rates of *all* routes - including the more difficult approaches.

Still how can one ever be 90-95% certain of anything? Had I not recently slipped and dangerously gashed my head in a slippery river bed in Cambodia and needed ten stitches in a rural Cambodian hospital to close the wound? Had I not not recently slipped on a rock in Waipi'o Valley on the Big Island and done serious harm to my confidence, legs and right shoulder? Might age be taking me in his firm grip and rendering me too infirm to undertake this effort? Indeed, it was time to be serious and listen to the pre-climb briefing carefully and motivate myself to access the full spectrum of the remaining abilities of my body. I was resolute - if there was going to be anyone amongst our group who was unable to complete the hike it was not going to be me. I filled myself somewhat convincingly with resolve. Not succeeding was not an option.

The climb of Kilimanjaro offered two challenges. First there was the arduousness including seven days of effort. This would be undertaken in a broad range of weather - including all possible forms of precipitation (rain, snow, fog, hail and sleet) and temperatures ranging from +29 °C to -12 °C. Add the potential for very strong winds near the summit - the wind chill could fall below -18 °C. This necessitated need for many layers of clothing and for the aforementioned heavy duty sleeping bag.

The second challenge was the altitude and potential for altitude sickness. The summit of Kilimanjaro placed it well up into the reaches of atmosphere where limited oxygen could become a health challenge. Oxygen at sea level comprises 20.9% of atmospheric volume whereas oxygen at 5,900 meters falls to an effective volume (or partial pressure) of 10% - greater than 50% a reduction. This reduction in oxygen availability falls into an extreme altitude category and altitude sickness becomes distinctly possible. We learned everyone reaching this altitude would experience shortness of breath however most could also experience varying degrees of the more severe clinical signs of altitude sickness including nausea, spontaneous vomiting, weakness, altered personality (including increased aggressiveness), perception of cold as heat and, in serious cases, lung and/or cerebral edema. These latter afflictions are termed High Altitude Pulmonary Edema (HAPE) and High Altitude Cerebral Edema (HACE) respectively. These are potentially deadly with the only known treatment being evacuation downward as quickly as possible. Between 1996 and 2003 fourteen people on Kilimanjaro died from HACE and five from HAPE. Other deaths arising from trauma (falls or rock slides) and heart attacks have also occurred (fourteen deaths in the same time period). The overall death rate on the mountain is reported to be 13.6 deaths/100,000 climbers/year. The probability of dying from gun violence in the US is 3.6/100,000 climbers/year. Kilimanjaro presented odds 3.8-fold of that.

According to published data, incidence of Acute Mountain Sickness (headaches, nausea, vomiting or loss of appetite) develops among 77% of all Kilimanjaro climbers. However, we were not apprised of this statistic at our pre-climb meeting. Instead we were lulled into acquiescence by Freddy's rosier view of the challenge - perhaps for good reason. To contribute to our collective lack of worry none of the nine of us seemed to have invested a great deal of time in researching the complications potentially arising from this effort.

Earlier this same year I had climbed to over 4,300 meters in Nepal without any health problems other than shortness of breath. To get over some menacing cumulus clouds I had flown my unpressurized airplane over North Dakota without supplemental oxygen to 5,000 meters with little ill effect except for exhaustion and a dead sleep upon landing in Bismarck and finding a nearby motel. The additional elevation of Uhuru Summit was concerning but, having experienced nothing serious nor terribly debilitating in Nepal nor while flying an airplane, I harbored confidence my physiology was sufficiently robust it would accommodate this more challenging elevation.

Because this climb was to an extreme altitude, we were to climb high and sleep low - during the day we would reach a certain high elevation but at night we would retreat somewhat down the mountain a few hundred meters to sleep. I don't understand the physiology underlying this however this strategy aided acclimation to high altitude (or at least delayed onset of AMS). Further, should we reach the summit, we would be permitted only a short time there after which we would need to descend quickly to a much lower Mweka Camp which rested at 3,050 meters (a descent of over 2,700 meters in a few hours). This too served to reduce likelihood of severe altitude sickness.

To further aid in high altitude acclimation we were required (or at least strongly encouraged) to consume Diamox (acetazolamide). Diamox alters oxygen-binding dynamics of hemoglobin so the likelihood of altitude sickness is delayed. This was available in the

US only via prescription. I could have discovered this recommendation in pre-climb literature but instead I arrived with the understanding Diamox would be provided by Kandoo. This information was hidden within one of the e-mails I had received from Rachel Bode. Alarmed I soon learned Trish had packed enough Diamox to support three hikers. Trish donated a blister-pack of Diamox to me to support my climb. Bless her heart.

Prior to this climb I had had one encounter with an individual afflicted with altitude sickness in Nepal. In Jomson just prior to striking-out for Lo Manthang our hiking group was enjoying a lunch in a rustic café. Once we were seated, a heavily-bundled middle-aged man arrived beside us and presented to us as weak and disoriented. A disturbance of sorts developed. He was with a child but was clearly no longer able to look after the child. Some of his friends reported to one of my companions they had just descended from Muktinath - a region of only moderate elevation (3,710 meters). One of our team doctors examined him, recognized he was possibly suffering from altitude sickness and insisted his friends get him down to lower elevations as quickly as possible. Without knowledge one could possibly make light of so-called "altitude sickness" - but in fact it can be fatal.

The Machame Route on Kilimanjaro was also known as the "Whiskey Route". This name had been assigned because the route is known as somewhat difficult but more expensive than the Marangu route. To celebrate the spirit of the route's name Richard and I had considered conveying a bottle of whiskey with us for the purpose of engaging in a regular evening celebratory night cap. However, upon learning of the expected arduousness of the climb we conceded we needed to instead commit our full energies to the hike and to abstain.

Other routes up Kilimanjaro had also been assigned descriptive names. For example, there was the shorter Coca Cola (Marangu) Route with a much lower likelihood of success. Other available routes included Umbwe, Rongai, Shira and Lemosho. Some of these offered better views. Some required more rapid ascents. Instead of ruing the decision we had not undertaken one of the more scenic approaches, I clung to the optimistic prediction "Machame had the highest likelihood of success". Natascha, the blonde-haired, Portsmouth-based organizer of the climb had arranged for us to hike this route without any consultation with the rest of the group and I was grateful. Given our inexperience and collective age, this approach seemed prudent.

During the group meeting, we also learned of the supportive aspects of the hike. There would be four English-proficient Kandoo guides (Lead Guide Freddy plus three other guides: "Obama", "Auguste" and "Raymond" - all Tanzanian), twenty-seven porters and two cooks; thereby creating a small community of forty-two which included ourselves. The numbers of porters and guides seemed clearly excessive but, then, no one had consulted me concerning the logistics. This support amounted to three porters/paying individual.

The proposed route to Uhuru peak on Kibo commenced at Machame Gate (1,800 m) with a climb on **Day 1** to Machame Camp (3,000 m), **Day 2** to Shira Camp (3,850 m), **Day 3** to Baranco Camp (3,950 m) via Lava Tower (4800 m), **Day 4** to Karanga Camp (3,930 m), **Day 5** to Barafu Camp (4,600 m), **Day 6** to Uhuru Peak (5,895 m) then back to Barafu then Mweka Camps (3,100 m) and finally **Day 7** to Mweka Gate (1,800 m). Seeing this route displayed on a flat wall did little to aid me in appreciating the undertaking. Total gain in five days was, therefore 4,829 meters, roughly five km in vertical gain. I ignored the descents, only to later find they were far more arduous than the ascents.

These various camps existed in the the differing climatic zones of Kilimanjaro with Machame Gate located in rainforest, Shira Camp in "moorland", Baranco and Karanga camps in a Low Alpine zone, Barafu in a High Alpine zone and the summit in a Glacial (Arctic-like) zone. A map I located post-climb described the climactic zones differently however. Included were six zones: a cultivated zone (to 1,750 m), a forested zone (to 2,700 m), a moorland zone (to 4,000 m), an Alpine Desert (to 4,900 m) and, finally, a Summit zone (to 6,000 m). Other means are also used to categorize the zones associated with the climb.

Unbeknownst to me prior to this meeting was that we were hiking "on the shoulder of the rainy season" - meaning ours would be the last hike of the season because rains became too prevalent in early-November through early-December to hike. Porters and guides used this one-month rain break to spend time with their families. Because of the threat of rain, we had been advised to bring all manner of clothing including good quality rain gear, water-proof boots and gloves and various thermal layers for multi-layering. Some of the clothing, the 15 kg aforementioned, would be carried by the porters.

Following a brief question and answer period, equipment was distributed to those who needed to rent it. Most rented the better-quality sleeping bags and some, including me, rented hiking poles. Others rented water-proof plastic ponchos, something I came to regret not doing. Freddy also assessed our heart rates and our blood oxygen saturation percentages using a device he attached to our index fingers. Pre-climb Kandoo literature indicated anyone with a resting heart rate exceeding 100 beats per minute (bpm) would not be permitted to climb. All of us fell below the exclusionary barrier. Oxygen saturation was measured with the same device. Based on the "redness" of our circulating hemoglobin, oxygen saturation was calculated by algorithm and displayed on the same device. At this altitude, a "normal" level should be above 95% and I believe all of those assembled scored >95%. Henceforth, we would be tested twice daily during the climb for heart rate and oxygen saturation - at breakfast and at dinner. As we climbed to higher elevations, it was expected oxygen saturation would decline and then hopefully, in adaptation, some individuals' saturation levels might, in fact, climb. Of concern to the guides however, were those whose oxygen saturation fell too low. Should that occur the afflicted individual would be evacuated from the mountain without recourse. I felt reasonably fit and hoped these extreme measures would not be applied to me.

Still, I harbored concerns regarding my cardiovascular, pulmonary and musculoskeletal capabilities. In the prior several months, I had developed a cardiac arrhythmia of some sort I believed was evidence of a pre-ventricular contraction (PVC) - an issue briefly developing 20-30 years earlier for a short period of time. I attributed the present arrhythmia to the stress associated with a particularly lengthy litigation process involving a former employee who had stolen reams of intellectual property and started a competing company in China. During this time my resting heart rate had increased from its normal 70-75 bpm to 85 +/- and I ascribed this to a less efficient heart needing to pump the same amount of blood per unit of time. Fortunately, I no longer harbor this affliction.

I understand one should be responsible and have this checked-out prior to undertaking a climb, but I didn't. Instead, I gave instructions to my wife on how best to divide-up the estate should I perish on the mountain.

Amongst the group a sense of order was appearing. Rich, the chiropodist, seemed to assume a type of "spokesperson-like role" as he seemed calm and collected - a non-excitable and intelligent sort. He also maintained a full head of hair. Richard became respected as a solid male member and levitator of the group. As I had expected, he filled the room with praise, optimism, enthusiasm, humor and mirth. I felt I was struggling with my newly-acquired identity as the orange-haired "sage" of the group. Amongst the women, Natascha, the trek's organizer, was the most animated, entertaining and talkative. This was directly in opposition to her younger red-haired sister Alex who was more quiet. I could imagine them growing up together with Natascha as the protective, sometimes more aggressive, older sister.

Debbie, our most athletic, appeared as the "baby" of the group with a mischievous smile and child-like voice. She periodically asked questions and asserted worries others were more than happy to indulge. Gillian, the pilot, impressed me as calm, serious and ready for the challenge. She did not seem to be a person who could be rattled easily. She considered her words carefully. Trish, Richard's former girlfriend, communicated via non-verbal cues her uncertainty with the undertaking. She, like me, appeared to have prepared little and her apprehension showed. Angie, younger, appeared buoyant and unconcerned. In fact, Angie initially seemed somewhat disconnected from the group - as if she harbored worries elsewhere.

Having been thoroughly and professionally apprised of the hike our group entertained a brief buffet dinner in an adjoining dining room then retreated to our individual rooms to begin the task of sorting gear into three piles: **a)** the *no more than* 15 kg duffle bag a porter would carry, **b)** a day pack (of unlimited weight but which most of us limited to near 7-8 kg) we would carry ourselves and **c)** supplies we could leave behind at the hotel in an unsecured cardboard box. With this accomplished I was fast asleep anticipating, somewhat apprehensively, a 10 AM departure.

Chapter Six
Machame Gate: Embarkation

Naturally a mountain as significant as Kilimanjaro possesses a storied history. Kilimanjaro is the tallest mountain in Africa and the largest free-standing mountain in the world thus making it a necessary destination among international mountain climbers who seek to climb each of the highest mountains on all seven continents - the so-called Seven Summits. This has been an intriguing quest but, after Kilimanjaro, I no longer retain any interest in it. Kilimanjaro consists of three volcanic cones: Kibo (the tallest), Mawenzi (to the East) and Shira to the west. The Kibo cone is 24 km across and its summit (Uhuru) stands at 5,900 meters above mean sea level (AMSL). In fact, the mountain used to be taller but the wall of the Kibo cone collapsed some time ago. "Uhuru" translates from Swahili as "Freedom" and was so-named when Tanzania won its freedom from the UK. When I first became aware of Uhuru Summit I was immediately reminded of Lieutenant Uhuru - an African-American actress in Star Trek and wondered whether her name was derived from Swahili and Kilimanjaro. A lot of thought went into Star Trek, we know.

Kilimanjaro last erupted 150,000 to 200,000 years ago and evidence remains obvious to the untrained geologic eye. Blackened, lichen-encrusted boulders of variable sizes lie scattered about the upper reaches of Kilimanjaro's lunar landscape - difficult to believe these boulders have been lying here undisturbed and quiescent for so long - maybe 10,000 human generations. But, what might be the alternative explanation for the existence of these patient boulders? In geologic time, Kilimanjaro is young and remains an active volcano. In geologic time, we are but the blink of an eye.

In written history Kilimanjaro was first climbed by Hans Meyer and Otto Ehler, both Germans, in 1889 (only 128 years prior to our group's attempt). Yet, Kilimanjaro has existed for millennia near the cradle of human civilization (the Rift Valley) and must certainly have been climbed by indigenous peoples, perhaps my distant ancestors, innumerable times prior. The German effort transpired only a few decades following its first report in Western literature in the mid-1800's. Tanzanian guides reported to me on the importance of Kilimanjaro and of the challenge it provided to young men as proof of their athletic prowess.

In the late-1800's East Africa was divided into German- and British-East Africa with Kilimanjaro lying approximately mid-way between the two colonies. Kilimanjaro became part of German East Africa in 1880. One commonly encountered story, believed a myth, asserts Queen Victoria carved-up the borders between modern day Kenya and Tanzania to give Kilimanjaro to her grandson: Kaiser Wilhelm II of Prussia.

Modern day Tanzania was assembled from a country that intrigued me when I studied classroom maps in grade school. Then the British Empire was depicted in pink on the world maps complementing every classroom. A vast assemblage of pink-colored countries convinced me of the magnanimity of the empire and filled me with pride Canada was part of the British extravagance. Those same maps improbably depicted a pink-colored "Tanganyika". What an esoteric and exotic-sounding place! Tanganyika! It rhymed with Eureka and engendered a somewhat similar emotion in me. Apparently the country's borders included modern-day Tanzania, Burundi and Rwanda. In 1964 modern-day Tanzania was born by the amalgamation of the English colony of British East Africa with the island Sultanate of Zanzibar - hence the name "Tanzania". I do not know why Burundi and Rwanda were jettisoned from this marriage. The combination of Tanganyika with the Zanzibari Sultanate resulted in a polyglot country of multiple languages and faiths - a country failing to present a common or obvious identity - an identity which might otherwise aid in the creation of a national galvanizing import. Borders which made "no sense" were the common result of English', and other nations', expiring colonialism.

In the short time I spent in Tanzania I saw churches, mosques and people who certainly retained more "primitive" faiths such as the traditionally - and colorfully-clad and more-than-elegant Masai children whom I observed tending to livestock next to highways. What sense "Tanzania" made as a singular entity remains enigmatic.

A dominating feature of Kilimanjaro is its snow- and glacier-covered summit. Early photos of Kilimanjaro show glaciers extending far further down the mountain than they do today. Like glaciers everywhere those of Kilimanjaro are in retreat. Eighty-five percent of the glacial cover of Kilimanjaro was lost between 1912 and 2011. Ice cover loss was 1.1%/year between 1912-1953, 1.4%/year in 1954-1989 and accelerated to 2.5%/year in 1990-2007. Because of global warming it is estimated the glaciers of Kilimanjaro will completely vanish by 2060. Our grandchildren may never witness the Snows of Kilimanjaro but will instead be resigned to considering old photographs - a crime of our preceding generations? Are we not all responsible to some extent for this? I drive too many cars, fly too often and my carbon footprint is too large. Yet I soldier onward as do most others - hoping for change.

The white glaciers rising to a crescendo at Uhuru inspired Earnest Hemingway to employ Kilimanjaro and an associated mythical white leopard as metaphors for goodness and for a spiritual journey toward good and immortality in "The Snows of Kilimanjaro". Had Hemingway lived one hundred years later there would have been insufficient snow and glacial cover on Kilimanjaro's summit to so inspire him. We harken to the older times but they are indeed gone. Or nearly gone.

Nowadays Kilimanjaro resides completely within Tanzania but this does not prevent Kenya from coveting Tanzania's trophy. The view of Kilimanjaro is said to be better from the Kenya side (*i.e.*, from the North) of the border and Kenya has naturally used the silhouette of Kilimanjaro in marketing of its abundant assets to tourists.

Aside from the physical aspect of Kilimanjaro, Tanzania is populated by a broad-spectrum of fascinating ethnicities and tribes. While the dominant national language is Swahili, English functions as the *lingua franca* of the nation (a result of British colonialism) with 126 additional extant tribal languages - some of which, like many other marginalized languages, will soon no longer be with us. Like Kilimanjaro's glaciers, rare languages have limited prospect for survival in an increasingly homogenous and populated world - a world that values modern concepts such Nike shoes, numbers of Facebook friends and the concept of Net Worth more than it values the traditions that propelled modern man into the 21st Century. These developments alone are worthy of a discussion I must avoid within the confines of this tome. But before I move on I do emphatically feel the diversities we are losing in languages, peoples, cultures and species are awful and very sad developments. Although the solutions to this challenge are already abundantly clear, most individuals and most nations are unwilling to make the changes needed to circumvent disaster. I count myself amongst the intransigent - maybe not the most intransigent but intransigent nevertheless.

As noted earlier, prior to arriving into Tanzania I was possessed by the irrational thought that I might be quite nervous and feel distinctly "alien" *in country*. But those thoughts never materialized. Instead Tanzanians were accommodating, gentle, fun-loving, humorous and kind. Perhaps these traits were best exemplified by Freddy our lead guide.

Freddy grew up near Moshi and conveyed an abundance of warmth and kindness. He stood at 1.8 meters and was slight - weighing only 60-65 kg. Certainly the rigors associated with the regular summiting of Kilimanjaro would have kept him slim. Freddy betrayed no evidence of extreme strength nor of endurance except he did project an obvious lightness about him. He moved effortlessly. He possessed an ease with himself any man would be proud of and was comfortable among his clients, his fellow guides and the large number of porters he supervised during the climb. There seemed no need for Freddy to resort to any type of coercion or intimidation to animate his acolytes. Instead his kindness and his care for both his clients and co-workers were more than sufficient for him to naturally fulfill the challenging and, for us, important role of lead guide. Of course I could not anticipate the role Freddy would play in helping me in particular. But his role surfaced when needed and I was grateful.

To drive those points home - consider the difficulty in delivering a successful climb to a broad spectrum of clients: young through old, through varying weather conditions, differing nationalities and languages, healthy through physically ill or injured, friendly, bitchy and argumentative, to the summit - all the while maintaining a welcoming, supportive and patient nature. Freddy exemplified the calmness, intelligence and maturity I came to associate with and appreciate about Tanzania - a remarkable amalgamation of over 100 tribes and cultures - somehow able to co-exist without overt conflict. I do not believe Freddy was a wealthy man but what he might have lacked in material wealth he more than made up for via the wealth of his humanity - a wealth I have struggled to emulate. Indeed, Freddy was a gem.

And Freddy was not unique. Each of our remaining guides, I would come to learn, was similarly endowed - so much so, I was quickly made comfortable with all of them. They mirrored my limited experience with the few Tanzanians I had already engaged with at the Bristol Cottages and downtown Moshi. I had met genuine people - people who “owned” far less than me yet were seemingly better people than I might realistically aspire to - people with more intrinsic wealth than me. Could I ever be so genuine? Indeed, the guides provided a daily reminder that we make impacts through our actions and with what we say - however small those actions may be.

After meeting Freddy, we slept early in our rooms at the Stella Rose but, drop by drop, dribble by dribble, I became aware and concerned Kilimanjaro's weather might be changing - and not for the better. At 5 AM I began to vaguely perceive a distinct staccato patter on the galvanized carport outside of my window. I tried to convince myself the sound could not possibly be the sound of rain. It must instead be wind twisting some ill-defined aspect of the hotel's exterior! However, within minutes a torrential downpour announced itself on the percussive zinc. I immediately understood - this might not be an entirely dry climb.

I was quickly upright and assessed the intensity of the rain from my balcony where I found Debbie also on her balcony next to my room - similarly ruing the sudden deterioration in weather. Resigned to the possibility of hiking in rain I retreated to my bed and managed to find some more sleep only to awake an hour later.

Breakfast was ready: pancakes, French toast, pineapple, papaya, scrambled eggs and sausage. There, I commiserated regarding the change in weather with my group. After checking the internet Rich reported poor weather was predicted for the week. I'm sure he was disappointed yet he remained outwardly resolute.

Richard absorbed Rich's warning and studied his plate of food. A crease crossed his forehead. He understood the implications of Rich's report but I understood he too was resolved to tolerate anything Mother Nature might direct his way. Such was Richard's optimistic habit. I tried to take my cues from Richard and Rich.

No one, if they were troubled or if they harbored doubts, voiced their concerns. Instead, to an individual, each projected a buoyant and confident demeanor. Our demeanor was infectious. If we individually entertained concerns, others' confidence aided in dispelling any reservations we might individually consider. What would one call this? Was this the definition of a team?

At 10 AM under threatening skies our group collected stoically in front of the Stella Rose, had our duffle bags weighed and, together with our guides and a few of our porters departed for the Moshi outdoor market to purchase some last minute supplies - water bottles, ponchos and drinks. Richard was cognizant he was going-off alcohol for a significant period of time and I agreed to set my Casio's stopwatch feature so we could monitor the hours Richard remained "off alcohol" in case he wished, at any point during the climb, to brag. We visited a jewelry store featuring Tanzanite - a locally-derived blue gemstone said to be 1/10,000th as common as diamonds and various other Tanzanian objects d'art. There, a rail-thin, shotgun-wielding and uniformed guard endured at the front entrance in a shabby navy uniform while we shopped. The purpose of visiting this store and thereby delaying our hike was not clear to me except any purchases might have involved added compensation directed toward either the guides or to the bus driver.

A note on Tanzanite: this gem is derived from a single mine in Tanzania, identified as "precious" by Tiffany's and marketed as Tanzanite beginning in the late 1960's. Indeed, Tanzanite is incredibly deep in color and beautiful. Its blue color is contributed by the presence of vanadium. An internet search reveals its abundant use as a "healing stone".

I had little interest in these pre-climb distractions. Mostly I was excited to get going, to get to the "jumping-off" spot: Machame Gate--- reputed to be a little over an hour away. It was the put-up or shut-up moment - the place where the rubber would meet the road, the moment I had anticipated for months. I knew this was going to be tough - possibly the toughest challenge of my life. I felt mentally prepared and wanted to start as soon as possible. I felt more than ready. All these delays were somewhat disturbing.

But once back on the shuttle I grew apprehensive. I became aware Gillian had arrived from Zambia harboring an effusive wet cold - a cold I absolutely understood to be highly contagious. Seated directly across from me on the bus she suffered miserably - sneezing, wiping at her runny nose with a well-used Kleenex and coughed. Any reasonable person would worry. I did not wish to catch a cold right at the beginning of an arduous climb. Hence, when opportunity first presented itself I escaped to the rear of the bus - to the quizzical attention of a few porters who had similarly situated themselves. I trusted the half hour I had already spent adjacent Gillian had not proved sufficient for her to transfer her aggressive and dripping viral infection to me.

Gillian's arrival with so virulent a contagion jeopardized the enjoyment of the climb for all of us. I questioned myself - was it petty of me to be so apprehensive? Was it selfish of her to not cancel her trip and arrive in so poor health? Gillian was the individual who had conceptualized the effort. That was important. But she was truly suffering despite trying to remain chipper. Nevertheless, I was on edge.

We wound our way on crowded streets to the outskirts of Moshi and then westward to the turn-off to Machame Gate - about 20 km along the two-lane Tanzania-Kenya highway - the same highway I had taken to Moshi from the airport three nights prior. From there our bus climbed in elevation through small towns - each surrounded by dry, cultivated fields and arid orchards. Inattentive children darted here and there, women ambled carrying sundry loads in baskets on their heads, straight backs with straight ebony necks, open-air store fronts made of cinder block painted pale blue, pink and taupe, Masai children, seemingly independent of the extended community, tending their stock in adjacent fields - their garments both flamboyant and elegant. The driver swerved to miss on-coming traffic, passed others and avoided motorcycles. All this caused the bus to sway back and forth in a rhythm found only in the developing world. Pendulous clouds hung perilously low to the road. I wanted to ask the driver to stop so I might take some photographs - especially of the Masai. But I understood photos would need to wait for another visit. We were all a little on edge -

anticipating the unknown. The scenery *en* route to Machame was not our goal. Instead we were privately considering what lay ahead and individually wished to get the effort underway.

By 12:30 PM we reached Machame Gate (1,800 meters AMSL) - an elevation constituting the base of Kilimanjaro's "Tropical Rain Forest". This zone extended from 1,800 meters up through 2,800 meters and would provide bookends to the bulk of our first day's effort. We disgorged enthusiastically from the bus and, amongst dozens of enthusiastic Tanzanian porters, made our way toward a nondescript government registration kiosk. There we signed-in with our names, occupations, ages, guide name, guide group and signatures. Because so many hiking groups had arrived at a similar time we were mandated to wait for our turn to embark in order to prevent larger assemblies of climbers from the necessity of overtaking one another during the more treacherous aspects of the first day's hike. Hence we lingered under a zinc-roofed shelter (it had started to sprinkle) and made the best of an unexceptional boxed lunch packed for each of us - cold fried chicken, a muffin, a chocolate bar and some tasteless powdery cookies. Upon our arrival our porters and cooks departed for Machame Camp - not subject to the same transit restrictions as us.

Adjacent to Machame Gate I was more than disappointed to find myself lingering amongst dozens of other white tourists - each displaying hundreds of dollars of equipment and each, including me, exhibiting the impatient attitude of wanting to get going as soon as possible. French tourists. British tourists. Italian tourists: mostly youthful - in their 20's. Until now I had been enjoying a fly-on-the-wall cultural experience in Moshi and in the Stella Rose. Now my cultural experience had been overwhelmingly diluted by these inconsiderate intruders. Kilimanjaro is mine I had thought. Machame Gate presented to me a measure of reverse, and unfortunate, culture shock. As quickly as possible I wished to divest myself with this reminder of the cultures from which I had derived.

We frittered-away time with photography and light banter. Nearby, at the entry to the starting point, a large rusted metal arch inscribed with the words "Machame Gate" stood over the road. Our trekking group (named "One Trek Mind") gathered beneath it and photographed one another to commemorate the beginning of our climb. As we did several Tanzanian men, seemingly held away from us by an invisible barrier lying across the road, fluttered colorful flags of various nations in our direction in the futile hope one of us might derive from the country of the flag they waved - their hope - upon reaching the summit we might claim our achievement in honor of our respective countries. In addition, a large well-constructed wooden sign, inscribed in brilliant yellow with names and distances required to attain to all further camps leading to Uhuru Summit, provided an additional excuse for more photos. Similar signs were situated in subsequent camps and were always employed as photo ops when we arrived into each camp.

In this manner an entire hour of idle time was consumed as we arranged and rearranged our hiking group for various photographs - with and without guides, shouting, as *per* our guides' requests - "Kili", "Pole Pole", "Jambo!" and "hakuna matata". For the moment we were a jolly lot.

Chapter Seven
Suffering

Just after noon we departed the steamy enclave where we had consumed our meagre lunch. A continuing light rain necessitated donning of rain gear. Being well-instructed by Freddy at our pre-climb meeting we had each crammed rain gear into our day packs. If rain asserted itself, appropriate attire would be at hand and not in a departed porter's duffle bag.

I wasn't worried about getting wet. My GoreTex kit was "state-of-the art" - with zippered legs, a zippered hood and miscellaneous pockets located wherever one might imagine one might need them. GoreTex was engineered to breathe - to not cloy like impermeable plastic gear. I had also packed rain-proof gloves and boots. At least I was going to be dry and comfortable if it should rain. Indeed, I felt badly for those who had resorted to renting non-breathable plastic rain gear at the Stella Rose.

The night prior I had not slept well. I had woken at 2:30 AM and re-packed my gear during the rain storm until 4:30 AM, slept again then finally rose near dawn - this being the remnant of my jet lag. Finding the hotel's erratic internet operating I texted with my parents, my sister and with a colleague in Indonesia (Yudha) in the intervening time prior to breakfast. Yudha had put together a sweet video of his students, ages 6-10, standing together under a mango tree shouting "I love you Pak Neil" ("Pak" being an Indonesian honorific for an "uncle"). This wish of good luck was followed by the well-coordinated placement of tiny hands on mouths and with the blowing of big wet Indonesian kisses toward the camera while simultaneously shouting "Mwahh!". Incredibly the Indonesian children were wishing me good luck on the climb! And no wonder Yudha had encouraged his acolytes to wish me luck. Two years prior I had climbed another volcano in Indonesia (Mt. Rinjani, in Lombok) with Yudha, his Indonesia friends and my marginally-capable

Malaysian nephew Juju. There I did not fare so well and needed to be supported for the last two km of a slippery and unforgiving footpath - this accompanied with torrential rain. I had buckled from exhaustion following three days of slipping and sliding amongst sinewy roots continually tripping me and causing me and others to fall into uninviting intervening crevasses. Yudha understood I was not invincible - hence his heartfelt video. The challenge of Kilimanjaro certainly exceeded Rinjani and I surmised he justifiably doubted my ability.

The first day's hike stretched 11.7 km with a 1,200-meter altitude gain and appropriated 5.5 increasingly-miserable hours of our lives. This effort equated to a slothful pace of 2.1 km/hr. Our four guides generously interspersed themselves amongst our group thus fashioning a twisting, caterpillar-like, single-file of thirteen hikers. While the Kandoo guides each wore a bright orange jacket the remainder of our group exhibited a broad spectrum of gloomy colors - shadowed blue, olive green, monochromatic gray and uninspired black. We noted later in the week other climbing groups, particularly those from Italy and France, had made more effort to both coordinate their colors and to wear more fashionable gear - as if their national pride was at stake. In this manner they presented a more striking, indeed one could argue, a more intimidating presence on the trails.

Periodically the sequence of our team members shifted and different conversations thereby sprung up between the newly-adjacent individuals. Some hiked quietly. Some never stopped talking. Amongst the women, conversations developed among not only between those who were directly adjacent but across our entire span of hikers - a distance of 20-40 meters! At times I was privy to two or three simultaneous conversations amongst them. In addition, the guides were always nearby and answered any questions we harbored regarding the day's effort - "How much longer?" "What is our altitude?" "When can we have a loo break?" I recall plenty of questions also concerning precipitation, altitude sickness, flora, fauna, and geology.

In many places the path had been well-constructed atop a spongy earthen base interrupted by diagonally-placed four- to five-cm bamboo stocks which prevented water from creating destructive rivulets from running vertically within the path. In this manner running water was diverted both downward and sideways and off the path: very clever.

Even without precipitation the rainforest was clammy. Elephant ear-sized emerald leaves hung low to the ground laboring with burdening moisture. The temperature seemed near the dew point because a stationary mist hung adjacent to the path and within the canopy of upper foliage. The path was soft - evidence of a recent downpour and of decaying detritus, and absorbed the impact of our steps without a sound. With so much moisture in the air breathing became labored. My clothing began to cloy.

Rain fell intermittently but as the day wore on it came in abundance - like a small waterfall. When breaks in the increasingly heavy precipitation appeared I fervently and naively prayed the downpour had concluded for good. There was otherwise plenty to see and enjoy along the path - bird life, a diverse spectra flowers (mostly very small and exhibiting delicate colors), rare Blue monkeys and a dense stand of green, yellow and brown foliage - some decaying. Accumulating moisture became so pervasive all I could focus on was the physical requirement of placing of one foot in front of the other and then repeating. It was becoming increasingly difficult to appreciate all of the beauty on offer.

As the afternoon progressed, accumulating moisture obligated a meditative state amongst us -we retreated into our own thoughts. Exertion and clamminess were becoming distinctively oppressive. I felt I was trapped in a greenhouse. Periodically I departed my body and gazed downward. I pitied the moist caterpillar-like labor of our group.

Within an hour of departing Machame Gate, the sleeves of my jacket were soaked through to my skin. I may as well have not been wearing the jacket at all. It made no sense. I had been led to believe GoreTex was completely waterproof and was able to "breathe"! Thereafter water continued to seep through to my chest and legs dampening the short-sleeve shirt and jeans I was wearing beneath. Angie, the Portsmouth lady who had bravely decided to quit smoking coincident with the initiation of the climb, had generously donated a waterproof daypack cover to me but this did not protect the portion of my pack adjacent to my neck. Water seeped down my neck and then down my back. The interior of my pack absorbed this and was becoming soggy. I was carrying my iPhone and Nikon camera in the pack and became concerned the moisture might damage them both. Hence, at a break I removed and wrapped both in a small cotton towel I had packed to wipe sweat from my face.

By the three-hour mark of the hike I was more than miserable. Rain had penetrated my jacket to a degree where I was no longer certain it was of any value at all. If I had removed the T-shirt I wore underneath I could have wrung water from it. It could not have accumulated more moisture if I had been swimming clothed in a lake. Because my lower extremities were less exposed to the direct rain they were not quite as saturated.

Also I was beginning to experience a sharp pain in the uppermost portions of both left and right quadriceps (thigh muscles). This grew in intensity - at four hours into the hike, each step invoked the sensation of red-hot knives, like kebab skewers, being thrust deep into my legs, to the femur, and then twisted. Every lift of each leg to plant another step had become excruciating- the worst discomfort imaginable - a ten on a scale of ten - searing white-hot. This was a level of agony I had not experienced in my legs prior.

It did not seem reasonable to me I could damage my quadriceps in so short a period of time. But what other explanation was there? I was certain I was shredding the contractile proteins of my skeletal muscles and would be unable to continue onward the next day. My spirits sagged. "This is *really* fucking miserable." "*What* was I thinking?" I thought of the comforts of my home; my red leather couch with a readily-activated, propane-powered fireplace nearby, dry, clean towels available anytime, my patient and understanding wife, accessible food, Malay cooking. My children close at hand; close enough to call or visit if need be. Friends. Friends I could go out with and drink beer and eat pizza with. "Never again I convinced myself." Indeed, this was lunacy.

Coincident with becoming completely water-logged and with the arrival of the intense pain in my quads, my ankles too began to twinge; first my left ankle and then my right. The hurt was originating from the point where the tibia meets the talus; a familiar problem of mine. In past hikes, I had taken appropriate doses of left-over hydrocodone to mitigate this; hydrocodone left over from root canals. This time I had forgotten to transport spare opioids to stave off discomfort.

Within another half hour, the small of my back, the sacrum also began to cramp sharply and object to each step. What muscles or tendons could possibly be connected to my sacrum? The ankle pain was expected, this was not. What might be the next part of my body to fail? I was feeling like a Chevy Vega, the ill-conceived and unreliable 1970s General Motors solution to expensive gasoline.

Wishing to find a silver lining in this otherwise dark cloud, I realized my deteriorating skeletal muscles were, at a minimum, fully distracting me from being wet and cold - like biting on a bullet prior to surgery in pre-anesthetic days.

I began to score each of my five weak points: left and right quads, left and right ankles and sacrum, by assigning each a pain score of

0-10 individually and then summing them. In this manner I could objectively determine whether I was experiencing stable pain or whether my body was deteriorating further. Both quads burned with scores of 10/10 while the score in my ankles and sacrum hovered near 5/10 each - leading to a combined score of 35/50 when I initially conceived of the method. To distract me, I considered whether my daughter, a patent attorney, might patent this scoring system. The thought was quickly discarded when I understood it contained no novelty.

Our team encountered some "technical climbing" aspects of the hike on Day 1 classified as moderately difficult - especially given the discomfort we were experiencing. In such "technical areas" we ascended treacherous, wet and untrustworthy rocks; this attended with pain scores of 35+. The technical challenges were not life-threatening but if one had fallen one could have done serious damage to one's self - perhaps broken an arm or leg. I removed my gloves in order to adequately feel the texture of the rock and thereby achieve some level of confidence in my purchase. It didn't matter whether my gloves were on or not. My gloves were already soaked through to my skin even though they, like my GoreTex kit, had been touted as "waterproof". Water, mixed with sweat, was running down my face, dripping off my chin and down across my chest.

Step-by-step, "Pole Pole", Step-by-Step, "Pole Pole". And on and on and on; like a dirge. In this manner, I lurched toward 1,200 meters in altitude gain making the best use of my unprepared, aging frame. I used techniques I had used on other hikes: in difficult terrain repeating "Ev-er-y Step A Safe Step" in cadence with each step consuming one syllable of the phase. "One, Two, Three, Four". "One, Two, Three, Four". "One, Two, Three, Four". In more vertiginous terrain I counted fifty steps then rested until my heart rate declined to less than 130 beats per minute. I could count my heart beats by the thumping in my chest - no direct contact with my carotid nor the radial artery in my wrist were needed. Indeed, my companions could likely have ascertained by heart rate by simply listening carefully from their distances or by observing my pulsating chest.

Then it began again. Over and over. “Pole Pole”. “One, Two, Three, Four”. “Ev-er-y Step A Safe Step”. I stayed with the group trying my best not to lag. Others seemed to be struggling as well. Trish was hanging back and was gratefully slowing down the entire group - like a trusted and invaluable anchor. This was turning into an incredible and horrible slog.

Looking backward and forward along the group it was clear no one was doing well. Heads were cast downward amid the foggy pall. We could as easily have been attending a funeral - such was the prevailing demeanor. The only items missing were the casket and an audible elegy. All outerwear was soaked and dripping. No one was talking. No one was deriving enjoyment from anything.

The rain became torrential. Plastic ware bore the sheen of moisture with water coursing from its lowermost edges. Water-proof clothing showed evidence of betraying its purpose - surfaces impregnated with moisture betrayed a more depressing hue. Our leather boots had taken on the darker colors of sodden and unhappy leather. Fog further enveloped us and daylight was diminishing - revealing only tedious grays and browns. The once vibrant greens of the adjacent foliage had retreated into a barely-perceptible drab olivine.

Two-thirds into the day’s climb I lost my footing. My boot slipped in the water-laden sod as I struggled, with the aid of a convenient tree trunk, to climb a steep earthen slope to regain access to a path. My inelegant collapse, the first recorded within our group, was witnessed by several and a few generously shouted “Are you OK?”. Of course I was OK! My dignity might have taken a “hit” but I was intact otherwise! The slip broke my GoreTex gear *in-* covering both my jacket and pants fully in mud from both knees and elbows downward. I didn't care. I had my mind firmly fixed upon the estimation of the remaining time our guides had intermittently provided and counted the hours and then minutes until the expected appearance of the promised destination: Machame Camp. It would be like arriving into heaven.

While others stopped periodically to devour carbohydrate-rich snacks, I was too miserable to do so. I had some biscuits and trail mix squirreled away within the bowels of my sodden day pack but did not have the energy nor the hunger to disassemble my kit and locate them. Opening my pack would have required more effort. Instead, during intermittent breaks, I rested, nay, brooded against a convenient rock. I lay my hiking poles down, closed my eyes, thought good thoughts and willed strength might return to my legs. When Rich or Richard came by to talk I worked at remaining chipper and optimistic. But I was struggling to avoid negative thoughts. Why had I paid *all* this money to fly *all* this way and do *this*? Might it not have been less expensive and more productive to consult a mental health professional instead? Should I not, at my age, learn to enjoy gardening? Or, crocheting?

As our first day's hike progressed into its fifth hour it had become increasingly obvious to me there was a high probability I would *not* be able to summit Kilimanjaro. I fought against this obvious assessment but could not eliminate it from my mind. It was a sad realization - like a defeat. Still, I had not experienced too many defeats in life and was reticent to accept this one.

My quadriceps were still burning with the worst imaginable pain with every step. Each stride was more than torture. My recently-improvised scale was exceeding 40/50. Every part of my body was beginning to hurt. A headache had set in. I concentrated again on good things in my life and imagined how quickly the remaining hour of the day's hike should evaporate. What was an hour? Nothing really. I ignored others and focused on getting through the hike. I had no choice. If I couldn't get to Machame Camp it would be a longer hike back to the start - back to Machame Gate. Getting to Machame Camp would be easier, at this point, than giving up. I willed my way forward. Tomorrow would be a new day - a day when I could evacuate back to the hotel.

Occasionally I assessed others' conditions. They too were not appearing to be at all joyful. Trish and Angie were both lagging - trailing well behind the group. Two guides walked with them offering encouragement and one relieved Trish of her day pack. No one had offered to take my pack and I'm not sure I would have surrendered it had they asked. I tried to appear sufficiently robust so there would be no question of my ability to carry my own pack. Richard and Rich appeared the be handling Day 1 handily. They inhabited a small damp knot near the head of the line - occasionally exchanging small words of encouragement - Richard in his baggy khaki shorts overlying black leggings. Despite the rigor, I would periodically hear Richard's loud chortle. Whether his heart was truly supportive of such levity or not was impossible for me to discern. But his enthusiasm helped me fight onward.

"<u>Ev-er-y</u> <u>Step</u> <u>a Safe</u> <u>Step</u>". "One, Two, Three, Four". "Pole Pole". "Pole Pole". And on and on we went.

I thought of the instinct of human survival. What we were doing was an effort; however, it was trivial compared to those other more well-known and more-heroic efforts - the Bataan and Sandakan Death Marches - those long jungle marches in WWII in the Philippines and on the Island of Borneo. On those marches one's collapse was a death sentence. Kilimanjaro is trifling in comparison. If I collapsed I knew they wouldn't shoot me.

By 5 PM light was becoming increasingly limited and a smothering, granular fog was settling in amongst us. Colors, reflecting our spirits, deteriorated further into a narrower range of dim gray and mildly tangible shit brown. Precipitation had retreated into a slow but steady drizzle. But it didn't matter if it rained or not. We were fully waterlogged. Even the guides hiked in a resigned manner - knowing their clients were suffering and there was little they could do to rekindle any optimism within us - optimism that had existed only six hours prior and which had been fully extinguished.

To provide succor, the guides would periodically announce "45 more minutes" or "30 more minutes" and I would cling to those predictions as if they had been chiseled into granite and then calculated the expected arrival times on my watch. I was timing the passing of each minute and as a result I became more discouraged when 15 minutes of a remaining 45-minute hike brought us to a subsequent prediction of "40 more minutes". The guides' times were slippery - possibly intentionally misleading to help us endure. Or was this "Tanzanian time?" Whichever it was I was not appreciating the guides' imprecise appreciation of time. I needed accurate timing to properly calibrate the expenditure of my limited remaining strength.

The sound of the rain was audible on our collective rain gear - a staccato sound of misery. We almost functioned as a collective - a wet ambulatory organism - like those black, half-meter long worms I came to loathe in Shikoku.

Ultimately we reached a muddy plateau and through the thickening fog I discerned the subdued colors of rust-colored tents in the muddled distance - perhaps one-quarter km away. Even though my quadriceps were drained of energy and continued to rage I experienced a glimmer of hope I might find a tent and have opportunity to remove my wet clothes and mercifully lie down. If I didn't "pass" during the night, in the morning I would decide whether I could continue or should more fittingly retreat. Perhaps there would be enough support available to carry me down to Machame Gate - supine on a stretcher. Or, if need be, shoot me like a dog. All that was imperative was getting into my tent, lying down, getting my boots off and replacing my wet clothing with something dry and warm. My duffle bag, should it be available, contained the promise of dry clothes. There should be a tent for me. Thank God I'm not sharing a tent.

Such was my diminishment.

We entered Machame Camp and regrettably needed to first sign-in at a government hut before making our ways to our individual tents. By this time light had almost completely deserted us - we were well beyond dusk. We clambered down a gentle 2-meter slope to the "Kandoo Adventures" camping area - each insufferable step downward reminding me acutely this - for better or worse - was the welcome end of my Kilimanjaro foolishness.

I was in my tent. I had been shown which tent was mine by one of the porters and was pleased to find my familiar black duffle bag secured safely inside. All was dry. I lay down in the diminishing light and stared vacantly upward. "What have I done?" "How am I going to extricate myself from this fucking mess?" "I don't belong here."

Like an exfoliating reptile I peeled-off my saturated leather boots, socks, pants, underwear and shirt and, except for my boots, replaced them with dry versions. I had worn a white silk interior layer of socks with a red exterior woolen layer - as *per* some on-line recommendation. The dampness that had passed through the leather of my boots (or perhaps the sweat from my feet) had caused the red woolen socks to bleed their color into my white socks leaving them a mottled pink.

My wet clothes had no chance of drying out overnight so I wrung what water I could from them outside of my tent and secured them in a few spare Ziploc bags- each bag weighing near one kg with their accumulated moisture. Without sun and opportunity to dry these clothes, I knew these items would mold over the ensuing several days. My duffle bag would certainly weigh over the 15 kg limit but I didn't care. The porters didn't carry scales on the mountain. They would likely not notice my duffle bag had gained in weight. I discarded concern and swallowed some Aleve - an analgesic I had some confidence in. I was in a sense moving toward "survival mode". Some anger had risen in me. Maybe I was just angry at myself.

Resting supine for thirty minutes, the throbbing in my left and right quadriceps, ankles and back began to subside. I was informed dinner would soon be ready in the "mess tent" - our first of many visits to this peculiar venue. There I reassuringly learned, as in "misery tends to love company", others had also suffered and had grown uncertain of their abilities to continue. Trish, Richard's ex-girlfriend was nauseous and cramping throughout her legs and back. Natascha, the blonde elder sister of Alex was gripped by a "severe" headache and felt disoriented. Debbie, the youngest and most athletic of our group, was "cold and miserable" and had decided quit - to retreat to Machame Gate in the morning. She was the first to have been defeated by Day 1. Trish, 10 minutes later informed the group she too was discontinuing her hike. I felt badly for her as I felt we had developed a meaningful bond the previous day. We all felt badly for both her and Debbie but no one wanted to reinforce any decision of theirs to quit. We were hopeful some buoyancy of spirit, some mending of the body, would return determination to both of them by sunrise. Still, I harbored a belief Day 1 of the hike might claim three of our group of nine: Debbie, Trish and me. Truth be told.

Gillian, the freckle-faced and energetic pilot from Zambia, still retained her dripping cold and felt miserable but otherwise did her best to extend support and mirth to the group. I have no record in my journal of Alex's, Richard's or Rich's conditions. Perhaps I did not have the energy required to observe. But a photograph of Richard in the mess tent in Machame Camp betrays a grim-faced and unenthusiastic man.

I did not express my own misgivings about continuing but I understood fully one-third of our initial cast of hikers was considering "baling" prior to continuing with Day 2. We each held our decisions close to our chests. None of us wished to quit. A decision to quit was anathema to our individual perceptions of our abilities and vigor. But our newly-acquired realities of our physical abilities were pressing down heavily upon us. I kept thinking "I am 63 years-old. What the fuck?": a repetitive theme of this narrative.

Dinner was served: hot chocolate and coffee with cucumber soup, tilapia, fried potatoes and vegetables after which we completed our "health check". That such an extravagant meal could be available after so ridiculous a day was inconceivable to me. My resting heart rate (RHR) was worryingly high (110 beats per minute, the highest of our group of nine) but my oxygen saturation remained reassuringly high (97%). I was hopeful my elevated resting heart rate had developed because I had consumed a coffee just prior to the assessment. We were informed concern with our RHR would develop when our resting heart rates exceeded 120 (not 100 as we had previously been informed). Displaying elevated heart rates we would be evacuated without recourse - like naughty children. We had each earlier agreed such afflicted people would not be allowed to argue about any decision the guides made. I felt I was already worryingly close to the mandatory evacuation threshold. "Might my evacuation happen tomorrow? Or might I endure a day or two longer?" Those were my private thoughts.

After dinner, we were given an overview of the next day's unfortunate challenge by Freddy and Auguste - two of our four guides. None of us were in a mood to hear this expedition might continue.

According to Freddy the second day of the hike was expected to be less demanding than today's. On this evening following the first day of hiking a less demanding hike was all that mattered to me. It was to be an 850-meter ascent to Shira camp; a 5- to 6-hour "lark".

Weather remained an unknown. We would rise early - 6:30 AM, have breakfast at 7 AM and try to leave camp by 8AM in order to complete our hike prior to the arrival of rain. Following this overview our demoralized group, like beaten dogs, retreated across a well-trodden and slippery portion of Machame Camp to our respective tents near 8:00 PM.

The group retained no interest in analysis nor in rehashing of the day's efforts. It had been universally understood by all to have been an awful experience; an unfortunate torture none of us could have anticipated. A wariness, nay, a strong apprehension had flourished amongst us. Had we all over-estimated our abilities?

Rich, Gillian and I possessed single tents. On this first night my tent was located right amongst others' tents and I harbored some concern my snoring might become an "issue". But I was also concerned others' snoring might similarly keep me awake - such was the proximity with which our tents had been pitched. Humorously Richard shared a tent with Trish- his ex-girlfriend. I detected no complaints from either as they made their way toward their cozy tent - a tent young lovers might consider too small. Debbie and Angie shared a tent as did Natascha and Alex- the somewhat enigmatic sisters. The three of us who slept as "singles" had adequate room to accommodate a 3-foot wide roll-out mat, duffle bag and backpack. However, the people who doubled-up must certainly have been cramped. Two roll-out mats would have consumed more than the entire floor area of the tents. This would necessitate sleeping in and around the added duffle bags and back packs. Still, Richard, Trish, Natascha and Alex endured without complaint - a stiff upper lip.

Once back in my tent I methodically assessed my physical and mental competencies. I knew I had unwittingly pushed myself beyond what I was capable of accomplishing.

Can I realistically continue?

The intense pain I had felt with every step in my quads had largely dissipated even though I understood I had damaged my quadriceps' muscle fibers appallingly.

Might I repair them overnight?

I knew contractile proteins were long-lived proteins and would require days (not hours) to repair. Muscle damage is not quickly repaired; that much I knew. My urine was still a proper color of pale yellow - betraying no traces of the rusts and browns of myoglobin degradation products associated with rhabdomyolysis - some solace. My physical degradation could be worse.

I was completely exhausted. I considered the distress and degradation of my psyche I had endured and estimated it arose from a combination of three factors: **a)** jetlag [I had been in-country for 3 days only and had slept poorly the night before], **b)** discomfort associated with being completely sopping wet and **c)** being in what I understood was marginal physical condition.

Searching for reasons for hopefulness, I considered **a)** any lingering jetlag should dissipate soon enough, **b)** it might not rain as heavily (or at all) on subsequent days and **c)** my "physical condition" should improve as the climb progressed (as long as I had not done irreparable harm to my thigh muscles). All this contributed to a limited sense of optimism.

Following two more Aleves, coffee, dinner, a little bit of jocularity and some rest I made a specific but unjustified optimistic note in my Kilimanjaro journal "I might survive Day 2". I estimated a substantial aspect of my leg pain might have arisen from inflammation. I willed the anti-inflammatory aspect of Aleve to work its magic as I slept.

Looking back, I am surprised I discovered any measure of confidence after such an awful day. Still I rued my decision to not seek out an opioid prior to departure. An doctor would argue the discomfort one wishes to cloak with an opioid is an important protectant - a signal - instead of medicating one's self and shielding one's self, one should rest instead. How could I disagree? But on this day had they been available in my kit I'd have gobbled them down in fistfuls.

I took my second half-Diamox of the day hoping it would help me more quickly acclimate to the increasing elevation. The warmth and dryness of my thick sleeping bag, my full stomach and the diminution of my nagging discomfort allowed me to quickly drift into a welcome and restorative slumber. Perhaps dreams were at hand.

Chapter Eight
A Reason for Optimism

Without equivocation Day 1 was more than awful. It was without a doubt the most miserable and painful experience I had ever endured. Sorrow and suffering- they must be related. But if one considers the ramifications of suffering, there may be value in challenging one's self and in learning to understand and accommodate the pain engendered by perceived heroic efforts. So many people climb mountains. And no one says it is easy.

What did I learn from enduring Day 1? There might be a time in the distant future where this suffering has become a distant memory but still informs me. Perhaps this can make me a better person. Perhaps some day I will be retired and will reflect on this exact story while resting on a floral-patterned rattan chair in Hawaii, enjoying my second cup of coffee of the morning or my third gin and tonic in the evening. There today's suffering may compel me to appreciate others' challenges, their miseries and my relative good fortune. I hope today's lessons might also compel me to reach out and attempt to lessen others' sufferings. Those were the "let's try to find a silver lining in this ordeal" thoughts I considered alone in my tent.

On this first night on Kilimanjaro I slept somewhat fitfully. Asleep at 8:15 PM I was awake from 2:30 until 4 AM and then slept a further two hours until 6 AM - a decent eight hours of sleep - enough I surmised to carry me through the day. Still, midway through the night I re-checked my resting heart rate and was alarmed to find it remained at a worryingly high 110 bpm - very near the 120 bpm mandatory evacuation, dignity-be-damned, imperative.

We woke to a heavy and gray overcast. Patches of mist swirled through camp like wary foxes hoping for a free meal. The temperature hovered near 11-12 °C. As the ceiling of my tent lightened into a burnt and luminescent orange, I was reassured to discover my resting heart rate had fallen to 88 bpm! Later, just prior to breakfast it had declined even more remarkably to 73 bpm. "Hell! At this rate of decline, it might not be beating at all within 24 hours!"

What a pleasant surprise! I had not yet become the decrepit old man I was beginning to contemplate only a few hours prior. Further, the severe pain I had experienced in my upper left and right quadriceps the day prior had vanished in totality! In totality! What could be the explanation for so rapid a recovery? Had I willed my legs to recover? Had the intake of eggs the day prior allowed the eggs' high quality proteins to efficiently repair the damaged contractile proteins in my legs? Perhaps I retained the ability, as Indian mystics do when they intentionally slow their heart rates, to direct my body's internal workings and to repair my legs. I was perplexed but satisfied. Whatever the explanation, I decided when I returned to home, I would bottle it and sell it.

A quiet night on this lower shoulder of Kilimanjaro had passed. Worries that had immobilized me the night prior were waning. As the sky lightened most of us had somehow regained a new and optimistic consciousness. Porters too, exhausted the night before, had become more animated. The camp was abuzz. We were alive. We were thriving. We were far from the securities offered by the comfortable confines provided by our couches, our chesterfields, our cots, our hammocks and our sofas. For the moment they were not missed.

Emerging larva-like from my tent I found the camp filled with an abundance of inquisitive and boisterous White-necked Ravens (*Corvus albicollis*) who were seemingly animated by a great deal of human conversation and booming East African music. Moving past the first day had transported all of us into a new and unexpected new world, possibly a better world.

The ravens, perched confidently on nearby rocks, observed the campers for anything food-like we might drop or toss in their direction - twisting their heads quizzically - their charcoal-colored eyes carefully attuned to any possibility of sustenance or perhaps opportunity to share survival skills. In this manner they made a living. These were large ravens- reaching almost 1 kg and a length of 40-50 cm. Their beaks were robust - well-designed for heavy work. Like crows they projected an abundant intellect and confidence. It was odd we had not noticed any of these stealthy birds the day before. Perhaps they had just arrived.

Conversation and laughter emanated not only from our camp but from the dozen or so other camps pitched on the same puddle-covered escarpment. A special blend of Tanzanian and Western music resonated from the assortment of camps and animated the porters' activities. Some porters danced - their Rastafarian hair flailing - all of them lithe. Most maintained an enduring and genuine smile as they went about their busy work - cooking, packing, piling, lugging and talking. They worked alone and in clusters.

Because this was the first I had seen of our encampment in the light I took time to study its layout. All of the structures I could discern had clearly been ferried by the porters the day prior. Within an hour each construction would be disassembled and transported to the next camp. I estimated each porter carried 20 kg - a weight ¼-1/3rd of their weight.

Our Kandoo Adventures enclave included six orange and beige Mountain Hardware tents arranged in neat rows and a sizable black "mess tent" with two 2-meter-long folding tables and nine chairs. Porters, guides and cooks shared similar large black tents - perhaps eight men to a tent, that were located 30-meters away. And finally we were blessed with a "toilet tent". This tent asserted itself imposingly amongst us as a sentinel - tall and stately. Its lowermost dimensions were approximately 1.5 meters square; however, it stood at over 2.5 meters tall and, with its entryway typically unzippered, it flapped unceremoniously in an ever-present soft mountain wind.

The toilet tent was erected in worryingly close proximity to the mess tent. To make appropriate use of it one needed to zip one's-self inside, complete one's business and then divine the method by which the device actually flushed. Various levers and handles were appended to accomplish a flush however I can't say I ever came to fully understand their individual functions adequately. A low-tech stick, always present near the base of the "device", apparently was provided to assist Luddites in the toilet's opaque operation.

The aforementioned technological marvel was tended to by the "toilet boy" and I presume his responsibilities included filling it with water, disposing of its contents, scrubbing it out, and, finally, carting it from camp to camp! He did not have a name. He was simply "the toilet boy". And despite the essentiality of the toilet to the happy operation of our camp and despite the difficulties associated with its operation, it engendered very little discussion amongst us - certainly not the discussion I felt it reasonably deserved. With abundant "hindsight", I believe it should have been a frequent topic of discussion. Chalk that up to the politeness of the British.

Still, a recalcitrant zipper on the portable toilet provided some entertainment to the group. First the zipper would not zip to the bottom thus leaving one's feet exposed when put to use. I reluctantly found myself able to identify the owner of the boots were *exposed* 'neath the faulty zipper. And second the zipper periodically stuck and thereby trapped enfeebled users inside. Debbie proved to be the person amongst our group who most often became trapped inside the toilet. Her wistful shouts for assistance provided us with an unexpected source of mirth. I believe it was Angie, her tent mate, who typically rescued her from the toilet tent.

One by one on this first morning on the mountain we reconnoitered in the mess tent. Richard stood with Rich and Angie outside of the tent, his navy blue balaclava pulled low over his forehead and his coffee steaming. All three were in good moods and welcomed me heartily as I approached. The night prior Debbie had presented as despondent whereas today she appeared gleeful - scampering about the campsite gathering belongings scattered here and there. Instead of a hat she wore a dark-colored headband to protect her ears and a thin T-shirt. The night of rest had convinced her to continue onward. However, Trish was less optimistic. Following breakfast, the two of us sat together and talked. She needed help in making a decision on whether to continue or not. I summoned Freddy and, following an extended conversation between them, they decided she would likely best depart our group.

An evacuation for Trish was not available from Machame Camp. Trish's choice was to either hike back *down* to Machame Gate or hike *up* to the next camp (Shira Camp, a challenging 850 meter gain in elevation) and be evacuated from there via an access road. No access road was available near this camp. Either of Trish's options would involve a further day's hike - either up or down. The latter gave her the opportunity of determining whether she might improve and therefore continue with the group. Further a climb *up* to Shira Camp was estimated to be easier than climbing back *down* to Machame Gate. Trish elected the latter option and I felt the "plan" had given Trish some confidence she had a way out if it became absolutely necessary. I felt good for having helped create a plan. Still, worry creased Trish's face - a visage contrasting with optimism the remaining eight in our group, including me, were sensing.

We assembled around a checkered table cloth for breakfast. A hearty offering of eggs, toast, fruit and coffee was on offer. Midway through the meal Freddy arrived with the heart/oxygenation monitor and with some misgivings we each submitted to his entreaties for cooperation. Each result (heart rate and oxygen saturation) was announced to the entire group then recorded and initialed by both the guide and the climber. There was no privacy nor HIPPA requirement up here!

My heart rate had declined overnight. It was a reassuring 88 bpm - a big drop from the night prior. However, my oxygen saturation had plummeted from 97% to 90% - a drop far greater than I had anticipated considering our limited altitude gain. But in comparison to others I seemed to be doing ok. Debbie, perhaps as expected, took on the role of "rock star of cardiac performance" within our group. Her heart rate remained in the low 60's and her oxygen saturation remained very high. She was the youngest within our group and certainly the most fit. In this manner she provided a good benchmark of cardiac and pulmonary health against which we could all appreciate our individual declines.

Following breakfast, I had a conversation with Rich, the chiropodist from London and long-term (44-years) friend of Richard. Rich was relaxed. He was casually sporting a few days of stubbly beard and a Tilley-style hat emblazoned with "Kilimanjaro" on the brow. After describing the problems in my quadriceps and their rapid improvement following the hike he surmised the cause had been lactic acid accumulation.

And of course! How could I have missed the possibility? I was (or at least had been) purportedly a "skeletal muscle biologist" for much of my adult life and fully understood the glycolytic pathway and the rationale for generation of lactic acid in muscle during extreme exercise. I understood as well the "lactic acid cycle (the Cori Cycle)" and the importance of the liver in clearing of muscle-generated lactic acid. But I had never experienced lactic acid accumulation in muscle prior and did not recognize it - despite at one time possessing an ability to run distances approaching half-marathons! What else could explain the rapid disappearance following the cessation of the climb and the complete absence of it the next day? Had I frayed my muscle proteins, as I had reluctantly surmised, the pain would remain. That could *not* be repaired overnight - unless divine intervention had occurred whilst I slept - divine intervention that I had no confidence in.

The complete absence of soreness today was the clearest evidence that lactic acid accumulation was the culprit for yesterday's infirmity. And knowing this I knew regular consumption of highly metabolizable carbohydrates during the climb, something that I was too distracted by pain to undertake the day prior, should prevent lactic acid accumulation on subsequent days. All I needed to do was ingest Fig Newtons or Snickers bars (or facsimiles) on subsequent days (even if I had no appetite for them). I resolved to do this and thereby derived some additional confidence in my ability to reach the summit.

The episode reminded me of a BC cartoon by cartoonist Al Hart. There was the anteater, emaciated and drawn, crawling across the desert, worried about its ability to ever find a meal of ants again. Then an ant crossed directly in front of him. The anteater gazed at the ant with dismay and sighed: "Aww it's just a *Hymenoptera formicidae*". As the ant walked beyond range and out of view of the cartoon panel the anteater realized, "Wait a minute! That's an ant". And then the dear anteater plaintively opined: "You get too much education, you starve to death". On this morning I personified the anteater.

Still, not knowing what the day's hike might entail and worried about the potential for challenges and further incapacity that lay in store, I ingested 2.5 Aleve as a prophylactic dose of analgesic prior to initiating the day's climb to Shira Camp.

I later learned we were collectively traveling with a veritable pharmacopeia of painkillers - others consumed Paracetamol, Ibuprofen and regular aspirin. Still, I regretted not spiriting hydrocodone into my kit - as I had done on less-challenging climbs in Patagonia.

I unloaded my heavy Nikon camera, lenses, yesterday's rain-saturated (and molding) shirts/socks and other odds and ends into the porter's duffle bag - feeling a little guilt-ridden but needing to protect myself from additional physical and mental degradation. This left me with an approximate 7 kg day pack, a drop of 2.5 kg. A very small glimmer of optimism rose in me. "Maybe."

Chapter Nine
Machame Onward to Shira Camp

Our drenched camp rested at near 3,000 meters of elevation and our destination (Shira Camp) lay at 3,850 meters of elevation - making for an anticipated net gain of 850 meters for the oncoming day. Unfortunately, when we rose the weather offered little to encourage us. Dark and pendant clouds were threatening, obscuring hoped-for views both summit-ward and downward. We were fully contained - sandwich-like between low overcast and our muddy escarpment. It was very possibly going to be another damp slog - except, propitiously, this would be above the moist tropical rain forest we had endured only yesterday. Hence one cause for optimism might have been today's effort should be less muggy.

At this altitude, vegetation had become noticeably scrubbier - a variety of tousled trees and forbs - none more than 5 meters in height. Lichen-covered and weather-worn boulders, presumably deposited by Kilimanjaro's last violent discharge millennia prior, littered the landscape like overturned and misshapen cars. The eruption of those boulders may have been witnessed by our African forbearers. But of course there is no record except, maybe, in our capacity for embracing anxiety.

The weather quickly deteriorated and a worry insinuated itself into our collective psyche. We were all a little nervous to get going - to leave this place for a hopefully better place - a place where we might gather more confidence - a need to leave behind the decidedly unpleasant experience of yesterday for something better.

Because we all anticipated rain would soon be amongst us we commenced our hike well-protected- donning ponchos, water-proof gear and warm hats. I was grateful for my blue Patagonia fleece hat. It fit snuggly, protected my ears and appeared impervious to the dampness and light rain. Richard was wearing a deep blue rain-proof slicker with his familiar, although improbable, baggy shorts and black tights. A rudimentary backpack, one lacking a supportive waistband, protruded from the cervical aspect of his back like a deformity. This was protected by a discarded white plastic bag he had retrieved from a trash bin back at the hotel. I found myself appreciating, on this and many other occasions, Richard's robust "devil may care" attitude.

The first five hours of the Day 2 hike consisted of a steady climb upon a narrow, muddy and boulder-strewn path. Like yesterday we hiked silently in single-file. But within a half hour, precipitation having not yet materialized, we began to strip away our rain gear and to stuff the excess protective clothing into our day packs. We were becoming too warm to hike so well-protected. We needed to dissipate heat.

Within the first hour I was *down* to my multi-zippered hiking pants and a T-shirt. But when we stopped for one of the frequent "loo" breaks I quickly became chilled. It was important to just keep going in order to maintain that requisite balance between heat generation and heat radiation. The frequent loo breaks interrupted our balance. During such breaks Rich, Richard, the guides and I remained behind reluctantly doffing our kit. We gave one another "knowing" eyes - all of us ruing the frequency of our stops.

Yet I was coming to enjoy our frequent breaks. We weren't here to set records. Even if we wished to set records it's doubtful our improbable group ever could have. There were views to imbibe, if not roses to smell.

A rhythm began to appear within our hike after about one hour from the commencement. The first hour would pass slowly as we adjusted, ant-like, to the unfamiliar terrain, to the mud, to the switchbacks and to the inefficient, some might say awkward, use of hiking poles. After the first hour, time would typically compress with the latter two-thirds to three-quarters of the hike passing more quickly than the first quarter to one-third. It was odd - but time always warped in this manner.

I spent time hiking near Gillian. Today's hike seemed effortless for her. Unlike me she carried no extra body weight and appeared in excellent shape - thin, lithe, athletic, optimistic. She wore good gear - well-designed, pale gray outerwear with potential to properly "breathe" with no hat. Her shoulder-length strawberry-blonde hair fluttered with the intermittent and changing winds. She retained telling aspects of her infectious cold and I maintained some intentional distance from her. I estimated the virtually unlimited dilution of the virus she was harboring provided by the outdoor air minimized the likelihood of its transfer to me.

Once again my muscles were beginning to object. I needed to focus on technique and to calm myself - to isolate myself mentally from the climb. I settled into internal counting of my steps and to repeating the Kilimanjaro mantra: pole pole [polay polay]; over and over. My mind wandered onto happy events in my life and troubles which commanded too much of my attention- my familiar PTSD-like civil litigation experiences. A hiking rhythm formed- step-by-step, pole pole, one-two-three-four, *ev-er-y-step-a-safe-step-* while considering the reveries and petty traumas - over and over. Alternatively, I counted my blessings- an endeavor requiring several minutes of contemplation and which typically ended when I reached the early-thirties of my blessings. I understood I was blessed. Simple conversations also helped to pass the time - of other hikes accomplished, of children, of how we would plan to eat during the day's hike, of our physical limitations, of last night's sleep. And in this manner we came to slowly know and trust ourselves and one another. In this manner the hours began to pass more easily - like the carefree and unadulterated days of our youths.

As we moved across the unfamiliar landscape the sun generously arched over us, almost undetectably, from the East - over our heads and toward the West. Our shadows shifted from laying to our right to laying on our left.

A riveting film - a cult classic from the 1970's came to mind:

> "And crawling, on the planet's face,
> Some insects, called the human race.
> Lost in time, and lost in space.
> And in meaning."

(*Richard, O'Brien, The Rocky Horror Picture Show*)

The climb to Uhuru Summit would take all of us, assuming we reached it, to an altitude far above anything we had individually reached previously. Hence we were all concerned about the possibility of altitude sickness. To minimize that likelihood, we each consumed Diamox (acetazolamide) twice/day. I was consuming two halves of the Diamox tablets had been provided to me by Trish whereas others within our troupe were ingesting as many as two full tablets per day. Having no prior experience with this medication, I was uncertain of its appropriate dose. I just didn't want to overdo it. I was aware of the contraindications: tingling fingers, hyperchloremic acidosis, low blood potassium, low blood sodium, adrenal insufficiency, impaired kidney function but most importantly increased urine output. Diamox unfortunately functions as a diuretic. Hence during the nights all of us, like 80 year-old men with enlarged prostrates, were having to wake every hour or two to urinate. And this was how I discovered the intrinsic value of the "pee bottle recommendation" accompanying Kandoo's climb preparation guide.

While the "pee bottle" was easily employed by Rich, Richard and me, the women struggled with implementation. Debbie travelled with a contraption which enabled her to pee within her tent whereas the others were compelled, as we were humorously reminded of each morning at breakfast, to wake several times each night and make their individual ways across uneven ground to the wind-whipped and fragrant “toilet tent” - not an easy task in the dark and with temperatures hovering near freezing.

Because I was not experiencing as much hurt on this second day I began to take a stronger interest in my surroundings and my circumstance. Unexpected thoughts naturally arose: “What the fuck am I doing in Africa on the side of a barren and inhospitable mountain?” “Is this truly Africa?” “Are my family members back in North America really oriented at almost 180-degree orientations to my perceived vertical; perhaps 11,000 km almost straight down below me?”

My surroundings didn’t impress me as being so different from what I would expect from a hike in the Oregon Cascades. The same dirt covered the ground. The same rocks protruded. Clouds delivered rain periodically as clouds do at home. The only indication suggesting an alternate geographical location to Oregon were our marvelous ebony-skinned Tanzanian guides and young Tanzanian porters who effortlessly sprinted past us in their worn-out first-world sneakers and recycled clothing - this while balancing 20 kg packs and 20-liter water bottles on their heads. No this was not Oregon.

“Jambo!” - the standard greeting the porters and guides exchanged amongst one another and with us as they passed on the trail. “Jambo!”- the equivalent of “Howdy!” or “How’s it going?” - the equivalent of Nepal’s “Namaste”. “Jambo!” was always accompanied with a broad, flashing white smile and with brief eye contact- sincere indications of fellowship and respect. So broad were the smiles the canines, pre-molars and molars were often visible.

Another Swahili maxim that we came to appreciate was “hakuna matata” (Meaning - it’s all right, nothing really matters, we’re all going to be just fine). The guides reminded us early in the hike of the preponderance of the phrase "hakuna matata" in the Disney movie "Lion King". Within a day of hiking the Swahili words - "Jambo", "pole pole" and "hakuna matata" had thereby naturally incorporated themselves into our group's lexicon. If one of us began to take too large a stride or exhibit a little too much enthusiasm to get ahead, the Swahili phrase of "pole pole" would emanate from others in the rear - as a "suggestion". If one became dispirited, damp or sore "hakuna matata" was proposed as solace - like an East African balm.

The day was progressing well. By mid-morning our collective thoughts of trepidation began to dissipate as the ponderous Kilimanjaro cloud layer began to lift upward and hesitatingly away from us - like the removal of a shroud. This allowed views of the flat plains lying to the south of Kilimanjaro. Moshi, the busy metropolis from which we had originated, now rested a couple thousand meters below us - on the flat. Still the density of the morning air, intermingled with an evaporating fog, prevented a clear definition.

Sunlight began to pierce the clouds sending warm yellow shafts of light to the ground. It was as if there was an entity cognizant of my need for optimism. The throbbing I had experienced in my legs the day prior had dissipated and I attributed this to my more frequent ingestion of refined carbohydrate-rich foods - biscuits, candies and juice. Those and analgesics.

A gentle breeze drifted downward from the summit and soothingly cooled us when we stopped. Day 1 had presented a brutal start to the adventure but now, in my heart, I was beginning to grasp at a fleeting optimism; like a baby alfalfa sprout - emerging from a dampened and fragrant soil.

Maybe I can do this. Sure I will admit it......I'm old, but my body was adapting and not telling me to give up. Maybe I'm not old yet. Yes, maybe I can do this. These were my private thoughts. I wondered if others were harboring similar thoughts.

Despite my growing optimism, I became aware the day was not stress-free for Trish. Even though Auguste, the most diminutive of our guides, now carried her day-pack and assisted her on the more challenging aspects of the trail, she, like a dispirited lamb, languished toward the rear of our troupe. When we encountered rock climbs or scrambles I could sense her need to dig down deep to access her near depleted energy stores. Mercifully her grit was apparent and she did not complain. When I slowed to talk with her, she remained lighthearted even though her face betrayed more than a little anguish. Whereas our group harbored the faith she would find the conviction and energy to continue with the hike, as the day wore on, she became more and more committed to evacuating from Shira Camp via the access road the next day.

Trish and I were near the same age. I was not in the best physical shape but, from brief conversations with her, I had come to the understanding I was possibly in a little better shape than her. I wanted her to go on. But more, it hurt to see her suffer. We hiked as a group and our progress was necessarily limited, as the weakest link in a chain, by the least capable of the group. Sad. But up here, true. If Trish continued I understood she might jeopardize the entirety of the hike.

Two other dynamics conspired against Trish. First, prior to the climb, Trish had known only one other member of our hiking group: Richard. As earlier outlined, Trish and Richard had intended to complete Kilimanjaro as a couple. However, Trish had unexpectedly broken-up with Richard a few weeks prior to the hike and I believe she had, in fact, hurt Richard's feelings. So, despite Richard's and Trish's agreement to complete their hike together, Richard was not inclined to be as sympathetic to Trish's plight as he might otherwise have been. That seemed to me to be fair. The attention of a supportive boyfriend/lover on the trail might have made a difference for her. In addition, the other five women on the hike (Gillian, Natascha, Angie, Debbie and Alex) had all known one another on-and-off for at least two decades. Prior to meeting in Moshi they had not been in regular contact (e.g., Gillian lived in Zambia) and this meant these five women, old friends, had experienced much water under their respective bridges - "water" needing to be shared and dissected with one another. Although everyone in the group including Richard spent time with Trish, much of the second day of the hike was dominated by the sharing of stories, some hilarious, others serious, among these five good friends. This left Trish as a little bit of an outsider to the group as a whole. Perhaps it was not so surprising then her interest in continuing waned. Still she showed absolute grit- the tenacity of the human spirit personified. I found myself hoping dearly she would continue. The guides did their best to offer encouragement and support - directly assisting her through tough, more technical, aspects of the climb and providing verbal encouragement. We all hoped for her success.

As the day wore on, the scrubby trees and shrubs present at Machame Camp became less abundant. Moist masses of orange-, vermillion- and rust-colored mosses began instead to proliferate as dominant plants. These hung from the eons-worn volcanic rocks irregularly assembled across and along our path. So dense were the mosses on these rocks they provided a welcome cushion against which we would lean during our periodic breaks. At the bases of erratic boulders colorful lichens also grew in profusion. Richard informed us "lichens only survive in areas with pristine air quality because so many nutrients they need must be extracted from air". Whether true or not, I accepted it and savored it as I drew Kilimanjaro's crisp cool air now deeper into my lungs; like an invigorating spray of pure clean energy. His observation made me reflect on growing-up in the late-1950s and early-60's in rural Saskatchewan, Canada. There, in early Spring, when the mauve-colored and velveteen prairie crocus first appeared, I contemplated the profuse lichens sprayed across the worn prairie granites; oranges, reds, pale pinks and olive greens. They appeared to be brittle. At the time, I took simple Northern beauty and its clean air for granted. Even as a kid, I had been drawn to the beauty of lichens. Now here they were again - an arch of 55 years.

And, in an odd development, I noticed the White-necked Ravens, when they were amongst us, also seemed to regard the lichens inquisitively - as if they too were appreciating the varied colors and patterns the lichens presented. They never perched directly on the lichens but, instead, always directly adjacent.

Richard enthusiastically shouldered a role as the group's resident naturalist - our private, land-based Jacques Cousteau thus providing descriptions of all manner of insects, plants and ecology. This helped us appreciate aspects of the hike we would have otherwise simply tread blithely past. Rich on the other hand took on twin roles as the group's geographer and foot doctor - the latter being of considerable import on a seven-day vertiginous hike. Rich had committed to memory the altitudes of each camp, the altitude gains and the distances lying between camps. Each of us needed to divine this information from him several times each per day! Rich was continually consulted for his insights into the proportion of the day's hike we had completed, the total elevation gain and the proportion of oxygen in the air relative to sea level. Added were stray comments on the importance of proper toenail care vis-à-vis hiking so as to avoid damage to one's toes. Knowing Richard and Rich possessed firm command of this information allowed the remainder of us to let our minds to wander more freely onto the less scientific and, instead, the more abstruse aspects of the climb. I was pleased to have packed toenail clippers and was pleased, because of Richard's insights, my low grade in first year Biology would not hinder me in understanding some of the esoterica of Kilimanjaro's unique ecology.

An hour of hiking was required for me to achieve a rhythm during each day's climb. And, I believe our group also reached a "group rhythm". Within 1-2 hours if all went well we settled into a group meditation and moved as a lesser-thinking primitive organism across the landscape - unified steps, limited conversation, absorbed in collective thoughts. Within our meditation time would inevitably bend and pass quickly. A full morning could thereby collapse into two hours. We reached this aspect of a group consciousness at roughly the same time and could have walked for hours in our elevated state. However, the state was fragile. A suddenly and unexpectedly announced need for a "loo break" shattered it. Of course those needing to pee blamed their need to urinate on Diamox.

All of us were cognizant of this Diamox-associated diuretic challenge and "held it" as long as possible thereby hoping another of the hikers might succumb first. But, more often than not it was Debbie who succumbed. She would announce "I need to pee" using so plaintive a voice it invoked a modicum of sympathy. Having little choice, the group would then grind to a halt, begin sloughing-off packs, lay down hiking poles against the moss- and lichen-covered rocks and somewhat begrudgingly exit the collective meditation. Once one person had asserted their need to pee many of the remaining hikers would similarly decide they needed to pee as well. The pee-ers would scatter hither and thither to find conveniently-sized boulders and bushes to hide behind. The remaining hikers would then loiter on the trail to kibbitz, drink water and ingest some carbohydrate-rich snacks. Often these pee breaks would extend into a full ten- or fifteen-minute break - to the growing frustration of the Tanzanian guides who clearly wished to reach camp before a mid-day rain shower. Our hike "on the shoulder of the rainy season" meant an early start and an aggressive hike with minimal pee breaks would deliver an essentially dry and collegial group to the next camp. Dillydallying meant the alternative - a sodden and miserable group, including sodden and miserable guides, would arrive instead. Further exacerbation of the frustration the pee breaks caused was provided by the French and the Italians when they overtook our dithering group. Our porters felt our tardiness reflected on them. By the end of the day our otherwise patient Tanzanian guides were giving the women five minutes (or less) to complete their bathroom duties and the guys were dutifully casting their collective gaze in the opposing direction to thereby enable the women to pee within sight of the trail.

Had we hiked efficiently we could have been in Shira Camp early. However, we were 1.5-2 hours from camp when the skies let loose with a horrendous insult of rain - like an expected slap in the face. This new onslaught of precipitation caught us so quickly we barely had time to don our rain gear.

To dry my GoreTex gear from the previous day's rain I had been hiking with both the outer jacket and the pants dangling from my day pack and by this time, with some exposure to sun, they were almost completely dry. I quickly donned these and I was grateful to Obama who then offered me a plastic poncho to be wrapped around my daypack so it would not become impregnated with moisture (as had happened the day prior). I stopped while he kindly wrapped my pack more completely - tucking in the edges of the poncho well behind my back. Then as a group we adopted our more-sullen demeanors, formed a quiet line and walked *pole pole* upward toward Shira Camp. As had happened yesterday the rain found its way through the GoreTex mesh of my hiking gear as if it was specifically-engineered to convey moisture efficiently and quickly to my skin, to soak me completely and to thereby completely rob me of my body heat. "How convenient" I thought. Others who wore cheap plastic ponchos became less sodden; however, their plastic did not "breathe" as did my ineffective GoreTex. While my hike, as a consequence, was wet and cold theirs were clammy. I'm not certain which was worse.

We continued upward until we reached a fog-shrouded ridge at 3,850 meters. From there through the haze we could divine the now familiar rusty colors of our tents and of the movement of porters who had already arrived in camp and who were busy, fortunately, with the preparation of a hearty dinner. We descended into the camp, had photos taken of the group at Shira Gate, signed in at the Ranger Station (our third) and, like dutiful moths to candles, swiftly found our ways to our tents. The tents were interchangeable, like my collection of red woolen socks. The characteristic distinguishing our individual tents was our duffle bag inside - now presenting as an old friend.

Arriving in camp - the beginning of a routine emerged. The same person who met me yesterday when I entered Machame Camp now met me at Shira Camp. I now understood he had been assigned to look after me. He knew my duffle bag and presumably had carried that bag into this camp, set up my tent and placed the duffle in the tent along with a sleeping mat and sleeping bag. He voiced no complaints about the extra few kg that he had carried-up the volcano on Day 2; a mild relief. I was pleased to encounter him and this time had enough energy to be hospitable and appreciative and to look him in the eye. Because I was apparently communicative following this day's hike he introduced himself as "Focus" by patting his chest with a closed fist and saying his name - "Focus". Focus I said. My name is Neil. I too placed my right fist to my heart as I stated my name - a universal form of communication and respect. Focus possessed no English skills with which to communicate with me but, via hand gestures indicated the direction of my tent. He unzipped it and I squatted awkwardly and entered while Focus crouched-down and secured my hiking poles under the tent - the beginning of a ritual. I lay back briefly on the sleeping mat to give myself some time to recover from and to consider the day's effort but unexpectedly Focus was aggressively *at* my boots - unlacing them, spreading the laces and straining to leverage them off. Embarrassed by what I thought was excessive assistance I sat up and half-heartedly tried to assist him with this process. But Focus shushed me away and completed the task himself. He then tied my shoe laces together and secured my boots in a dry corner under the overhanging "fly" of my tent. I proffered my thanks - two men - the same needs - air, food, warmth and love - an understanding was flourishing. Still - such an imbalance in our "means". A circumstance where an older white man was having his boots removed by a younger Tanzanian man. This was an imbalance I was not comfortable with and thought about throughout the hike. Our eyes, his yellowing and distant, met briefly and communicated an acknowledgement of sorts. And then he was then gone for the evening - like an evaporating morning dream.

It was 3PP - we'd been hiking for eight hours. Including the various breaks, this hike was two hours longer, and considerably more sodden, than what we had been promised. The shoulder of the rainy season? I began to wonder how challenging the rain was going to be. I didn't mind the cold. I could dress for cold. The rain, however, presented challenges I had not adequately prepared for.

Once again we were situated within a uninspiring muddy campground - a re-visitation of yesterday's nightmare. Perhaps thirty tents had been set up - the endeavors of the same international excursion companies we had observed at Machame Camp. A light rain misted onto the camp and like yesterday, the cloying, gray fog fully enveloped and chilled us. I didn't care. I was relieved the day's efforts were completed and warm dry clothes were at hand. I now possessed fifteen luscious hours, my reprieve, to rest and repair the damage I had imposed once again onto my unaccustomed and ancient body. My tent had become my only refuge - my cocoon. I was pupating and would emerge in the morning as a metamorphosed entity - hopefully more capable of the third day on the mountain. My tent's fading orange and beige, a visual opioid, comforted me in the waning light. I was alive and had survived another day.

Abruptly following arrival most of our hiking group convened, like communication-starved depression-era farmers, within the mess tent to kibbitz. Richard's familiar chuckle resonated through the thin wall of my tent like a familiar friend - bursting forth with its reassuring cadence. The women chattered amongst themselves with Natascha's periodic hoots being the most identifiable. Periodically I could hear her sister (Alex) chime in with a reassuring and steadying laugh. Guides and porters came and went - setting-up their tents, preparing food and joking amongst themselves. Even though we were exhausted we were indeed a joyful camp. What a difference a day can make!

I lay comatose for three hours before being roused for our regular health check and for dinner. There I struggled to present an optimistic demeanor. My heart rate was 88 bpm (somewhat elevated) and my blood oxygen saturation had remained at 90% - still acceptable and well within the range of others. Similar to our previous health checks, Debbie proved again to be our most fit - maintaining a resting heart rate in the low-60's and an oxygen saturation well above 90%. Debbie had no difficulty basking in our gentle adulation - her smile contagious. We were happy to stroke her ego.

Whereas Gillian had presented as healthy during today's hike she remained in obvious distress because of her cold. In the two days we had hiked there had been no diminution in her clinical respiratory signs. Her crimson-tinged nose, Rudolph-like, dripped and she dabbed at it with a knotted and well-used Kleenex unremittingly. Periodically she sneezed and coughed. Within the close confines of our mess tent, which measured 3 X 5 meters, I grew more concerned she would infect the rest of us. Hence I made every reasonable effort to sit as far from her during meals as possible. Others though seemed unconcerned about her illness as if they were fully unaware of "germ theory". Why would that be, I wondered. I take the suffering associated with colds very seriously and have observed many times others do not worry about them as much as me. Why is this? I reasoned acquiring a cold on this mountain would be more than awful and could potentially rob any possible enjoyment from it - if there was going to be any enjoyment of it. Am I too petty? I studied myself inwardly. I didn't come up with an answer.

Trish on the other hand had reached the point of "throwing-in the towel". Certainly she had shown incredible determination by completing Day 2 - especially given Day 1 had been the hardest on her of all of us and given she was very ill on the morning of Day 2. All of our team had encouraged her and the Tanzanian guides did everything they could to encourage and support her including carrying her day pack and supporting her on difficult transits over treacherous aspects of the trail. However, upon her arrival into Shira Camp Trish had made what appeared to be the irrevocable decision to depart to the nearest access road the next day. One of our four guides (Auguste) was selected as the one who would accompany her. If Trish did depart we would be down to three (from the original four) guides. The three remaining would be our lead guide Freddy, the somewhat brusque Obama and the soft-spoken Raymond. The possibility of Trish's imminent departure hung over us ominously for the remainder of the evening.

Dinner was an extravagant affair especially again considering our location - a new flavor of vegetable soup (pumpkin), pancakes, rice with greens, stir-fried beef and vegetables. On hand were several jams, jellies and hazelnut-flavored Nutella to supplement our energy reserves. I maintained a robust appetite and ate as much as possible - especially the beef so as to effect repair and re-building of my recalcitrant leg muscles. I willed the metabolizable carbohydrate to the rebuilding of my liver and muscle glycogen stores. I was appreciative of my appetite - recognizing it as my ally.

I was becoming an opportunistic eater- eating whatever I could to help me get through the next day - whether it be eggs, nuts or meat. Like Kilimanjaro's rapacious ravens I scavenged anything proteinaceous on offer - hoping it would help me quickly rebuild and restore my questionable musculoskeletal capabilities.

Following dinner, a preview of our next day's hike was provided by Raymond, a mellifluous, trim and kind-hearted guide. From Raymond's his soft and measured tones we learned tomorrow's hike would be the longest and possibly the most strenuous of the entire effort (9-10 hours in duration). His term "possibly the most strenuous", I was to eventually fathom, was not true. Far worse would come later. Indeed, the guides interspersed our hike with well-rehearsed falsehoods and misrepresentations; falsehoods and misrepresentations served to both protect us and to encourage us. With hindsight I now understand the fabrications and deceits the guides regularly employed to cajole us into continuing upward. They were like well-trained sales people - people trained to sell us on the belief we were all capable. None of us were sophisticated enough to see through their mendacity. Instead, our need to believe in our abilities enabled their strategies that cajoled us upward. But to be fair their goal was to deliver us to Uhuru....and they had clearly developed lines of logic and other stories convinced us we were capable- a well-honed canard.

Tomorrow we were to climb from Shira Camp (3,800 meters) eastward to Lava Tower (4,600 meters) and to then descend southeastward into Baranco Camp (3,960 meters)- a basket-like depression resting between two sharp ridges. The philosophy underlying this plan was, as noted earlier, to "climb high and sleep low". This strategy assisted in our physiological acclimation to high altitude (considered to be anything over 3,000 meters) and permitted our otherwise excessively rapid ascent of Kilimanjaro - an ascent rate that could exacerbate risk of altitude-related illnesses.

A general recommendation in the climbing literature is once one reaches 3,000 meters one should not ascend more than 350 meters/day thereafter. Now, months removed from the Kilimanjaro effort, this recommendation seems to be excessively cautious. "Climbing high and sleeping low" permits a more aggressive overall ascent. Upon climbing up to Lava Tower and then down into Baranco Camp we were warned we might begin to experience clinical signs of altitude sickness- possibly nausea. Most of us, like would-be antelopes were beginning to anticipate the challenge.

By 7:30 PM we had finished dinner and were chatting agreeably amongst ourselves. We were now warm, dry and satiated. I was slouched comfortably in an aluminum-framed lawn chair in the extreme interior corner of the mess tent not really participating in conversation. Natascha and Alex dominated - joking for most of the dinner - a mixture of some mildly bawdy humor (which I appreciated) and interesting stories of their growing-up together - stories made more endearing by hearing both of each others' recriminations.

Exiting the mess tent we found Kilimanjaro's oppressive cloud cover had completely, and in very short order, evaporated. The night sky in all of its luminous intensity radiated kind promise down upon us. Billions of stars - each glittering individually in inky darkness - each with its unique power and color - each surrounded by its own worlds - worlds we could never know. A dense and creamy stretch of the Milky Way stood out against the blue-blackness of the night sky like a swath of filamentous gauze while a patient and waxing orange moon began to warm the Eastern sky - the moon a vulnerable and expectant mother. I tilted my head back to drink and breathe it all in. To breathe it all in like I had never done prior. The thin air. The blackness. The stars. The cheese-colored moon. It had taken two days to reach this place of enchantment and it was more than worth it.

Filled with optimism I retreated to my tent and listened to the dwindling social reverberations of our camp. Sleep came upon me quickly and I was engaged in a dream within ten minutes.

The stars of Kilimanjaro. I had just inhaled them. Pulled them deep into my lungs. Indeed, they were transcendent. That an entity could imbibe and appreciate them was a revelation I knew was important. To make sense of them was an even greater task. That I appreciated these things gave me confidence my "phenomenological self", my consciousness, my sense of "self" was contained within a capable physical body. "I'm not so old!" "My mind remains at least marginally capable", I mused. The optimism I had begun to feel early on the second morning had not dissipated. Like an acorn landing and finding refuge in nourishing soil I was beginning to grasp potential.

As I slept Kilimanjaro's glistening and dense stars, no longer strangers, spiraled across the indigo heavens - like a reliable old world clock. No one informed me of this because all of us had slept through it. But when I woke I knew it had been just like that. And knowing this while finding a new day delivered to me I felt renewed and confident. Amongst the stars I understood I was part of the plans of the heavens.

Chapter Ten
On Finding One's Self Alive in Shira Camp

****
*

Snowfall On Kilimanjaro (Geno Cattouse, 2013)

The Ashes of a million souls drift down to the Baranco Wall and Moorland.

Seventeen thousand feet is All
Deep and dead is the cap on Kilimanjaro.

If a tree falls in the Forrest. You will hear it on Kilimanjaro.

Haunting stones on Easter Island whisper in the dead of night
and speak to Kilimanjaro.

Pitcairn Island far and lost.

Fletcher Christians mournful ghost wails and screams as the Bounty burned
a light seen from The Kilimanjaro.

Supai City Arizona in the bowels of the gaping gorge
looks out to Kilimanjaro.

Oymyakon Siberia. Minus 93 degrees. Chatter and freeze
akin to The Kilimanjaro

World ends in the stratosphere
Fight for breath face your fears.
Where minutes pass like plodding years

in grasp of Kilimanjaro.

+++++++++++++++++++

I often thought of my family while hiking on Kilimanjaro. The hike can become monotonous and one relies upon various "devices" to pass the time. I was approximately twelve time zones removed from North America and I often imagined what my families in Oregon and Canada were doing in their 160- to 180-degree orientations relative to me. They thrived nearly 11,000 km beneath me with their feet pointed upwards toward me - my father, my mother, my sister, my wife, my two dear children - Amelia and Johan.

My father in the past few years had developed a disease termed "COPD": Chronic Obstructive Pulmonary Disease triggered by a 30-year addiction to cigarettes. Now at home with my mother in a condo in Canada he was experiencing difficulty in undertaking simple tasks such as walking to and from the bedroom. That I was so vibrant and so aggressive I might climb one of the Seven Summits at age 63 reminded me often of how circumscribed his world had now become compared to mine. How I wish I could have transferred to him some of my pulmonary capability. How I wished he could have accompanied me on this effort. Throughout the climb for this reason and many others he and the rest of my family were always with me.

It was a climb I undertook for personal and opportunistic reasons but I also came to understand that this should be a climb for my Dad because I knew how much it could have meant to him. I knew that he was proud of my efforts - not only this mountaineering effort but other more intellectual efforts. Each day the thought would pass through me several times that "indeed, this climb, if I can make it, would be dedicated to my dear father - a father who had made, as our fathers do, so many sacrifices in his own life so his children might enjoy opportunities in their lives." Sacrifice. That's what my Dad did. I could and can still learn from him.

Dads. As important as they are to us, they don't last forever.

Appreciate them when you have them.

++

I knew Richard had lost his Dad many years ago. When we both worked at Sultan Qaboos University in Oman 19 years earlier he had had to return to the UK for his father's funeral. Others too on this hike likely hiked without fathers in their lives. I didn't ask. Let's take a moment to appreciate and thank them as imperfect as they may individually be or have been..

And then, too, there will be that time when I am no longer here and perhaps my children or their children might read this. Well, let me just say that you gave me far more that I could have ever given you. Thank you for having had the chance to be your Dad. Nothing was/is more important.

These were the thoughts engendered by Kilimanjaro. Simple and obvious thoughts to be certain. But important thoughts nonetheless.

++

The camp woke at 6AM- the unexpected but welcome glow of a brightening day projected against the thin and undulating taupe fabric of my cocoon. I had slept nearly ten hours - a time fully needed to mend some of the damage done, again, to my climbing muscles over the past two days. My sleeping bag was thick - sumptuously 7-8 cm thick- and perfectly warm. It was as if I was under a goose down-filled duvet on a similarly lenient mattress. Such was the intensity of the warm pleasure my body delivered to me on this morning in my sleeping bag - every heat receptor and every pleasure receptor in my skin were communicating deep satisfaction. I stretched, absorbed the comforting warmth, considered the soreness of my body and came to the determination today I could be expected to be reasonably ambulatory. A day at a time.

Members of our trekking group had one by one materialized from their respective tents and were huddling together near the mess tent - drinking coffee or tea from Kandoo's utilitarian plastic mugs. During the night dew had condensed on the tents and then frozen. Sheets of ice coated each of them. Or perhaps the ice originated as much from the moisture we had respired during the night. Irrespective - thumping the surfaces of our tents caused these icy sheets to shatter into thin glass-like panes, to slide onto the ground and to fragment into knife-like crystal shards.

The sun had yet to rise. But already the Eastern sky was coloring into mouthwatering strawberry pinks, peaches and banana-oranges. Nary a cloud was present and this circumstance for the first time afforded us our first observation Northeastward toward the summit of Kilimanjaro. The lowermost edges of its snow-capped peak could now be discerned. Rocky outcroppings below the peak, in this muted light, appeared as blue-grey and featureless. Isolated and serene. Not worth approaching. Nothing. Important. Was. Evident. Here we just existed as living and breathing entities.

Still - with a measure of uncertainty we gazed upward.

Natascha, Angie and I stood together in a small klatch - clutching mugs in our bare hands in order to warm them. Alex, a late-arrival, quietly joined our group. Moisture from our breaths hung in the frigid morning air and comingled before dissipating. I was reminded of John Donne's imagery from "Ode to a Flea" - learned decades ago in my Freshman English class: "and in this flea our two bloods mingled be." Yes, it was a romantic thought.

We made small talk. Natascha with her snug, navy-colored stocking cap and bright smile - quietened. Angie, with her streaked, blonde, unkempt hair- grinning and happy, giddy perhaps - anticipating the day. Alex chattering quietly and cheerfully. Nearby Richard and Rich stood stiffly side-by-side- still shivering in the dull early morning chill - facing toward the summit- waiting for the sky to lighten and further define its dimensions and the day's imperatives. Indeed, they were caught irretrievably in their decades-long friendship and by their small reflective stories. Periodically we would look around and appreciate the intensity of the full spectrum colors of the rapidly evolving morning sky - colors stretching forever - from monochromatic blues and greys in the West to a full palette of luminous orange, yellow and mauve pastels in the East - a palette we rarely witness.

Shira Camp was located abruptly above the Rainforest Zone and was surrounded only by sparse "alpine vegetation". The occasional trees near us were scraggly - standing no more than 3-4 meters tall. Their twisted rheumatic branches indicated they had struggled to attain even these modest heights. Their foliage was the deepest of greens.

Rocks, scree and dozens of observant White-necked ravens, our ever-present and sometimes excessively-inquisitive companions, occupied the camp. Our scraps of food and handouts appeared to sustain the birds. Perhaps we entertained them. Or perhaps they felt they had something meaningful to contribute to our hike. One could not be certain. They exhibited confidence. This was their home.

We were located on a large escarpment on the West side of Kilimanjaro with thirty other tents and possibly fifty other internationally-derived hikers. Porters from all camps were crammed together in their nomadic "Tanzanian village" off to the East, toward the summit. I imagined they had little loyalty to the individual organizers of the trip. Instead I imagined they were mercenaries - they worked for whomever hired them for their 7-8 day climbs and would find themselves among the same community of porters on no matter which climb they undertook. Like the ravens this was their community. This too is where they lived - a far cry from my red leather couch which now lay vacant at home.

The twin benefits of a golden morning light and a cloudless cobalt sky pervaded camp. I thus wanted to seize opportunity to capture the vibrant beauty and diversity of the "Tanzanian face". Indeed, Tanzanian men exhibited mouthfuls of well-formed glistening white teeth and harbored no reticence in displaying them. Many accepted my grizzled visage and my entreaties for photographs.

As the sky lightened Freddy announced our porters would put on a welcoming presentation prior to breakfast. So encouraged - our porters assembled into a semi-circle along with our four guides and each introduced himself to us or, if they were unable to express themselves in English, were introduced by one of our four guides (Freddy, Obama, Raymond or Auguste).

The porters were each dressed unassumingly - in blue jeans and a T-shirt with rudimentary and well-worn sports shoes - a hoodie possibly emblazoned with the name of an American university ("Franklin and Marshall" being the most obscure). And of the large assembled group I recalled the names only of two - Focus (my porter) and the "toilet boy".

It was an important ceremony. These were the men who worked harder than any of us and who were making our ascents possible. In mornings their responsibilities were to strike all tents and gear (tables, chairs, toilet, food, sleeping bags and pads, remaining water, tarps and other kit) and then scramble to the next camp and reverse what they had completed in the morning. We would typically depart camp at 8 AM and within ninety minutes our porters would have struck our camp and would be sprinting past us, gazelle-like - this despite the obvious fact they carried at least twice if not three times the weights we individually carried. Further the construction of their loads was not elegant. Instead they transported their loads as haphazard accumulations of jugs, boxes, chairs and bags often wrapped with black or blue plastic tarps for rain protection. As they passed we were reminded by our guides we needed to clear a path for them so they were not impeded. With each passing - greetings and smiles were enthusiastically exchanged: "pole pole" and more often, "Jambo!".

While living in the Sultanate of Oman many years ago a Zanzibari Omani named Rahma who worked as my secretary taught me some Swahili. This, because prior to 1970 the Omani intelligentsia had escaped the previous intemperate and backward-looking Sultan by moving to Zanzibar. Their return to Oman following ascension of the present Sultan Qaboos bin Said introduced a Zanzibari Swahili dialect into Oman's lexicon. The only Swahili word I recalled from Rahma's language lessons was "Jambo!", or "Hello". Rahma taught me the correct response to "Jambo!" was "Jambo si Jambo!". When I began responding to the porters' greetings of "Jambo" with Rahma's recommended "Jambo si Jambo!" and accompanied it with a broad and enthusiastic smile and a wave I was able to elicit consistent laughs and happy broad smiles. Apparently "Jambo si Jambo!" is either archaic or uniquely Zanzibari. That a North American Caucasian would be using a Zanzibari Swahili dialect would be surprising. And the porters' surprise didn't deter me from this habit. In fact, I was emboldened with this knowledge and attempted to use it to my advantage - evidence I was a humorous and endearing participant in this jaunt.

Following our mutual introduction, the porters broke into a traditional Tanzanian dance performance I began to recognize and actively appreciate. The dancing consisted of one porter amongst his semi-circle of friends capering while singing a primary verse - a verse to which all the remaining porters would then chime-in with a chorus. It didn't take too much practice for my Western colleagues and me to recognize we too could chime-in on the chorus, clap our hands, sway our hips and boogey with the remaining porters. After a minute or so the dancer in the center would switch-out with another porter who would continue with a different primary verse but always the chorus returned to the same chant - often centered on "hakuna matata". I surmised the dancer would sing a well-known Swahili song after which the assembled porters and we would chime-in with a sad but hopeful chorus of "hakuna matata". I took it to mean nothing matters, it's ok, the sun will still rise in the East tomorrow no matter what - a laid-back Tanzanian philosophy - Yes life is hard, shit happens, your wife leaves you, you don't have much money...but it's ok - hakuna matata. This went on for an enjoyable twenty minutes and involved the entire assembly of porters, guides and hikers - an authentic experience I won't forget.

Yes - we've all had difficulties in our lives but in the end we'll get by. What really matters? Nothing matters! We have friends and family who love us. And they are with us. Beer is cheap. There's always pizza at hand. We're all going to die anyway. Hakuna matata.

Even as we danced the ravens observed us - perhaps only 8-10 meters away. They too had formed a semi-circle extending away from us. In a way they had completed the circle. They gawked sideways at us and shook their stout white-tipped beaks and strutted. In fact, they appeared to be grinning. Their eyes sparkled - reflecting the nascent morning sun back toward us.

The Grateful Dead. My friend Gary Merrill's go-to music - "I will get by. I will survive". Every society likely possesses a similar nihilistic solace in its music - usually presented in a minor key in the West. So too here on Kilimanjaro's shoulder.

This morning presented a clear passionfruit-pink and citrus sky - a sun rising and promising a warm day with views of the Tanzanian escarpment lying well below. There remained a close memory of the suffering we had collectively endured on the hike two days prior - but also a memory of the star-filled night and the fathomless density of the Milky Way the night prior. I was hiking with a dear friend I had first met two decades ago. I was witnessing the developing friendships and meeting those who had been friends for years and being given opportunity to glimpse the magic of those durable friendships. I had awoken in an ice-covered tent and found hot coffee and cocoa waiting for me in thermoses. I warmed my hands with mugs as the sky lightened. I felt my body strengthening in response to Kilimanjaro's challenge. The assembled porters, the guests, the ravens and guides shared smiles and universally-held positive emotions in their dance, smiles and songs. Life could not become better than this. Life was good. It was an honor to be here. The day would be hard. But it would also be good. My Dad would be proud of his son.

Chapter Eleven
The Departure of Trish and the Climb to Lava Tower

Following the porters' dance and breakfast it became clear Trish would be departing our group. A night of rest and our fervent prayers for her recuperation had been insufficient for her body and mind to recover from the exacting first two days.

Trish moved quietly from person to person amongst our group and gave each a hug - accompanied by Auguste, the guide who would accompany her to the access road which lay, apparently, within reasonable a distance from Shira Camp. I paused to consider Trish before she reached me - a kind lady whom I would miss. I wanted her to stay.

When Trish reached to me our eyes met reluctantly. We hugged and then further fanfare she kissed me on the cheek - perhaps a European gesture - perhaps a gesture of genuine affection. I took it more as evidence of the latter - a brief but close relationship we had forged both prior to the climb and during the past two days - an intense and challenging time for all of us. I felt honored to have known her even for this short time.

We were all disappointed to see Trish vanish tentatively over the adjacent ridge with Auguste. Trish was without doubt a kind-hearted and genuine person. But she had underestimated the effort and to my understanding had not adequately prepared physically for the climb. She had done less than I had to prepare. And my efforts had been inadequate too. Nothing could have been done to help her forge onward. Sadly, we understood it was best for her to depart.

Trish's departure left us as eight climbers- three men and five women. Of the eight remaining climbers I was the oldest and without much doubt the least physically capable. Like Trish I had admitted to myself an inadequate preparation. But others had infirmities too. Angie was struggling with quitting smoking and Gillian continued to suffer with her infectious cold. Richard's cough was becoming more pronounced as the air thinned but that did not seem to interfere with his hike. He, at 54, remained outwardly and reassuringly vibrant. Three of the others (Rich, Natascha, and Debbie) exhibited no outward evidence of illness or incapability. Alex, even though she was an avid "vaper" and often surrounded with clouds of acrid nicotine-filled smoke, displayed no evidence of disability. The spectrum of our abilities and health, even without Trish, remained quite broad.

Breakfast consisted of scrambled and boiled eggs, toast (with assorted jams and jellies), pork sausages and porridge accompanied by copious amounts of instant coffee and tea. Again, I ate extra dollops of anything high in protein to support the rebuilding of my damaged muscles and informed the group of the importance of maintaining a high protein intake - the beginning of my role as the nutritionist and pseudo-medical expert for the group. I knew on average, an adult required 40-55 grams of protein intake/day just to maintain existing body protein mass. With our added exertion I was certain this was elevated to near 100 g/d. Considering a boiled egg contained only 6-7 g of protein one needed to work diligently to reach one's elevated protein needs (not to mention one's elevated caloric needs).

Refreshingly Richard was continuing to develop his reputation as our naturalist and convivialist - this despite the departure of his former girl friend. No, there appeared to be no grief displayed on his countenance by her absence. Indeed, Richard became more animated and insightful and was reasonably able to identify many genus' of trees, insects and lichens and discuss interesting aspects of their biology and taxonomy. This ability was in part derived from his training as an entomologist and from field excursions he had made to various exotic locales - the Atlas Mountains in Morocco and Oman for example.

It needs to be said Richard had not experienced a perfect life, as none of us have, and his ability to therefore find humor and optimism, to show his broad, toothy smile and to communicate his genuine laugh convincingly in many challenging situations inspired us. Richard and his friend Rich's forty-year friendship was a respected foundation around which all of us rallied as we also rallied around Gillian's decades-long relationships with Natascha and Angie. The glinting-eyed Natascha, the organizer of the hike, had quickly established herself the jokester/entertainer/center-of-energy of the group with her ability to maintain levity during meals in the face of both difficulty and poor weather. Natascha helped buoy the group in times of stress and make our meals fun-filled - the center of attention always. Debbie was everyone's younger sister - a fit woman who nevertheless emanated an intriguing fecundity and who easily accumulated the attentions of both men and women in the group. Debbie's affectation consisted of a youthful demeanor and voice - neither of which needed to be feigned. She was playful and buoyant - eminently appreciated and fun. Angie was somewhat quiet and pensive, disheveled and out of her element but clearly a thinker and perhaps was evolving into a role as a secondary stabilizing force - a counterpoint to Rich. We needed to consider Angie's position in our decisions. She was thoughtful and her opinions were well-formed. By Day Two the only member of our group who did not yet have an obvious "role" was Alex - Natascha's reserved, younger, red-haired sister. But, she came to the fore as an important stabilizing and mirthful presence later. It just required time for her to emerge from the long shadow of Natascha - her eminently lovable and more gregarious sister.

Our intent had been to depart from Shira Camp for Lava Tower at 7:30 AM. But our increasingly-apparent level of disorganization delayed our departure until 7:50 AM. Today's disorder consisted of the inability of Debbie to finish the packing her bag in her tent while the rest of us ate our breakfast and her delayed time in the toilet tent - needs for which we all forgave her and simply waited whilst appreciating the warm sun she was thereby generously allowing us.

After departing camp, we walked in single file - interspersed with the remaining three guides and headed Eastward along an open grassy and lightly-treed plateau. We gained altitude slowly - an easy start to the day. Lava Tower would be a 822 meter climb and would require an estimated 5-6 hours to reach. Our legs were fresh. Our stomachs were full. The air was clean and crisp. The sun beat down upon us and benevolently warmed us. We were amongst people whom we trusted. Optimism thereby prevailed.

As noted earlier approximately one hour of hiking was required before we were able to mentally "enter" the hike and establish a rhythm. That first hour required adjustment of gear, getting the legs working, waiting for the effects of painkillers to kick-in and scouring the mind for the appropriate meditative pattern of thought - all needed to fully enter and engage with the landscape and with the meditation. I was not an avid hiker but by Day 3 this pattern was readily apparent to me. I was anticipating it - the palliative that would carry me upward.

Hence, it was with considerable dismay that within fifteen minutes of departure Debbie announced to no one in particular she needed to pee! No sooner had she doffed her kit than the remaining women also expressed to the group their similar physiological needs. Poles and backpacks were discarded haphazardly along and within the foot-wide path. Our originating camp remained only 0.5 km away.

Each being modest the women scattered haphazardly toward adequately-sized and distant boulders and bushes. The remaining three men and three guides said nothing to one another. Instead, our heads, if accurately gauged would have been tilted a few degrees downward in disappointment.

Within 5-10 minutes the women had returned and quickly determined they were too hot - they had over-dressed for the day. There had been too much activity. A glorious and warming sun had risen from behind the adjacent Eastward summit - only a T-shirt was needed. Clothes then needed to be removed and repacked into backpacks and gear adjusted.

The Italians and French appeared from the ridge behind us and strode confidently past us paying us no heed. By necessity and with some chagrin our guides dragged the women's doffed gear away from the hiking trail to clear the way for these more capable yet galling passing teams. We watched begrudgingly as they vanished from view - up and over an adjacent rise - their cadence and uniformity remarkable. Perhaps those were the people who would successfully reach the summit whereas we might not.

Members of the Italian group - even the guides - were clad in identical fashionable green ponchos perhaps a characteristic one might anticipate with Italians. Richard speculated "whereas the Italians might be the best dressed the French likely hiked with the best food". When I queried Richard about what our UK-based group might be best known for, Richard quipped "the least organized". The chaos associated with "Brexit" suggests he might be right.

Debbie - aware she was holding-up the group appeared anxious. She was struggling with her gear and then admitted she had forgotten to don her belt. She informed us this is what had accounted for her pants sliding down earlier. She had been unable to locate her belt in her tent at camp. A guide-assisted search of the dozen or so zippered pockets on the exterior and interior of Debbie's backpack eventually revealed her belt and once donned the uppermost aspect of her pants became well-located around her waist. We were soon underway - a delay of 30 minutes following a 15-minute start.

As we moved onward the frequency of bathroom breaks and other distractions diminished - thereby allowing us to regain some of the lost time and to redevelop our rhythms. The path lead slightly upward toward Lava Tower through a wide open vista of volcanic boulders- boulders spewed skyward millennia ago perhaps coincident with the exogenesis of primitive man. In the intervening time the boulders - ranging in sizes from fist-sized lump to camper vans - had worn, had blackened and as noted the day prior - had sprouted impressive accumulations of colorful and dense mosses. These hung from their moorings like ringlets and provided cushions against which we could rest.

Until now the easily-identifiable “Lava Tower” loomed ahead of us. However, by mid-morning masses of threatening clouds began to approach us from both the West - from where we had derived - and from the East, (*i.e.,* from above). Hence, visibility of the tower began to diminish. The latter bank of clouds grew increasingly menacing and we understood within one-half hour we would be fully enveloped in fog and not so improbably - rain. Above us, on a distant and upper ridge we could divine the Italians striding quickly in order, no doubt, to evade the oncoming deluge.

The Tower was no longer visible. The upper bank of dark clouds was moving rapidly down to greet us. Freddy chattered about the rapidly changing weather in metaphorical detail referring to it as “The Kilimanjaro Cocktail” - with the rain representing the “pineapple juice” and the sun representing “the rum” - the two creating the Tanzanian version of a “Mai Tai”. None of it made sense but it was humorous.

By 11 AM the familiar coarse mist was heavily amongst us. It pried its way inside of my clothing and moistened my T-shirt. It worked its way into my psyche. We stopped to retrieve our rain gear from our back packs and reluctantly endeavored to put it on. The three-hour reprieve we had enjoyed in the sun passed - we steeled ourselves to a sticky and uncomfortable remaining climb.

Had we departed on time. Had we taken fewer breaks Had Debbie worn her belt, Had the French and the Italians not diminished us.......... these unhelpful thoughts periodically asserted their ugly heads within me.

Early in this moist aspect of the hike I joined Gillian at the lead just behind Obama and we again talked story about piloting for a good hour. While married and living with her husband at age 20 in a camper van in the UK Gillian had struck-out for Zambia to visit a friend and discovered a more interesting life she wanted - a life differing drastically from what she was then experiencing in the UK. In a short two weeks she left her husband - packed-up all of her gear and moved permanently to Zambia. That was nearly 30 years ago. In the intervening time Gillian obtained her pilot's license and became employed by a Zambian airline - flying throughout the country and coming to know all of Zambia's larger and smaller airports. She flew propeller planes- ones that could accommodate 6-8 passengers - often tourists. Some of her trips were routine airport-to-airport connections whereas others were flights to and from venerable tourist destinations - like Victoria Falls.

As pilots are wont to do we exchanged stories of the more harrowing experiences we had each experienced as pilots. On one flight she lost her only engine near Victoria Falls and had glided safely onto a sandy bank along a river near a ranch. She and her passenger were invited to stay overnight at a rancher's nearby home from where she called her office and a mechanic was flown out the next day to repair the aircraft such Gillian could fly it home. I had my stories too. But Gillian's were more varied and interesting. The addition of the African color (Wildebeest stories, Zambizi River rafting stories) added a dense richness and romance to her aeronautical adventures. She was calm intelligent and careful - qualities you would want in a pilot and clearly her various landings *sans* operating engine were evidence of her abilities. I understood and appreciated her heroics because I had miraculously accomplished the same feat next to a cemetery in a pasture back home. Presently Gillian owned a ranch raised cattle and was supported by Zambian maids and ranch hands. This conversation lasted a good hour and brought us closer together for, as reported earlier, I had been avoiding Gillian for fear of acquiring her cold.

I thought of the choices we make in life and how Gillian had made such an adventurous choice very early in life - to build a life in one of the most improbable of locations - Zambia. Perhaps this was easier or more accessible for a Brit - someone who might feel a relationship with the developing world via closer proximity to a colonial past. Any of us could have made such bold choices in our lives but somehow our inexperience and lack of imagination limits our views of what *is* possible - especially when we are young when our decisions carry so much import. Think about the arbitrary selection of a college major and the impact that decision imparts on one's life. Think about the choice of a partner and its impact. So much is possible when we are young. Who could have imagined Zambia in one's future? Who really has so much courage?

To my kids - (or any other young person reading this) - be bold. There's a big world out there and there's no one way to experience it! Decisions we make in our teens and 20's - even our 30's carry outsized import.

Gillian and I could have talked longer however Obama began playing music from an obtrusive Bluetooth speaker affixed to the rear of his pack - a speaker directed toward me. I was dismayed. First I felt music did not fit our pristine - almost sacred - environment and – second - Obama's choice of music bordered on the banal. Think "Queen". Reluctantly I stepped aside and away and established a hiking position at some distance from both Obama and Gillian. I did not want my experience to be diluted or intruded upon.

Each day contained some humorous incidents - something we could all laugh about as a group. On this day we had stopped for a brief rest beneath Lava Tower when Richard - thinking he remained a safe distance from the group - blasted out a hellacious fart - heard for dozens of meters. Unfortunately for him he had not noticed Debbie was adjacent to him and had bent over immediately behind him whilst retrieving something from her pack - with her ear located no more than two hand-lengths from his back end.

Debbie's reaction was priceless. She emitted a colossal shriek and ran from Richard at top speed - claiming not only was it loud but the odor was atrocious. And Richard being a good bloke took it all in good stride with his laughter resonating within our group and with our guides. From there Richard's threats of even worse flatulence at the next rest stop persisted for a good ten- to fifteen-minutes.

I ruminated on the gas laws and how they pertained to Richard's flatulence. At these upper elevations the gases produced by gastrointestinal microbes would be under less pressure and thereby be of considerably larger volume compared to volumes at lower elevations. I estimated the volume of flatulence generated per unit of time would be roughly double that of "normal" up here. Certainly altitude must have contributed to Richard's remarkable achievement. As to the odor, however, I'd blame the eggs not the elevation.

At this elevation (3,900 m) - amongst dense fog - we entered a new climactic zone. Depending upon one's source of information this was referred to as either "moorland" or "upper woodland". And as our new moorland trail became steeper an eccentric Kilimanjaro-specific "tree" (*Dendrosenecio kilimanjari* - Giant groundsel) came to prevail.

Coming from the Canadian prairies I'd not experienced anything quite like this "tree" before. A member of the sunflower family - *Dendrosenecio* are native to higher altitudes in mountainous regions of East Africa. They are characterized by stout 10 -15 cm woody stems that subdivide into several smaller branches - each of which presents a rich accumulation of desiccated russet-colored detritus along its stalk and a burst of olivine new growth at an apex. The younger plants stood at near 2 meters whereas the older plants reached 5-8 meters.

Richard, bless his heart, knew some of the the botanical names of the *Senecio* and other species and this enabled me to record and retrieve some of the above-noted information.

The novelty of this strange vegetation and the eeriness of hiking in so dense a fog distracted us from the moisture beginning to inch its way into and, unfortunately, under our hiking gear.

We reached Lava Tower at 1:15 PM - 5.5 hours following departure from Shira Camp. Had we been as efficient in hiking as the more-competent Italians or the French we would certainly have dodged the rain altogether. Pre-climb literature had indicated the climb from Shira Camp to Lava Tower should have taken four- to five-hours. We had arrived toward the laggard's end of that approximation.

Due of the rain and fog, visibility at Lava Tower had diminished to less than fifty meters. Upon arrival we were quickly directed by our guides toward our familiar "mess tent" and devoured the full nutritious lunch on offer.

Our elevation was 4,630 meters - the "climb high" aspect of Kandoo's "climb high, sleep slow" philosophy. This was the highest elevation to which any of us had hiked. Here we were beginning to assess our individual susceptibilities to altitude illnesses. We trusted the "climb high-sleep low" philosophy however we would soon learn strict adherence to this philosophy was brutal.

Little time was wasted with kibitzing over lunch. The mess tent was dark and desultory. We gobbled down our meal and then departed. We wanted to get ahead of the rain. Further, a significant hike was required of us to reach our evening camp - an anticipated two- to three-hour slog downward into Baranco Camp. This new destination rested at 3,976 meters- a drop of over several hundred meters - the "sleep low" aspect of Kandoo's hiking strategy. Baranco Camp lay only slightly above our previous night's camp in Shira. And while one might anticipate hiking *down* would be easier than hiking *up* I came to fully appreciate the reverse was true. Hiking down involves gravitationally-induced acceleration downward must be countered with additional involvement of one's quadriceps.

Vegetation- and climate-wise our descent into Baranco Camp was essentially the reverse of our ascent from Shira Camp to Lava Tower. We were circumscribed for almost the entire hike downward by a palpable gray fog which circumambulated the familiar *Senecio* forests, over-sized boulders and sage-colored brush - all of this with the silence accompanying the world's largest volcano. The path was well-marked and stony but not terribly dangerous or technical at any point. It was simply a continuous and reasonably steep downward trudge. The path was moist and a little slippery as well. We continued to wear our rain gear because the fog was so dense it mimicked a light rain. Without it our clothing would have become drenched. Visibility remained limited.

From Lava Tower we entered a deep natural valley adjacent to a nondescript Western wall and the "Baranco Wall" to the East. Elevations of both grew as we descended. It was through this valley where much of the rain that fell onto Kilimanjaro was channeled downward. Periodically we crisscrossed a burgeoning stream carrying the moisture from the higher elevations of Kilimanjaro to the agricultural plain near Moshi - southward and a few thousand meters below us.

Of the remaining eight climbers only Angie suffered overtly. She had quit smoking on the day of departure from Machame Camp - a decision although heroic jeopardized her enjoyment of the effort. Late on this day we would learn one of her knees had revolted - a common affliction of a downward hike. She languished far behind the lead group. Fortunately, she was accompanied by Raymond - our gentle soft-spoken guide. The remaining seven of us were acutely aware of Angie's withdrawal from the group and developed some concern. She was not catching up with us nor becoming visible behind us during our infrequent breaks. What is going on? Debbie asked. We were all concerned but could do little to help. Might this day claim our second hiker? Tomorrow, would we be down to seven able-bodied hikers?

This being our first descent I began to understand the import of preparing for a climb and in particular in developing one's quads adequately. Similar to Day 1 my quads began to ache. I understood the biology and physics of the pain but there was little I could do beyond ingest more painkillers and unlike Day 1, stop to periodically consume easily-metabolizable carbohydrate-rich foods. The hurt on this day did not reach the levels I had experienced on Day 1 where I needed to begin quantifying the level of misery I was experiencing. But to be certain the hike down was less than enjoyable. Within a few hours I had tired of the novelty of the *Senecio*, the blackened boulders, the multi-colored lichens and the sage-colored forbs. Instead I concentrated on the weak points of my body. Perhaps we were all concentrating on this aspect of the challenge.

We had departed Lava Tower at 2:15 PM and miraculously arrived into Baranco Camp four hours later. I was sweating so profusely that I had stripped down to a T-shirt. All of us, lacking Angie, then coalesced for photos at the Baranco Camp sign following documentation of our arrivals at the Baranco Ranger Station. We individually began recording "unusual" occupations into the Ranger Station ledger - a couple of us entering "male model" as our occupations (maybe it was the altitude). Angie arrived 45 minutes later looking bedraggled and was suffering in one knee. Her normally lighter demeanor had been replaced with a heavily-furrowed brow and an obvious unvoiced worry. She was concerned and asked "Was there an evacuation site available at Baranco?" It seemed unlikely given the remote precipice upon which we resided.

During the last hour of our downward hike from Lava Tower, the sky lightened, the exotic *Senecio* vegetation vanished, the clouds retreated and when we entered Baranco Camp proper we encountered an unexpectedly magnificent and welcome sunset! The sun was setting behind the Westward ridge with its softening golden light - illuminating the nearby Baranco Wall - a wall we were to climb tomorrow - with increasingly psychedelic colors. As the sun further retreated the wall itself shifted from brilliant oranges and rusty-reds to soft, earthen browns - the sky resplendent and shifting into various hues of oranges, pinks, peaches, yellows, blues and sapphires. I scrambled about with my wide-angle lens doing my best to capture the magic of the colors and the effervescence that my friends were expressing in having reached so remarkable a night's accommodation.

Baranco Camp lay on an abbreviated red-rocked plateau on a Southern craggy exposure of Kilimanjaro - snuggly nestled between the aforementioned two ridges. The camp commanded an astonishing vista southward toward the agricultural lands surrounding Moshi and of an adjacent leaden lake. As the evening progressed the lights of Moshi materialized and Freddy joked "the red light there is my house". However, of the thousands of lights emanating from Moshi none of us could divine a single red one.

So began the rhythm of Kilimanjaro...days would dawn into thin air with a clear cold sun and with ice cloaking our tent - we woke to warm ourselves with mugs of hot coffee or chocolate - a few clouds and a warming three- to four-hours after which clouds would form, fog would encroach and rain showers would prevail after which, near dusk, the clouds would retreat and warm dry air coupled with compassionate evening colors returned. Indeed, this was the "Kilimanjaro cocktail".

Dusk enveloped our insular camp and we withdrew into lesser motion. Three days had elapsed - it felt like three weeks. We had reached 3,945 meters of elevation but, more impressively, we had entered the lofty elevation of 4,600 meters at lunch. I rested in the darkening mess tent listening to conversations but could not warm my body. Alex realized I was non-communicative and quite shaky and suggested I retrieve warmer clothes from my tent. Perhaps I was unknowingly chilled. I followed her advice and immediately began to feel better.

As foretold by our guides the first sign of altitude illness announced itself within me. In addition to the physical pain I manifested a wretched nausea and could not muster much appetite at dinner. I ate only four cashews a small amount of spaghetti with ketchup and half a bowl of thin pumpkin soup - this despite an abundant repast on offer and a high caloric need. The thought of consuming more food revolted me. Amongst my friends though some retained a robust appetite. Others too felt poorly. Our arrival at Baranco presented a mixed capability. Gillian retained her wet cold. Angie was doubting her knees.

Despite the day's effort and the elevation all of us passed our health check. My heart rate was 98 bpm but my oxygen saturation had increased to 91%. I was the first in our group to exhibit an upward deflection in oxygen saturation and interpreted my meager improvement as evidence of the plasticity of my physiology. At least this was an improvement I could hang my hat on and thereby derive some solace.

We withdrew to our tents beneath an intense spray of Kilimanjaro's abundant and glittering stars - so intense they cast distinct shadows of our tired bodies against the stony camp floor and upon the walls of our silent tents. Before I entered my cocoon I looked skyward to imbibe their magic and the charm of the many spinning galaxies. They radiated their steely blues, their soft yellows and their apricots. Without hesitation I reached heavenward and moved my hands amongst them - their masses stinging like cold needles against my hands. Unexpectedly the stars were loosened gently from their moorings and swirled in familiar Van Gogh-like spirals.

Refrains from Don McLean's "Starry Starry Night" ran through my mind with its alternating major and minor keys - from then and until I slept. One man confronting infinity.

++

"Vincent (Starry, Starry Night)"
-Don McLean

Starry, starry nlght
Paint your palette blue and gray
Look out on a summer's day
With eyes that know the darkness in my soul

Shadows on the hills
Sketch the trees and the daffodils
Catch the breeze and the winter chills
In colors on the snowy linen land

Now I understand
What you tried to say to me
And how you suffered for your sanity
And how you tried to set them free

They would not listen, they did not know how
Perhaps they'll listen now

Starry, starry night
Flaming flowers that brightly blaze
Swirling clouds in violet haze
Reflect in Vincent's eyes of china blue

Colors changing hue
Morning fields of amber grain
Weathered faces lined in pain
Are soothed beneath the artist's loving hand

Now I understand
What you tried to say to me
And how you suffered for your sanity
And how you tried to set them free

They would not listen, they did not know how
Perhaps they'll listen now

For they could not love you
But still your love was true
And when no hope was left in sight
On that starry, starry night

You took your life, as lovers often do
But I could've told you Vincent
This world was never meant for
One as beautiful as you

Starry, starry night
Portraits hung in empty halls
Frame-less heads on nameless walls
With eyes that watch the world and can't forget

Like the strangers that you've met
The ragged men in ragged clothes
The silver thorn of bloody rose
Lie crushed and broken on the virgin snow

Now I think I know
What you tried to say to me
And how you suffered for your sanity
And how you tried to set them free

They would not listen, they're not listening still
Perhaps they never will

Chapter Twelve
Baranco Camp Lore

Rise (Pheko Mothaung, 2016)

Rise
Mount Kilimanjaro
Kiss the sky

Camp animated itself at 6 AM to the irritating sounds high-pitched metal zippers. When I unzipped my own tent cold heavy air awoke in me the precarious awareness of confronting another day. The sun lay far below Baranco Wall and had yet to begin its enlightenment of the adjacent creamy Western ridge. Temperatures were well below freezing. One by one our team members unfolded from their tents - collecting mugs of steaming coffee tea or cocoa. We huddled in small clusters and warmed our hands and stomachs - rehydrating and steeling against the cold and the anticipated day. Nary a breeze touched us. Our expired air hung fleetingly then vanished quietly – ephemerally - into the chilled morning air.

Conversations were short and UK-polite - "Good morning, how are you? Fine, Thank-you, and you?" and "Did you sleep well?". These abbreviated meditations progressed into more complex conversations and became more animated as Richard's good-natured laugh gained ascendancy. We were developing friendships and confidence. So began our days.

The atmosphere far beneath us lingered as mist. A comprehensive view of the primordial Moshi plain was thereby obscured. But as the sun gained elevation the view beneath us transitioned into vaporous mauves and peaches and the floor of the Moshi plain began to take form. To the East- the sky- crimson at Baranco's summit - shifted incrementally into more vibrant hues - blood orange, canary yellow and searing white. As the sun cracked the Eastern horizon at the zenith of Baranco its warm energy enlightened the uppermost reaches of a chilled and still sleepy Western ridge. A sharp shadow cast by the jagged Baranco summit advanced down the Western wall and crept toward our still dimly-lit elevation. Forthrightly our nearest celestial star warmed us directly. We then lingered and absorbed its warmth - like stationary insects on a cold morning - despite the beckoning of our guides from the still dark mess tent.

The assignment today promised to be both treacherous and arduous but if weather cooperated - potentially scenic. Parallel ridges radiated downward from Kilimanjaro's summit toward its expansive base near Moshi. Each of the valleys provided unique habitats with potential for unique species. One of these habitats sanctioned growth of Africa's tallest tree (*Entandrophragma excelsum*) - a tree for which no "English name" seems available. However, three local languages (Luganda, Rukonjo and Rutoro) refer to the tree as "Muyovu". Three extant Tanzanian languages use other names for the same species. Discovered only in the last few years it stands at 81.5 meters and at its base is 2.5 meters thick. These are rare trees and are threatened within Africa. Aspects of the tree have traditionally been harvested to treat gonorrhea and cough. I hoped to encounter Muyovu - not to treat either of these two maladies but for biological interest.

On today's hike - *Hymenopterae*-like - we would traverse several of Kilimanjaro's ridges perpendicularly. First we were to scale the adjacent Baranco Wall then descend into its neighboring valley. From thence we were to mount a second ridge and again descend into a second valley. There was to be a third ridge and a third descent and finally one final ascent into Karanga Camp. Today's hike would navigate the southern exposure of Kilimanjaro at altitudes varying from 3,600 meters to 4,200 meters and deliver us to a vantage point where we might view Mt. Mawenzi - a spectacular but extinct volcano lying to the East of Kilimanjaro proper.

Baranco Camp lay at 3,600 meters whereas Karanga Camp lay at 4,000 meters. Hence, the day's effort would net us a 400-meter gain in altitude - this despite many more hundreds of meters of climbs and descents. I imagined this minimal gain in altitude served the purpose of aiding our adaptation to altitude. One was not supposed to be gain altitude too recklessly in these environs.

Amongst a bevy of communicative Ravens, we gravitated toward the mess tent - joining the guides at 7:00 AM. Clearly the ravens anticipated the arrival of food as eagerly as we. They beseeched us via their beady expressive eyes and their downcast wings. When we tossed a piece of toast or sausage in their direction they would all rush toward it - nodding and cawing their pleasure - fighting one another for a share of the morsel. I wondered if these were the same ravens who met us in Machame Camp and who then followed us upward. Or were there distinct populations of ravens populating each camp? Irrespective - theirs could not be an easy life - scavenging what little the climbers and the mountain might collectively surrender.

Reassuringly my appetite had returned following its unexpected departure the evening prior. The lack of food last evening and the intervening twelve hours - during which time my muscles were left aching for nourishment - had translated into a rapacious interest in eating whatever I could place my eyes and hands upon. But today's offerings were less plentiful with only soup, toast, eggs and bacon on offer.

By now I was becoming used to the more-polite ways of people who derived from the UK. Breakfast requests typically consisted of "Could you please pass the...", "thank you" and "excuse my reach". Perhaps the most striking example of politeness though was in methods used to consume soup. Whereas I - bohemian-like - simply lifted my soup bowl to my lips and drank the soup directly - *i.e.,* Japanese-style - the remaining members of my group consumed their soup with spoons. How unnecessary I thought! However, Gillian went so far as to use a more most-polite technique - she spooned her soup away from her body and lifted it, spoonful by spoonful, from the opposing aspect of her bowl! While impressed with her adherence to decorum I felt our circumstances did not warrant it.

Today I made bacon sandwiches with warm toast and orange marmalade. I willed all of the protein toward my aching leg muscles with the ardent prayer my musculature might regain some of the structural integrity it had lost during the first three days of the hike. I know - this is a recurring theme. But I had become fixated on this each time I had access to any recognizable form of protein.

Our group was upbeat - possibly arising from the magnificent sunrise we had shared. Angie, having struggled mightily with her knee the day prior presented as determined, gregarious and buoyant. Rich and Richard arrived together enthusiastic- like fidgety horses - champing at their bits. I was growing to enjoy their reference to each other as "mate" and beginning to employ this term of endearment when addressing them. Natascha remained boisterous and happy. Her sparkling blue eyes and unkempt long blonde hair betrayed an infectious high-spirit. Alex was opening-up and becoming more cheerful - talking and smiling broadly. Debbie, her thick hair held back in a ubiquitous blue elastic bandana was chattering with everyone and laughing - the freckles on her face dancing as the stars had the night prior. Gillian though still suffered from her cold and although she remained stoic she remained cowed. Her affliction seemed to not have abated whatsoever - surprising to me because it had persisted four full days! Further, Richard had a runny nose and commented privately to me he may have "caught Gillian's cold". His news reinforced my resolution to continue to maintain as much distance from Gillian as I possibly could - at least when contained within the mess tent. It appeared to be one of those insidiously tenacious colds - like an angry dog - growling and refusing to give up its bone. It was not lessening in severity. If anything it was taking an even greater hold upon her than when she had initiated the hike.

We all felt badly for Gillian but out of our need to maintain a collective high spirit and optimism we never discussed the malady in Gillian's presence - unless she brought it up first.

We were to depart at 8 AM. No one quibbled with early departures because we fully appreciated the importance of staying ahead of the rain. Kilimanjaro punished laggards with inclement weather. Nevertheless, Debbie decided at the predetermined time of embarkation she "needed to go to the 'loo'". Thus delayed - hikers and guides waited "patiently" adjacent to the commencement of the Baranco trail. The narrow circus-like toilet tent again rattled to and fro as Debbie thrashed within its narrow confines. The design of the toilet tent caused any motion initiated toward its base to be entertainingly amplified several-fold at its apex. It could only have been more humorous if a flag had been attached to the top.

The commencement of trail led downward across a well-trodden gravel slope. Twenty-to-thirty other brightly-clad French and Italian hikers well ahead of us - zig-zagging their way down into a pristine river valley and then up along and onto the still-darkened West-facing Wall. At a distance these hikers appeared as animated strings of Nepalese flags - decorating an otherwise nondescript wall with dancing colors.

At the base of the Wall- perhaps thirty meters below camp - we forded a small stream. We gingerly leapt from rock to rock eschewing the water threatening to seep into our boots. Once across we entered the cool protective shade of Baranco Wall. I was grateful for the shade because the two-hour climb of the Wall would be much easier if we were not exposed to the sun's direct rays.

As if anticipating our move, the ravens departed camp *en* masse and followed us - this time circling us in ever-widening arcs - 20-30 meters above us. Even from this distance I noted their heads twisted from side-to-side- each eyeing us for possible signs of sustenance. Or perhaps their purpose lay beyond this primal need. Certainly no one was feeding them. Instead they genuinely appeared to be just watching us - maybe enjoying us. "Why do these little people labor so hard when they could more simply float on the winds?" they were thinking.

Perhaps this was a symbiosis whereby we first fed the ravens and then they then took-on roles of protectors - perhaps showing us the way of Baranco Wall. Teachers maybe. Or possibly they were curious. Or they might be satiated but bored.

We re-entered the "alpine/high desert" zone of Kilimanjaro - a zone extending upward from our current altitude to 4,875 meters. Here plant-life was greatly diminished and the air noticeably thinner - slipping in and out of my chest effortlessly. Searing but refreshingly effortless. That my lungs were still able to extract sufficient oxygen from this thin air made me proud.

Baranco Wall represented the most treacherous physical aspect of the entire Kilimanjaro experience - a near vertical 400 meter +/- ascent. To scale the wall, we followed well-worn switchbacks - snaking left then right - unforgivingly upward. We were unable to use hiking poles for this ascent because we instead needed free hands to gain purchase of the convenient rocky outcrops littering the climb. I adhered to a self-taught belief - at all times I should maintain three points of attachment to the wall. When contacts were reduced to two - I experienced some anxiety - the palms of my hands would moisten and my heart would quicken. During the most treacherous parts - where the trail was narrow and steep and where a fall could easily have resulted in death - our guides distributed themselves above and below us and were ready to grab at us or to extend a hand to assist in minimizing risk. The truth however was, if one of us did fall, there'd have been little they could have done to arrest a fall. The best they might have done was to wave and wish us a safe non-lethal landing.

I was certainly aware of this risk but was not terribly worried. I retained confidence in my ability to undertake such risks. I could feel the shape of the uneven path unmistakably through the Vibram soles of my boots. My bare hands trusted the morning-chilled and immovable rocks standing alongside our path.

Angie became petrified by the challenges presented by several treacherous portions of the wall - perhaps unreasonably so. Her eyes narrowed and she isolated herself from the rest of us whenever she needed to focus on these challenges. To me - her fear bordered on acrophobia. At difficult sections of the trail guides assisted her - one on her left and one on her right - sometimes one behind her. They used verbal encouragement to wheedle and cajole her into believing the wall was well within her capabilities. She was fighting fears she had not known she harbored. The rest of us were pleased to have the guides help her because we needed to give full attention to our own ascents. We were in no position to offer assistance. Our fears were reinforced when one of the porters from a leading hiking group lost his footing and fell at a dangerous section of the trail. He lost the entirety of his load but fortuitously managed to prevent himself from sliding over a precipitous edge following its lead. The load tumbled 200-300 meters below us - bouncing unpredictably - shredding *en* route and came to rest in the river valley we had departed not so long ago. That a young and experienced porter could slip and fall.......

Aspects of the young porters' lives were quite sad. They had individually derived from many of Tanzania's impoverished villages. Few spoke English, the *lingua franca* of Tanzania. Ferrying tourists' kit up and back down Kilimanjaro was the best they could do to earn money for themselves and for their families - a physically-demanding and possibly dangerous job. All of the porters appeared to be less than thirty-five years-old. Most were in their early- to mid-twenties. Sometimes their limited means meant their gear was inadequate and I have correspondingly read reports since returning from Tanzania a few porters die every year from hypothermia at the higher elevations of Kilimanjaro. Some guide companies - as Kandoo does - make efforts to assure customers of their concern for their porters' well-being. Some companies do not. These latter companies charge correspondingly less for a guide-assisted ascent. This is how the world *is* and always will be. But it does underscore the power of the decisions we each have opportunity to make - decisions can either bring harm or bring benefit others.

On the wall - every step and every handhold needed to be tested and secured. During the more lackadaisical aspects of the other day's hike - the rambles - my mind would wander far and wide. On the wall - I had to focus - blocking out thoughts of people back home and thoughts of my various petty traumas and insults. But, I enjoyed the requisite concentration immeasurably. I felt my body laboring capably. There was freedom - the freedom from everything normally consuming one's consciousness - a type of meditation. On the Wall we existed individually and in the present. Here we understood and appreciated ourselves as the living, respiring hymenopterans we were. If we weren't careful the mountain would take us and squash us. And like the insects we also thoughtlessly squash without giving second thought - little would change in the world if any of us were similarly taken.

Whereas we had been promised the ascent would require two hours - the actual ascent required two hours and 45 minutes; a sizeable chunk of the anticipated four- to five-hour entirety of the day's hike. And while an added three-quarters of an hour may sound trivial to the lay reader - in the moment it represented an important addition to our effort. With no extraneous bushes nor large boulders accessible the Diamox-challenged members of our group had miraculously accommodated this duration without a single pee break. Further no complaints were voiced. Why would that be? On prior days the best we had endured without a pee break had been one hour. What the human spirit may overcome when choices are absent!

Baranco Summit materialized as an expansive, undulating, granite-floored ledge with potential for dramatic views to both the South and Southeast. However, by the time we had arrived outsized grumbling clouds were fomenting anarchy just beneath us. Catching view of us on the ledge they began to assert themselves aggressively. It was another dramatic example of Freddy's allusion to the "Kilimanjaro Cocktail" - the rum - as is its wont- was again in need of the pineapple juice.

At Baranco Summit the porters supporting the French and Italian efforts had prepared a coffee and tea reception in anticipation of their guests' arrival. I was relieved to find almond-filled croissants were not on offer for them. Our porters were notably absent. I estimated that our porters might already be in Karanga Camp-possibly enjoying their own restorative coffee and tea-unencumbered - for the time-being - by their needy charges. While our continental contemporaries did not overtly rub our noses in our poverty we could not help but feel further diminished and incapable.

Stil - animated by the confidence engendered by our success on "the Wall" - we posed for group and individual photos on a precipice overlooking a weather-obscured expanse of northern Tanzania. Our packs and poles had been discarded - much like tattered Groundsel detritus. Such was our flexibility and satisfaction with the day's effort that no one would have complained if Freddy had equivocated - "Change of plans! We're camping here tonight!". Jokes about this possibility were made. But we knew. Our porters and our gear were in fact long gone. No such announcement was nigh. The French and the Italians had departed without a respectful glance in our direction. We understood a protracted day - perhaps a more difficult aspect of the day - lay ahead.

Following a twenty-minute break a dense fog enveloped us. It swirled around in patchy rivulets of wind-whipped airborne vapor. Visibility was fifty meters. Gritty biting sleet impregnated itself and harassed exposed skin. Wind howled in and amongst oversized boulders. It was rapidly chilling - well below freezing. Prior to departing I retrieved my blue felt Patagonia hat from my pack, snugged it comfortably down over my ears and cheeks and then wrapped a buff around my neck and mouth. In our real and metaphorical packs - we have these blessings.

We continued downward into the first valley - a descent of nearly 150 meters - re-entering the familiar "moorland and heather" zone. Not unexpectedly the adjacent valley comprised dense *Senecio* forests again accented by a thick texture of sage-inspired shrubbery - boulders blanketed by dense carpets of maroon-colored mosses and patchy lichens - red, brown and pale orange. All of this partially cloaked by errant sprites of fog.

The day's ascents crested the more ascetic alpine aspects of Kilimanjaro. At each apex biting winds whipped around and through us and compelled us to never linger- but to sally into the more-protected valleys. We hiked the duration of the day - in and out of these remarkable transitions - becoming less enamored with the changing climactic and vegetative phenomena as the day wore on - a combination of habituation and exhaustion.

Because more moisture was contained within the lower valley altitudes the clay footpaths were more slippery than I appreciated. Our team employed all manner of strategies to safely descend without slipping. We put our hiking poles to good use to break our downward momenta and used of the branches projecting across the path for hand-holds - particularly on the switch-backs - the steeper portions of our descents. As evidence we were not the first to struggle on these slippery trails - the vermillion bark of madrone bushes had been polished smooth by the oils derived from the grips of repeated use by passing hikers. Without poles and these handholds my toes would have arrived in even worse condition than they otherwise did arrive into Karanga a few hours later.

This was Day Four. Each of us was doing well and developing confidence in his/her abilities to "summit". Summiting was in the back of all our minds. The concept had been introduced to us in Kandoo climbing literature and bandied about throughout the hike. Kandoo had touted a "greater-than-90% success rate" in getting climbers to the summit. None of us allowed ourselves to doubt our abilities and our guides provided continuous reassurance we were all capable of summiting. Whether this was a true confidence or was wishful thinking is still not clear. Notwithstanding - while we were developing confidence in our athletic prowess we had not tested our abilities to withstand altitude. None of us had previously hiked over 4,000 meters. Some of us had not climbed over 3,000 meters. We were well above 3,000 meters and had far more to go. Kilimanjaro's summit lay at near 6,000 meters. Uncertainty remained.

The day wore on and I had forgotten my interest in Africa's tallest tree - the Muyovu. The lankiest trees we encountered were the Groundsel. We no longer considered these exotic nor terribly interesting. Based on my reading the Muyovu existed nearby. I just did not know which valley they inhabited.

The last valley - the third fold of Kilimanjaro's Southern cloak - presented near noon. It required another descent of a few hundred meters, a crossing of a shallow boulder-strewn river and then an ascent into our refuge for the night - Karanga Camp. Approaching camp, I discovered one could approximate the location of the succeeding camp by the distant arc of ravens. That we had seen no ravens since our departure this morning and came upon a circling population hinted each camp maintained its own resident population.

We tentatively approached Karanga's lofty radio antennae - framed against blustery leaden skies. Freddy informed me the antennae's function was to communicate between the Ranger Station and the authorities below. Perhaps a helicopter could be called in to address a severe injury or illness. The antennae and ravens were welcome harbingers of Focus and all else they portended - a tent, a sleeping pad, an unfurled sleeping bag and a duffle bag filled with dry clothes - those coupled with good food and conviviality.

Coincident with reaching a ridge overlooking the day's final valley I discerned musters of porters descending from the opposing ridge - down toward a small river lying between these two neighboring ridges. Rather than employing an obvious path the porters clambered down a steep wall - moving hesitatingly - leaping like sure-footed goats from one safe position to the next. Upon reaching the river they collected water into 20-liter jugs. The weight of water they carried was impressive considering the water represented ¼ - 1/3 of our porters' weight. The water the porters ferried - upon its arrival back into camp - was treated with chlorine or iodine so it would be safe to drink upon our arrival - perhaps 2 hours later.

The final ascent into Karanga Camp was virtually beyond us. We were collectively beaten and downcast. The long day of ascents and descents had taken its toll. Looking upward, ravens circled effortlessly, their wings stationary and as they orbited they again taunted us: "Ha ha you ungainly, pitiful creatures!" "You have so much more work to do!" "But if you had our wisdom and talents, you could rise on the wind and frolic with us. Ha ha." With that they circled away and vanished behind the Karanga ridge. I was too tired to damn them for mocking us.

We were exhausted but I found myself at the front of the pack - perhaps eagerly anticipating arrival and the collapse into the warm canvas embrace of my bivouac. My quadriceps seared with as much discomfort as they had on the first day of the hike. But here I addressed the problem with a double dose of painkillers. No one was communicating. Whereas the day had started easy and light-hearted with plenty of banter and excitement concerning Baranco Wall we were diminished both physically and emotionally - all operating on fumes. Our marginal breakfast had proven insufficient to meet the day's caloric need. We were rapidly mobilizing body mass to reach this remote and desolate camp. Some of us were packing more body mass than others. Perhaps my access to metabolizable energy was why I found myself at the front of the pack!

After resting three or four times we arrived into Karanga at 1:15 PM. The hike had taken 5.25 hours - only marginally longer than the anticipated duration of four to five hours.

Kilimanjaro Summit - above us and to the Northwest - endured behind a dense cloak of steely gray clouds. A silent Mt. Mawenzi remained similarly shrouded. However, transcendent downward views - both to the South and to the South-east compensated for those twin disappointments.

After registering at the Ranger Station I met up with Focus and he directed me again to my familiar abode. On the past two nights my tent had been pitched at the outermost edge of our group's camp and I wondered whether this extreme location was associated with my reputation for - at a minimum - excessive snoring. When I had awoken during previous nights I was assaulted by a cacophony of ungainly reverberations produced by my teammates- snoring, unzipping, thrashing about and coughing. Could my own commotions have been so much worse that I needed to be so located? I never asked. Nor was this possibility ever discussed in my presence. Just to be safe, however, I recommended to Rich- the occupant of the closest tent- to wear ear plugs on this and subsequent nights.

Thankfully Focus assisted me in unlacing and removal of my hiking boots and in storing my hiking poles beneath the floor of my tent- perhaps acknowledging I was – indeed - an older man. I tipped him with a $20 US bill and discerned from his face and cloudy red-stained eyes he appreciated the gesture. Whether it was his thin smile or the slight dilation of his pupils which communicated gratitude - I can't be certain.

My legs ached and I ingested more painkillers - this an hour after my last intake. After a few minutes of rest, I gingerly removed my mildewed socks and discovered three toes on my right foot were freshly inflamed - swelling bordering on blistering - a sign of wear and tear arising from the three descents of the day and previous day's descent from Lava Tower into Baranco. My big toe in particular was expressing particular dismay. Fortunately, as *per* Kandoo recommendations I had packed all manner of support materials for this development - moleskin, medical tape, triple antibiotic ointment, nail clippers and bandages. I had hoped they would prove unnecessary.

Boots are critical to a successful hike. This pair had served me well in Nepal, Patagonia and elsewhere. I had confidence in them. Because of this I had not anticipated their degradation. In Karanga I discovered the stitching on the lower inside arch of my right boot was beginning to loosen and give way. Hence the cupping or gripping feature of my right boot holding my heel back toward the rear of the boot during descents was beginning to fail. I had no access to the stout stitching required to effect a repair.

Resolved to continue, I wrapped my inflamed toes with protective barriers of Neosporin, medical tape and moleskin.

I had brought my son's solar charger with which one could - via a USB connector - charge an iPhone or other device. As I was increasingly using my iPhone for quick and easy photography I set-up a charging station beside my tent for my phone and - when Richard discovered my innovation- for his iPhone via a second USB port. To keep the feather-light charger from blowing away we anchored its base with lava rocks and angled its face toward the sun. Porters came and went noting this novelty and I was briefly made to feel like a sophisticated and knowledgeable hiker. Via intermittent late-afternoon sun we achieved near 25% charges on our devices.

The camp - anchored in the arid Alpine Zone of Kilimanjaro - was nearly devoid of vegetation. It occupied a precipice on the darkening Southeast face of Kilimanjaro and was populated by misshapen, wind-worn boulders of varying sizes. The few plants amongst us were small, woody and robust - no more than a few centimeters in height. Insects were notably absent. As the sun's light waned - the camp's few ravens lay hidden in protected crevices - their silvery neck feathers betraying them. Yet, they watched us and waited.

The sun emerged intermittently from behind fast-moving thickets of fog. The razor sharp wind whipped briskly. Untethered tent flaps flailed defenselessly - producing hostile thrashing sounds. I recalled the comforts I felt indoors when blizzards captured our resolute Canadian prairie homes.

The temperature was at freezing - promising a cold night. Sleet began to assail us and was beginning to accumulate in cracks in the ground and next to rocks and tents. And thereupon we were beckoned for dinner.

Like the ravens we huddled in the mess tent exchanging small stories while the protective tarp vibrated and snapped threateningly in the wind. Periodic blasts of durable sleet produced a sharp staccato against the rigid, undulating cover.

The cook had made an unusual effort - bestowing upon us crepes chock-full with tangy Nutella, sliced bananas and rice - all carbohydrate-rich and potentially storable as liver and muscle glycogen. As usual amity prevailed but it was clear Gillian had finally transferred her viral respiratory infection to Richard. He was sniveling. We offered whichever decongestants and antihistamines we harbored in our packs. No recriminations were directed in Gillian's direction. Such was the gentle and forgiving nature of our group.

Freddy gingerly entered the mess tent to complete the daily health check and provide some information on the upcoming day. Yet our team refused to pay him any heed. Exuberant back-and-forth conversation continued unabated until Freddy - using a more insistent voice asserted "May I borrow your silence?" Seven of the eight of us then quietened and directed our capricious attentions expectantly toward Freddy. Richard however took no notice of Freddy and continued on with his gleeful banter as our ever-patient Freddy stood silent – waiting - eyes darting among the newly-silent. Rich finally nudged Richard gently in Freddy's direction to aid

Freddy in gaining Richard's full attention. Freddy's medical check proceeded without concern - all of us easily passing both the heart rate and hemoglobin oxygenation assessments.

It was malevolently dark - more so than expected for this time of day. Cloud cover was solid and the unremitting sleet continued to pound aggressively against the thin tarped walls and roof of the mess tent. We were fully satiated but none of us were eager to retire. It was still too early and - in addition - none of us were willing to confront the aggressive sleet storm raging immediately outside. Richard - flushed from excessive sun - recounted his day with Rich's broad smile, encouragement and interest. Rich opined on all manner of Kilimanjaro trivia and - appropriate to his profession - the impact of the hike on foot health. Gillian had become animated - more so than prior and I considered she was beginning to shake her cold. Her face was less taught and her eyes glistened with more mirth than I had observed previously. Alex and her sister were clowning - much to our entertainment and to the attendant guides'. Natascha's remarks were becoming increasingly bawdy and - as a group - we were loud when we laughed with her. Other hiking groups - perhaps the French and the Italians - must certainly have heard us.

Yes - it was chilly and inordinately inhospitable outside - however the tarp isolating us from the inclement weather proved sufficient for humanity to gain a small foothold on this unprotected flank of Kilimanjaro. How many similar evenings has this mountain engendered - engendered among people who were firstly strangers?

Within an hour the sleet storm abated and its attendant cloud cover was bullied rapidly Northward. Accompanying this fortuitous development - the sky lightened. The lofty summit of Kilimanjaro's tallest cone (Kibo) became visible. And when news of the visibility of the Kibo summit arrived we evacuated the mess tent *en* masse and gazed heavenward - agog. Kibo towered - a snow and glacier-striped dome - the tallest of Kilimanjaro's three peaks - brooding blue-grey and white - foreboding yet regal in the darkening wind-whipped evening sky.

The uninviting steel-gray pallor of the peak alerted us to the proximity of tomorrow's effort. Tomorrow we would assail the dome- an effort none of us had come close to attempting prior. There it was - Kibo- in cold blues and grays.

Despite Freddy's insistent earlier briefing some rather important details were omitted. Had we been adequately apprised of the next two day's effort we might justifiably had lost confidence in ourselves. Further - none of this information had been provided in Kandoo product literature nor in the trek's pre-hike briefing - the briefing delivered only a few days earlier at the Stella Rose Hotel. This omission - I believe - was likely an intentional omission because it allowed a measure of optimism - albeit misguided - to prevail amongst us prior to undertaking the challenge of Kibo directly.

The expectations for Day Five - as outlined by Freddy - are briefly detailed below:

> We would depart early the next morning from Karanga Camp (*ca.* 4,000 meters) and hike to Barafu Camp (4,673 meters) - arriving near noon. Barafu would function as our "base camp". This represented a net gain of 670 meters for the first hike of the day. Of note, this would be the highest elevation to which any of us had hiked previously. Then we would hibernate in our tents till near 10 PM - a 9-hour hiatus - which allowed us to re-collect strength, reconsider our

limitations and then undertake the second hike of the day. For the latter effort we would strike-out for the Uhuru summit of Kibo (5,995 meters) at 11 PM, hike through the night and - without incident - arrive at the summit near 8 AM- nine hours later. This would be undertaken following a night with no sleep and a 1,200-meter additional altitude gain. The net gain in vertical elevation for the twenty four hours would therefore approximate 1,900 meters. This effort would allow us to witness "a glorious Tanzanian sunrise". The rising sun would climb over the Eastern Tanzanian landscape, illuminate neighboring Mt. Mawenzi and Mt. Meru and would be visually stunning - a phenomenon said to be worth the effort alone. Because of altitude sickness concerns our time at the summit would be limited to less than one hour after which we would descend to Base Camp and after a brief stop and lunch hike eight more hours down a dry river bed to a lower elevation (Mweka Camp, 3,983 meters) so the earlier rapid ascent to Uhuru Summit did not result in any untoward elevation-associated and life-threatening maladies such as HAPE or HACE. The drop from Uhuru Summit on Kibo to Mweka Camp was 1,913 meters - roughly equivalent to the elevation gain existing between Karanga Camp and the Summit. The hike downward from Base Camp to Mweka would be completed between 1 PM and 6 PM following lunch. Those were the unexpected nuts and bolts of it.

That none of our group had grasped the effort required of us to reach the summit prior to embarking on this ambitious day was remarkable. We had been more concerned with food and getting a decent night's sleep.

Chapter Thirteen
To Barafu Camp

The boy in mount kilimanjaro (by Ary)

the boy in mount kilimanjaro,
I was told.
how he sits on blissful soil
with head up in clouds
looking at mixtures of azul.
under ravishing lights.

the boy in mount kilimanjaro
his eyes I was also told.
how the sun would turn away
or how the comets whisper
in shame-
luminous perhaps?
that's the boy in mount kilimanjaro

tonight, under no starry skies
I met the boy in mount kilimanjaro.
eyes closed, he was looking up
but in one breathe I made-
he opened them.
rays of galaxies shone
making pathway for the stars
from his eyes.
above us, the skies reflected his eyes-
stars appearing & dancing like fire,
flickering & twinkling in the skies
of sapphire.

in a wind's gush
the boy turned to me,

his eyes still glistening
from the stars that left his eyes
and onto the never ending night.
therefore, as the story goes & told
secrets of the night unfold.
in the eyes of the boy from mount kilimanjaro
lies the wishes of what the night skies
borrow-
the kilimanjaro stars.

****

We woke to cheerful moods engendered by a clear sapphire sky, a crisp breeze, hot coffee, enthusiastic friends and a magnificent vista. From Karanga Camp we looked down upon pinnacles and valleys of soft clouds spread across Moshi plain and Westward toward Mt. Meru (4,562 meters) - the second tallest mountain in Tanzania and one of three of Kilimanjaro's peaks. Meru used to be taller but lost much of its altitude eight millennia ago when its summit collapsed. Rich, Richard and I took turns photographing each other on a precipice overlooking all of this - to the considerable interest of the itinerant ravens. They cocked their heads side to side and - emboldened by their colleagues - mocked us again. "Caw Caw" they crowed. "Caw caw!" But this time their voices seemed to be more strident.

We departed camp near 8AM after a morning consisting of the usual stimulatory hot drinks, casual conversations, adjustments to gear, breakfast and collection of our day's water ration.

Water.....life's most essential nutrient.....unless you count oxygen.....

We conveyed our daily water (1.5-2 liters each) in our backpacks and accessed it via a plastic tube extending outside of the pack - a "camel pack". For the past two days I had been supplementing my water with powdered electrolytes to prevent my perspiration from depleting my body of essential salts - sodium, potassium, chloride and phosphorus. This innovation added the nauseating artificial flavors of mango, strawberry and melon to my hydration. That a mango flavor - whether authentic or ersatz - appeared on Kilimanjaro in the first place........

Our hydration was challenged by three concerns. First, Diamox increased our urinary output two-fold. Second, we sweat a lot, even at altitude. Finally, the air was dry. Water disappeared from our bodies without our awareness. To maintain our hydration, the guides - every fifteen minutes - reminded us to drink by hollering "Sippy Sippy". As child-like an admonition as the expression was - we were grateful for the frequent reminders.

Reassuringly this morning's hike began in clear cool air. The sky remained brilliant sapphire and- as we clambered over a small stony rise adjacent our camp- we imbibed our first vision of Mt. Mawenzi - an unusually-shaped extinct volcano to the immediate East of Kilimanjaro.

Mawenzi is one of three of Kilimanjaro's peaks - the other two - Kibo and Shira. Whereas Kilimanjaro's tallest peak (Kibo) is rounded and worn with snow- and glacier-covered ridges- Mawenzi asserts itself vigorously skyward and is immensely more rugged than Kibo or Meru - perhaps a younger sibling of both. Mawenzi's massive slabs of summit rock- each hundreds of meters - appeared to have been piled upon one another haphazardly to create a sharply-defined, serrated, snow-peppered cylindrical cone - a summit like none other I had ever seen in person nor in print. Mawenzi remained visible throughout the day - an improbable but inspiring backdrop to our labors.

This was Day Five. My body had begun to acclimate both to the altitude and to the climb's elevated caloric demands. Further, today's climb was gradual. I was comfortable. My legs were stronger - like those of a rambunctious colt - finding pleasure in frolic - eager for a greater challenge. Because there was no downward aspect to the day's trek my well-bandaged and Neosporin-slathered toes did not object with further blistering. I prayed this day's reprieve might allow a modicum of their recovery. Because there was no rain I stripped down to a T-shirt and light jeans. The scenery South and Eastward and up toward the summit was spectacular and the pleasant chatter from my fellow hikers was reassuring and buoyant. I periodically engaged with my friends but at other times retreated into my own comforting thoughts.

I thought of my Mom and Dad at home. I had been out of contact with them for several days and worried about their health. I thought about my wife – Azizah - in Oregon and what she might be doing at this moment. I missed her. My two children (Amelia, age 30 and Johan, age 23) were on a tour and in Morocco - a remarkable coincidence given none of us had ever visited any part of the African continent prior.

We traversed Kilimanjaro's Kibo flank in a Northeasterly direction for nearly an hour and then encountered a raw toothy plateau extending across three to four km - Mawenzi still to our right. The route leading to the distant aspect of the plateau meandered gently left - then right and further upward. At the furthest distance of this escarpment the well-worn footpath took a sharp upward turn and vanished over a spiny sunburnt ridge. Beyond, the path twisted Northwestward toward "Base Camp" (Barafu).

Terrain on this day's hike took on an other-worldly appearance - a near monochromatic iron-laden rock - frothy and raw. Rocks varied in size from those easily held in one's hand to those the size of a beckoning full-sized leather couch. Our understanding these had been ejected in a cataclysmic event - occurring eons ago - registered impressively - a geologist's dream.

Even at this altitude flamboyant lichens - yellow, brunet and pink - colonized the otherwise inhospitable texture of Kilimanjaro's Eastward exposure lavishly. The geology reminded me of that which I had noted in the Sultanate of Oman two decades prior - but perhaps two or three shades darker. This ejecta was derived from beneath Earth's solid mantle - a molten and compressed iron-rich interior - an interior still swirling dizzyingly and menacingly directly beneath us.

Inspired by this geology and perhaps blessed with clement weather - preceding hikers had assembled rocky shrines of varying degrees of sophistication - each stacked as a precarious tower- each an optimistic statement arguing against ephemerality - each erected despite their obvious fragile transience when juxtaposed against the dominance of geologic time.

Hundreds of these edifices had been erected. And even though we appreciated the efforts others had made none in our group attempted to fashion a structure of their own. Instead we rested amongst them - commented on them and collected photographs.

As we had gained altitude the air had thinned but - already - some of our oxygen saturation profiles - including mine - had crept upward - back into the 90's. My oxygen saturation had dipped at Lava Tower into the high 80's however I was back up into the low 90's - a reassuring development. Not only was my oxygen saturation improving my heart rate at 88 bpm was no longer worryingly elevated. I harbored no sense I might need to be evacuated, using “He’s an old man. He should have known better.” as a reproach. Our nascent understanding the body could acclimate in so short a time is worth remembering - at least while ambulatory we are never too far away from an improved physical condition.

Unfortunately, when I am not “on the mountain” my red leather couch and other sundry beckoning and comfortable horizontal spaces in my homes in Oregon and Hawaii hold greater sway over my behavior. We all could do more both physically and mentally. Next week if we took the right steps perhaps we could run a marathon!

Such was the day - virtuous weather - a dazzling sky - an inspiring Mt. Mawenzi - frothy, un-weathered and rust-colored volcanic rocks – camaraderie, cool air and fresh legs.

The air was thin and moved effortlessly into and out of my lungs - its coolness refreshing- like Diet Coke on a parched throat. Indeed, my physiology – remarkably - appeared unaffected by the altitude.

Such were the portents. My mind lifted away from the confines my body typically insisted upon. My consciousness became somewhat transcendent - beyond reverie. With some apprehension I followed my itinerant mind.

I again thought of my family and of what they might be undertaking. My Wife, My Kids, My Mother, My Father, My Sister. I needed to convince myself they were protected in order to explore further - even though I had no real way of divining their condition. Perhaps I harbored a concern - that if I followed my impetuous mind - I might not return to see them again - at least as the person I was or as they knew.

My friends' conversations no longer registered as sounds nor did I find those conversations of interest. My path was the same as my friends' however we no longer hiked exactly on the same plane nor in the same dimension. My mind and body loosened from the Earth as they have irregularly loosened previously - always when confronted with an intense experience with nature.

A vaguely-familiar sensation of weightlessness enveloped me. I drifted upward - perhaps twenty-five meters above the path my friends were following and trailed behind them without effort.

The froth of the Earth's surface took on a warmer tone. The sun penetrated and warmed me. I looked at my hands. A coffee-colored aging integument encased my hands and I felt some sadness in the realization. My hands were maturing – hardening - in front of my eyes. They were no longer the hands of a young man. Indeed, I was contemplating the time-worn hands of my father.

The veins carrying blood from my fingers - across the back of my hands and upward toward my heart appeared a deeper blue than typical. On closer inspection I discerned individual erythrocytes within my vasculature spinning and tumbling as they plaintively sought their individual ways back toward my core in search of life-giving oxygen - those fatigued erythrocytes laden with carbon dioxide – the carbon dioxide respiration generated as I struggled to experience and survive the world. How hard they battle! How hard we all battle!

My legs still seemed to move. My arms still seemed to swing freely by my side - my left and right hands intermittently cooled by the light breeze winding its way amongst and through my father's sturdy fingers.

The absence of the burden of gravity not only freed my legs from effort but freed my mind as well. What does one do with freedom like this? I recalled an earlier time where a differing set of challenges had similarly freed me from Earth's surly bonds.

It was in Japan, in 1991, twenty-six years ago, where I had confronted the trials of living in a foreign culture without the support family and familiarity provide. I began to flounder but, no longer supported by the familiar talismans I had used to maintain my stability I grasped at other supports - supports I had not ever needed nor been aware of prior.

I was in Rikugien Koen near Komagome Eki in Tokyo – alone - lying on a park bench hidden amongst bamboo - gazing upward examining the complexity of a tree. Unexpectedly I encountered a burst of transcendence - of leaving my body and having access to a broader range of thinking. My Eastern Asian effort at thought had been inconsequential - maybe a blind alley. However, the novelty of the experience had remained with me. I had learned the mind can exist beyond the body, reach beyond its familiar environs and enter unexplored caverns within it. What seemed to enable transcendence was the elimination of the mundane, the absence of the familiar handholds we have grown used to - to sustain our lives. Without doubt this came as a surprise to my unsophisticated Saskatchewan prairie boy mind.

There I came to understand the depth of experience in life is determined by the degree of organization existing within an entity. For example, a rock lacking intrinsic organization has little perception of a "life". Whereas humans, who are substantially “organized” with specific cellular functions, tissue functions, organ functions and even societal functions have gained an understanding of a small slice of sentience and of the nature and power of the universe. What then might a well-organized entity understand about life and its meaning - especially given our insights are severely circumscribed by our few senses. Indeed, modern physics predicts existence of multiple dimensions of the universe humans have no proximate capability of divining. Given our perception of reality is limited to so few dimensions any knowledge of truth rendered by human consciousness would be circumscribed with those limitations. How then could any rendering of a human answer to the big questions approximate truth?

What was Kilimanjaro? If not an immediately-perceived large heap of rock which could be considered by our six distinct senses might it also provide the metaphor of challenge we individually confront in coming to an understanding of truth - of a “meaning to life”? We climb on this mystery. We wonder why we are here. We can’t know if we might summit and if we do what we might discover in doing so.

It struck me these were the uncertainties I should dwell on given my mind was somewhat liberated and more capable. “What truly *is* the meaning of life?” “Why *are* we here?” These may appear as trite or silly questions given they should have been fully resolved hundreds if not thousands of times prior by intellects greater than mine over millennia of opportunity.

In addressing the question of the meaning of life one advantage I potentially held was I was not a religious man. Certainly I had been influenced by Western and Eastern civilizations largely grounded upon the world’s foremost religions (Christianity, Buddhism and Islam in particular). However, as a non-adherent (some might say an apostate) I was free of the strictures those beliefs would have imposed on me. But perhaps I was also lacking the head starts they might individually have given me. No, I was alone.

Flickering heat waves were rising insistently across the corroded plateau. Mawenzi, still weighty and unperturbed, shifted in proportion while its peak drifted intermittently behind dreamy clouds. My friends continued to ambulate below me and share stories. However, I was fully isolated from them - perhaps 100 meters above them. Floating. I could no longer hear them. Among them, I could no longer determine who was whom.

A solitary White-necked Raven approached and soared effortlessly to my right- intermittently cocking its head this way and that- he - like me- held aloft by an unseen upwelling of warm, desiccated air. Although the raven seemed at first bewildered I had entered its dominion, it also projected a welcoming and calm demeanor - like he had soared with others prior.

Effortlessly Raven and I slipped further away from the immediate environs of the path and rapidly gained altitude - each of us buffeted by the same ragged updrafts. Raven's left wingtip was immediately beside me - to my right and it oftentimes brushed my right shoulder. A single point of light reproducing the sun in miniature gleamed from its beady left eye while iridescent colors danced from the tips of his otherwise inky-black trailing plumage.

Raven was larger than I had appreciated - reaching more than one-meter across - its graceful arched wings fully extended. I found myself appreciating it rocking from side to side as the unpredictable up- and down-drafts seized its mass. How dreary was our sedentary Earth-based existence - an existence filled with the mundane and unimaginative!

My friends appeared insect-like - far below - their limbs moving herky-jerky like an ant's. Even though I was a kilometer removed from them I knew - should any of the guides request it - I could quickly leave Raven's jurisdiction and rejoin the group effortlessly. But I felt no need. I was safe.

As my colleagues scuttled haphazardly upward I was left to consider my thoughts from my newly-acquired perspective. I was conscious of my juxtaposition and began to accept it and exploit it. My companions seemed unconcerned - possibly unaware - of both my location and the coincident arrival of Raven. It was exciting to begin to see new avenues of thoughts available to me. Indeed, I was free to explore.

What might be the "meaning of life"? It was a question I was aware of and had asked of many. Trite answers were abundant as were many well-considered answers. Years ago I had hosted a Palestinian named Mohammad Alayan to work in my laboratory as a graduate student. His family had derived from Jordan but spent most of their professional lives in Kuwait. Mohammad was a devout Muslim - so devout on many occasions I encountered him washing his feet in our departmental bathroom's sink before prostrating himself before Allah in my unaccustomed radioisotope- and toxin-filled laboratory. His succinct answer to the question was: "The meaning of life is to worship Allah". And all well and good. But if one does not believe in a benevolent, observant and transcendent higher power this philosophy becomes an unfulfilling answer. Large swaths of our ocean-dominated planet consist of non-believers. Further, religions conflict. If they conflict, then how does one ascertain the truths and falsehoods within each? Is there not a "meaning of life" that pertains to them globally? Is meaning only a property of a believer but irrelevant to a non-believer? What about the fish? Do they not have meaning?

I respected Mohammad's devotion even though I thought he was misguided and wasting his time with such a high level of devotion. With my transactional way of viewing things, I would expect devotion to a God would yield specific benefits. But in the end what did Mohammad's exceptional piousness and devotion to Allah deliver to him? He was one of fifty Muslims shot in the Canterbury, New Zealand mosque attack in March, 2019. He spent time in critical condition in a New Zealand hospital. His son Atta Elayyan (with a differing spelling of the last name) who was praying with him and whom I knew as a boy was shot and died from his wounds. The Economist featured his son's obituary in Spring, 2019. That tragedy would occur 16.5 months following the Kilimanjaro hike. Why would a caring omniscient God permit that travesty to happen? Especially to one who believed in Him so devoutly? When I queried Mohammad in April, 2019 regarding the tragedy he still held firmly to his understanding of life's meaning by responding *"As you know we Muslims have to accept death as an article of faith in the hereafter and Qadar. Al-hamdu li Allah Atta* (Mohammad's dead son) *has fulfilled the true purpose of life as per verse 56 of chapter 51 of the Holy Quran: 'And I (Allah) created not the jinns and humans except they should worship Me (Alone)'."*

Even the tragic loss of his son could not shake Mohammad's faith nor his understanding of the meaning of life. Such is the power of faith - something I will never grasp. Of course religion helped Mohammad carry him through what must be the most awful event one could experience in life - the violent and senseless loss of a child. There was also a biblical story of Abraham - a father who - in deference to God's willingly lay his son Issac on a rock to slay him. No matter what I ever encounter, my son would never be laid on a rock. I would die first in protecting him.

Many are not pious. Might there be a "meaning" transcending the narrow strictures of faith imposed by religions and which would bring about an equal or greater benefit to human societies? A benefit, perhaps, not associated the harsh aspects of hatred and isolationism associated with religious cultism?

Years prior I had queried my mother - part in jest and part in seriousness. I had hoped for her answer even though we had not had this type of a conversation prior. She espoused no answer and this led me to believe my mother may be a nihilist - that nothing really matters, that there is no basic philosophy underpinning the progress - or lack thereof - of humanity. My mother grew up in Saskatchewan. One would almost need to be a nihilist to survive the Depression in Saskatchewan! Certainly a large streak of nihilism moves through me and my mother might be the wellspring of this philosophy.

My father's answer to the question was *"You just gotta keep on living!"*. He stated his philosophy to me when he was 88 or 89 years of age. His philosophy resonated to such an extent that during a sojourn in Hawaii I painted an acrylic image of this philosophy. I added to it by penning a more complete mantra- *"You just gotta keep on living --- and listen to Pink Floyd"*. This conceptual piece incorporated a single beam of white light piercing a Dark Side of the Moon-like glass prism - a beam subsequently splitting into the familiar full spectrum of visible light - red, orange, yellow, green, blue, violet. Between my Dad and me, maybe we had it figured out! He was the beam of white light. I was the prism splitting the beam into its constituent elements. Still, there were wavelengths in the white beam we could not divine - infrared and ultraviolet on opposing ends of the spectrum - and more wavelengths beyond those. But we did the best with the senses and equipment we possessed. This is how generations progress.

I hiked with my daughter through the Upper Mustang region of Northern Nepal only a few km from Tibet earlier in 2017 - with an entirely different group of travelers. The arid Upper Mustang-nourished by the muddy yet Holy Kali Gandaki - is the last of the Himalayan Kingdoms which joined present-day Nepal - a small Tibetan-influenced valley opening itself up to exploration and to tourism only in the early-1990s. Its insularity allowed it to maintain much of the culture it maintained prior to unification with the greater Nepal. Even today contamination by outside influence has been limited because the Nepalese government restricts tourism into the area with onerous daily fees. These fees prevent many of the less well-off younger international hikers from undertaking entry into this ancient Kingdom and thereby tainting local culture. Hence the knowledge the mighty Kali Gandaki might impart is limited to those with both money and a lust for travel.

The Upper Mustang was interesting in many respects but one aspect of this region particularly stood out to me. Because it lies just south of Tibet it functioned as an escape route Tibetans, including the current Dalai Lama, used to avoid the harsh intolerance of the monolithic - some might say despotic - Chinese regime. While there I had opportunity to tour monasteries and to freely read - when translated - some of the underpinning philosophies of Tibetan and Upper Mustang cultures.

Perhaps the most spectacular of my Upper Mustang memories occurred in the most fantastic of settings - a centuries-old brick red monastery. There, amongst thousands of painted golden Buddha's, their eyes downcast, their legs crossed, amongst hundreds of creamy lamb fat candles respiring - their smell acrid and animal-like, amongst palpable and dense golden shafts of sunlight betraying an inadequate roof, among dusty shelves of hundreds of hand-worn hand – inscribed scrolls - scrolls of an ancient language containing a wisdom accumulated and assimilated by generations and which allowed adherents to thrive as a culture within an unforgiving and spare environment - I felt levitated. Who would not be so elevated? Of course I could not read any of the scrolls sheltered in the monastery but I understood that pious second-born males would spend years, lifetimes perhaps, studying the writings of the long-dead ascetics who prepared these gilded parchments. In this way they would gain an understanding of a meaning of life supporting and creating all needed dimensions of a culture in this remarkable context. And I somehow understood the interpretations of the documents by these believers were important and held universal value. But I also understood there must be culture-specific aspects to "meaning" - some of the "meanings" contained within those scrolls - values supporting a strong and impressive people in a unique and unfortunately harsh environment for centuries might not find relevance to other cultures - to our modern, some might say "fucked-up" situation. Instead, I wondered - might there be a universal meaning to life with relevance to all humankind irrespective of time and location - a 'meaning' transcending culture and representing the property of being human?

Or perhaps the "meaning of life" fully depends on context- the circumstances of the individual who aspires to understand meaning. These were the thoughts that Raven seemed to be willing to share with me.

A child who grows-up in Los Angeles or Odessa and who never leaves - what can that person hope to "know"? A child who grows up Baptist and who remains a Baptist. A child who grows and stays in the slums of Damascus, Syria. What can they come to know of the full human condition? Donald Trump and his sycophants. All so limited mentally and easy to exploit.

While in Nepal in early-2017 I had made mental notes of some of the writings and oral statements of the current Dalai Lama. These were infrequently available on English language documents provided at the various Upper Mustang monasteries - but particularly at the Zangpo Namsum, Lowo Monthang Dragkar Thekchen Ling monastery near the uppermost reach of the Mustang Valley. And I make note of this because I believe this monastery and other lesser monasteries influenced me - providing information to me and may have delivered some of the bases for my own formulations I present above and below - interpretations made on the slopes of Kilimanjaro where I had managed to almost fully dissociate myself from my colleagues and from immediate contact with my usual - occasionally tiring - human circumstance.

In Nepal a hiking colleague - a Canadian neurosurgeon - reported to me neuronal structures had been discovered in the brain that were possibly quantum in nature. Might quantum structures within the neurons enable humans to reach higher levels of thought? Might quantum brains be connected - all part of one master organism? - like the ants or bees of a colony or hive. Might these unseen connections exist in the unseen dimensions that physicists believe exist? Dimensions we can't directly experience but only infer? Dimensions that *must* exist for sense to be made of reality.

With Raven jostling thoughtfully and patiently beside me it struck me - maybe we do manifest quantum elements of our brain by connecting to others in terms of friendship, in terms of love and in wanting to do 'good' for others - by appreciating diversity. Perhaps *empathy* is a quantum experience. Those with fewer quantum aspects to their brains, those with less 'organization' to their brains, may have lesser ability to connect and to understand others' circumstances and needs. Like all other biological traits perhaps people vary in their quantum connections to others - their quantum capacity (QC). There's a hypothesis I would love to test!

The exterior world intruded on Raven and me unexpectedly. Mawenzi - with is coarseness - reminded me of its purpose as a harbinger of honesty and perhaps fidelity- to my right- ice-covered slabs, upended mantle - its summit – intense - slate gray but still forgiving and open. Stoic. Like my Scandinavian grandfather and presumably my Great-Grandfather Israel as well.

Uhuru Summit - upward and to my left - portended challenges we would soon undertake in divining a purpose to life and of the strivings we individually undertake. Its reality was a dead-weight.

Mt. Meru - unobtrusive - lay to the Southwest- a gentle dome protruding unobtrusively above a thin pastel layer of mauve and moist pink clouds reminded me there is softness and forgiveness in our lives- life need not always be harsh - when we fail there is always recourse.

Perhaps our lives lie scattered amongst those three portents: of hardness, of challenge and of softness - as we strive for fulfillment - on this rocky and unpredictable road we call "life".

From Meru I understood no matter what I believed there would be tolerance of my meagre and likely wholly inadequate assessment of the purpose of one's life. I did not possess the mind of a Hawking - a Hawking who reported posthumously "There is no God". Nor did I possess the mind near any of the Great Thinkers - Einstein, Galileo, Nietzsche or Archimedes.

No I was and remained wholly inadequate to the task-at-hand intellectually - the Canadian prairie boy. A boy who liked to rise early on cold Spring mornings – excited to observe the lethargy of chilled flies and to catch frogs and magpies.

What might my entirely inadequate quantum mind conjure and what could my aging osteoarthritic body achieve in the face of so many mental and physical limitations?

Again I centered on the same pattern of thoughts. Was not 'the mountain' the perfect metaphor? Was I not stretching and testing my physical limitations? Why not similarly test my mental boundaries? Would my thoughts be trite because my intellect was limited? Would I be able to summit Uhuru physically and as intellectual metaphor? Was deeper thought worth the effort? Was it worth the effort to scale a mountain? Should one follow one's own beliefs, however implausibly engendered, or should one rely more upon history's greater thinkers and religions? Perhaps an empiricist to an extreme I was reluctant to rely wholly upon others' contemplations or upon their purportedly divine inspirations.

From my distance I realized my group had quietened - laboring as one on a slope leading progressively toward the rugged Southeast shoulder of Kilimanjaro. It was mid-morning and as usual cessations in the effort had been taken here and there - breaks where my friends - individually and in groups - assembled with the magnificent Uhuru Summit beckoning even more insistently. Vegetation apart from a few struggling forbs and the pastel-colored lichens was virtually non-existent.

The dimensions of my mind were clear and easily accessible. I learned I could - at will - explore my mind and ruminate on the thoughts each portion independently generated.

What is real? What is trash? I would discard the latter, cling to the former and combine rational thoughts into an increasingly coherent distillation of truth - the amalgam hardened into a trusted handhold - a sturdy cleat for a steep climb. When my thoughts bordered on what I could comprehend but began to slip away- as in a vanishing late-morning dream - I lashed a sturdy line to them in order to hold them and reconsider them until they congealed into accessible belief. As was clear- this was a journey - a physical journey to be certain but also a mental and metaphorical journey in which the mind took control of the body and willed it to execute. Similarly, the mind surveilled itself and compelled it to dwell on concepts ordinarily difficult to contemplate. This was an effort revealing one's physical and mental strengths. To tap into these strengths and to share these insights with my *self* was an opportunity I had never fully encountered prior. I had not anticipated this opportunity. To this point I had only wanted to summit and survive and to have a story to tell.

What is universally meaningful?

Raven remained alongside. His eyes signaled approvingly of my question but then he twisted his neck, looked directly toward me and gave me an impatient look - like he doubted I had the fortitude to find an answer – to get off my couch. His two attentive eyes communicated two foci of light- each eye a brilliant pinpoint of blindingly white sun. Raven's feathers rustled as he vibrated unevenly beside me - the still unpredictable up- and down-drafts again rocking him sharply from side to side. As my mass was far greater than his, the drafts exerted lesser effect on me. Indeed, I was proving to be more stable than Raven. I knew he envied me. His struggle was greater than mine.

At this proximity I noted Raven did not have so much a white band of feathers at its neck but, instead, a collection of white feathers unevenly distributed within a region approximating its neck. It was not as organized as it first presented in Machame Camp. Indeed, things were not as they first appeared to me. Perhaps Raven was less organized than I had believed and was counting on me to help him assimilate the thoughts it too struggled with. Perhaps this too was a symbiosis- another quantum connection.

Instinctively and without effort I skidded diagonally and merged directly with Raven's corporeal mass. His fully enveloping body was a welcome and warm embrace- a father's embrace- a mother's embrace- the embrace of a friend. We were one. Elation rose in me as I felt our hearts beat together.

I took full control of flight. I dipped my right wing downward, lifted my left, twisted my neck slightly toward Mawenzi and accelerated earthward and across the vast Eastern flank of Kilimanjaro. It was a graceful and instinctual move. The jagged ochre-colored surface of the Earth raced below me as I departed my colleagues for Mawenzi. And just as the power of the wind against my outstretched wings reached a force I could no longer fight I lowered the trailing feathers on both of my wings and tilted back toward Uhuru gaining altitude quickly - possibly 100 meters of gain in elevation in a matter of seconds. And as the power of my momentum dissipated I extended both wings to their extreme, grasped a slight upwelling of warm air and held my altitude. I stabilized and arched to my left - circling. The updraft, while modest, remained sufficient to not only support me but to gently lift me skyward. I could feel the sun warming my dark feather-covered back and neck. It was comforting and I felt confident.

I understood birds had animated others. My Dad carved birds because he saw the beauty of life in birds. Robins as harbingers of Spring were his favorite birds. He often lived within the beauty birds provide. My son had a Robin tattooed onto his ribs, one of the most painful sites to receive a tattoo, in recognition of my Dad's favorite bird. My Dad tried to capture his love of birds and to share with others - his gesture of love and friendship. He tried to bring happiness to others via the sharing of his art through his abilities as an artist. It was his way.

“Now I understand - what you tried to say to me”. The familiar refrain of a favorite and sad yet comforting song.

I came along a tangle of nondescript awkwardly clumped neurons I had overlooked many times prior - always in a hurry - so much of a hurry I never spent time with them. I took a moment to deviate and explore them - their twisted passageways and cavernous reserves. Their stalactites and stalagmites. Their quantum elements I could not fully divine. They were deeper and more extensive than I expected. I was wishing I had brought a better quantum light.

I took a moment to consider a massive ochre-hued stalagmite. It became almost luminous in my light and I peered into its mottled core. Without fanfare, *it* came to me quickly and easily; like *it* had always existed within me. I had only needed to look for *it* and ask myself. *It* was right beside me. Inside me.

There *it* lay. The meaning of life was simple. *It* was three-fold: *“to know friendship, to know love* and *to bring happiness to others”*. It was as if someone or something had withdrawn drapes and revealed something always there.

Indignant equivocation presented itself to me - one could not *always* ‘know love’, *always* ‘experience friendship’ and *always* ‘bring happiness to others’. With some thought it became apparent one could only *periodically* experience the joys of friendship, love and of bringing happiness to others. And, *those* needed to be good enough.

I rocked to my left and then downward, thrust my trailing feathers downward and again felt the cooling rush of air across the upper surface my wings. I didn't wish to lose sight of my colleagues. After turning and accelerating toward them I dipped my trailing feathers again on both wings and lifted skyward as I came over them. I circled clockwise over them still on a light updraft. My friends periodically glanced skyward and considered me but did not seem alarmed. They moved in one direction while I floated as the second-hand of a clock.

I surprised myself. Updrafts were not difficult to locate. The shimmering associated with the uneven mixing of cooler and warmer air betrayed their location - like Schlieran optics occurring within the mixing of cooler and warmer waters. The air was cool and refreshing. Without the rushing air I knew the heat from the sun would overwarm my plumage and I would need to find refuge amongst the shadows of the stony outcroppings below. Either that or ascend to even greater and cooler heights.

I was pleased to have stumbled across a simple formulation. That I understood "meaningfulness" could not be continuous let me understand there was value in the valleys - the sadnesses we experience. Life is filled with obstacles. But the prospect of knowing friendship, of knowing love and of bringing happiness to others is always there - those can lift us.

It struck me this insight derived from my Dad's example - an example he struggled as a shy man to communicate via his art, via the look in his eyes and via his firm handshake. He communicated friendship. He communicated his love for others. And he brought those dear to him happiness. He had exemplified a successful life. I was looking forward to seeing him again. I was looking forward to better live by his example.

Eager to share new insight I located my outstretched arms – the humerus, the radius and the ulna - and brought them together. I reached toward my heart - co-joined with Raven's. Our heart was hot and beating rapidly - well above exclusionary rates proscribed by Kandoo. Placing my palms- my carpals - firmly against our pulsating atria and ventricles I pushed myself free - spiraling leftward awkwardly - away and outside of Raven's corporeal existence - at first uncontrollably. But then a familiar buoyancy returned to me and I stabilized several hundred meters above my hiking partners - my legs dangling downward and my upper body oriented upward.

Raven had announced no indication he was tiring of me. I had the impression I might never have departed - I might have taken up permanent residence. Yet even while contained within his body I knew I had an important life elsewhere - important challenges and further opportunities to greet in my other life. Like a patient on a surgical table who is drawn back from above the table by the mysterious warm glow which beckons one heavenward - I understood the imperative to return.

Raven rolled sideways and with a few light beats of his wings rapidly gained altitude and slid sideways away toward Mawenzi - the rugged aspect of Kilimanjaro. I followed his trajectory as he diminished in size - no more discernable than any of Kilimanjaro's stars.

I regarded my friends as they continued to labor upward. I remained 100 meters above them but felt the imperative that had pulled me away from them was gone. Without conscious effort I descended to their path and rejoined them. My legs felt contact with the earth and began to move and propel my body forward.

Again I was part of the team. None of my friends showed any interest in the fact I had departed and moved away, soared away, from them for the better part of an hour. Such were their own efforts and contemplations - they had not noticed.

At the next rest stop I described my nascent revelations to Rich and Natascha but I was disappointed when they did not find my insights to be particularly interesting. Perhaps I did not articulate my insights with the proper fervor. And so I retreated. My ideas were too new and ill-formed to share. I understood there may not be only one "meaning of life" but one for every person. Further I understood Rich and Natascha may not be possessed by a similar quest - at least for now. Perhaps their "quantum brains" were not in tune with mine. These might be the thoughts one becomes consumed with once one reaches 63 years. My companions were still relatively young.

A philosopher unknown to me surmised the experience of true happiness is so fleeting it is not worth pursuing. The same could pertain to a need to appreciate the nature of "meaning". Yet I would posit fleeting moments of knowing friendship, of knowing love and of bringing happiness to others are sufficient. There can be boredom in day-to-day living - drudgeries between the summits. But know, at the summits one can reach out, grasp and understand the stars.

Chapter Fourteen
Base Camp

I reflected on my physical state. I had not showered in five days - sweating copiously for hours daily. I presumed I reeked like a vast Antarctic penguin rookery. My hair retained its unseemly orange hue and what little I had left was matted appallingly to my scalp. My quality of dental care had also diminished. People say "one cannot smell one's self" and Kilimanjaro proved it true. Call it self-preservation. Whereas at home I am loathe to wear the same clothing two days in a row, here it had been five days and I had no sense of presenting as offensive. Perhaps we were all similarly unpleasant.

One fascinating aspect of the hike involved discovering the curious aphorisms that Brits use. The women frequently attended the "loo" or "went for a wee". They announced they were "knackered" at the end of each hiking effort. Instead of French toast in the morning we ate "eggy bread". Upscale or stylish items were "posh". When one went to the toilet tent one took "bum wipes". I've noted earlier the term "brilliant" - an expression used to describe anything one might say or do that was surprisingly insightful or helpful. Richard made good use of this term to an extent it has found a way into my own lexicon. When a troupe of stranded Thai boys were recently rescued in a cave, video of the discovery revealed a UK diver who exclaimed "brilliant!" upon learning all thirteen lost boys remained alive. His exclamation immediately reminded me of Richard and gave me confidence the boys would be well taken care of. Then there was the term "bollocks" (literally, testicles) - used to express contempt or disbelief. Small efforts or small amounts were referred to as "a wee bit". For these and other reasons I was becoming increasingly enamored with my friends.

Near 1PM we entered Barafu Base Camp. Our demeanor had been buoyed by perfect hiking weather and our limited gain in altitude for the day meant we were not as tired as when we had arrived at previous camps. Hence we remained moderately animated. Because other hiking groups including the French and the Italians had arrived in camp coincidently a back-log of twenty to thirty hikers milled around the ranger station awaiting their individual opportunities to sign in. The temperature was near freezing but felt comfortable. We chattered amiably. No one was displaying or admitting to any evidence of oxygen deprivation. The dome of Kilimanjaro had grown in size- capped with a delicious tiara of gleaming silver snow and blue ice. Optimism was sailing through our hearts like a fluttering butterfly. None of us were in a rush to reach our tents - we were euphoric.

As quickly had our buoyancy developed it began to dissipate. It drained from us as blood drains from one's face when confronted by any unpalatable or unexpected shock. Loose collections of shabby hikers had arrived to wade zombie-like in, amongst and through us - eyes glazed, faces sunburned and gear haphazardly affixed to gaunt frames. Little energy animated their limbs. Instead these hikers were simply lifting their feet a few cm off the ground and then letting gravity swing their calves forward on the downslope in order to effect individual footsteps. In doing so they swayed side to side as they plodded by. None were talking nor joyous. One by one our group understood these were climbers who had been just attempted "the summit" and who were retreating downward. They were one day ahead of us.

From amongst our midst Natascha shouted "How was it?" Her comment was not directed to anyone in particular but rather to the entirety of the straggling commiseration of hikers amid us. Only one woman replied but I covered my ears. I didn't want to know. Perhaps I already knew. I was pleased when there were no follow-up questions. The French and the Italians had remained silent and only watched.

"Focus" was patiently waiting for me beside the ranger station. He too had remained swathed in the same clothes since departing Machame Gate several days earlier. Endearingly he was still wearing his improbable Nepalese-style woolen hat with two long woolen braids suspended past his ears. The vitreous of his eyes remained jaundiced and I wondered what that indicated. As always he said nothing - only indicating he recognized me via eye contact and then using hand signals to indicate the direction of my tent.

"Focus" led me to my shelter - a shelter located an inordinate distance - possibly two km from the registration site. I lumbered inside and let him again unlace and pull off my boots and store my hiking poles. My feet were suddenly free and felt cool as moisture evaporated from them. And then I just rested staring at the lightly billowing roof of my tent as one might watch cumulus clouds drift on an idle summer day - listening to its calming fluttering. I inhaled and exhaled slowly and monitored the steady and confident beating of my heart. Lunch would be ready in 15-20 minutes and I resolved to relax every muscle fiber in my legs, arms and feet and to rest my mind and body fully.

I began to consider the effort coming our way. To recapitulate - we were to depart from this camp (Barafu) for the summit at 11 PM (ten hours hence), hike through the night, reach the summit at near 8 AM, stay for perhaps thirty to sixty minutes then retreat hastily to this same camp - possibly reaching it by noon - a 13-hour hike round-trip. Because we were all focused on the climb and on the chances of our individual success none of us had paid much if any attention to what might happen following our arrival at Base Camp for the second time - a second time in twenty-four hours. Unregistered in our collective consciousness was the need to quickly depart this camp an hour after reaching it and hike to the much lower "Mweka Camp" ten to fifteen km away. That was forgotten. That part seemed so trivial in the overall scheme of things it was relegated to an afterthought - if it was ascribed any importance at all. No this was about the climb and summiting - of finding the place where we would certainly come closest to Kilimanjaro's stars - the place where any revelations meant for us would certainly be on offer. The descent was a "given" and would be quick, anticlimactic and unmemorable.

While I rested I noted the porters were surprisingly noisy - their music blasting on portable Bluetooth speakers accompanied by boisterous shouts and laughter. Of course! I realized - they are not climbing higher and only need to maintain the camp while *we* attempt to summit. They're on a 24-hour vacation! After all of the efforts they had expended, efforts considerably greater than ours, who could blame them? Still our three guides - Freddy, Obama and Raymond would accompany us on the ascent. They failed to attend the festivities.

Today's lunch, although a largely perfunctory affair, was exceptionally vibrant. Rich and Richard were in joyous moods despite Richard's deepening chest infection. Rich peppered us with all sorts of facts about the coming evening's ascent. Natascha and her friends were laughing gleefully throughout lunch - their sibling familiarity endearing. Alex was beaming and looking calm and confident. One could not have imagined a group possessing a countenance of greater confidence and solidarity.

Freddy entered the mess tent carrying with him a much more serious demeanor than what we had become used to. As a consequence, our conversation ebbed and quickly extinguished. There was a heaviness on his shoulders. He leaned inside, splayed his reedy fingers across the checkered tablecloth and in a sober tone provided us with his updates. He informed us the weather was good and we would be attempting to summit this evening. This came as a surprise because I had never considered we might reach this stage of our climb and then be turned back because of weather. He instructed us to go to our tents and try to sleep until dinner at 5PM. We needed to complete sorting of gear to ensure we carried only what was necessary (water, snacks and warm clothing). We were to report any of the well-known clinical signs of altitude sickness (e.g., vomiting, nausea, headache) to him. Our oxygen saturation profiles and heart rates were assessed and we were encouraged to sleep. There was to be no sleeping after 10PM tonight and - I was to learn - for an inordinately long period thereafter.

I had slept well the night prior and today's hike had not been arduous. Hence I was not heavy-eyed. I lay down and instead let my mind ramble. Momentarily I recognized my entrance into a blissful albeit rare state of reverie. I visualized myself looking down from several km above Tanzania proper- again from Raven's perspective. There was a speck of a camp on an abbreviated plane, circling the sun, the sun only one of many billions making up the Milky Way arm of our galaxy. And then at the center of the galaxy a black hole was actively devouring everything near to it. I watched as all matter in our galaxy- even the atoms constituting my corporeal existence were be torn asunder as they were accelerated irreversibly into the black hole. And then, I saw our galaxy was only one of many billions of galaxies in our visible universe and knew infinite numbers of black holes exist. In this stark context of absolute diminishment - I understood any need or wish or any want or angst I might sense - could only be small! How unimportant I truly was in this great cosmic festival we call "existence"! It wasn't an original thought. I'd believed in this and thought about this frequently since my late teens. And so had many others. And never during any of these prior deliberations had I conjured anything particularly illuminating negating cognizance of the obvious futility of life. No, not much we might experience nor undertake in a short human life can be enduringly meaningful. But what may be considered meaningful in context of a human experience is we undertake to experience love and friendship and try to bring happiness to others - to make a "go" of it nonetheless. And, why not?

Time passed. It was 3 o'clock. I'd been lying motionless for an hour still contemplating my tent, my intermittent thoughts and my recalcitrant extremities. Still the possibility of sleep seemed remote. Because the porters were so loud I affixed my ear plugs and also donned an eye mask in the vain hope I might embrace sleep. But alas. I was rousted for dinner at the proscribed time - 5 PM - having not slept at all.

Dinner was not a lively affair. My colleagues had become very serious and were deep in thought. Out of nervousness I admitted to no one in particular I was concerned about my ability to hike through the complete night with nary any sleep. I had never stayed awake for an entire night *let alone* hike through a night. This would be the first time I combined both. Rich was worried about hiking in the dark itself - something he had never done. Debbie and Natascha sat next to me and discussed the challenges of peeing privately on a path described alternatively as narrow, winding, snow/ice-covered and, at times, near vertical. Alex periodically and sagely took a "hit" off of her vape and I believe I saw Richard take a hit or two off of it as well. With each draw the two of them appeared to experience brief moments of clarity but the thoughts calming them were never shared. The smoke billowing from their lungs with each expiration filled our tent - fruity and pleasingly acrid.

An engagingly-large burnt-orange sun was sinking into the adjacent ridge of the South-west side of a violet Kilimanjaro. It cast a somber and peculiar yellow-grey light into our camp. We were aware of it acutely. The icy wind slowed and the gust-animated tents quietened just as our guides entered our mess tent for a final Q+A session. Again we reviewed the equipment we needed. "No one is going to check your gear!" we were admonished. We would be woken promptly at 10 PM, have "early breakfast" (9 hours early!) then depart for the summit at 11 PM, "prompt". This was becoming like the military! Grim gallows humor was beginning to prevail amongst us.

We reviewed the warning signs of altitude sickness. What would be done should any one of us not be able to "make it"? Details on how an evacuation could be managed. And of course what the actual hike would consist of. With nary additional warning nor encouragement we were summarily dispatched to our respective tents in the waning light at 5:30 PM and encouraged to "sleep" until 10 PM - as if sleeping could be so willed.

The sun had not yet set. Once in my tent I heard no kibitzing between members of our group. Everyone was doing their utmost to remain quiet and to be considerate of their neighbors' efforts to rest.

My mind wandered. My families are in Oregon and Manitoba! The sun is just rising in North America and they were standing upside down relative to Tanzania on the other side of this planet. I'm far away from home. I'm lying on the African Continent on the shoulder of Kilimanjaro! It's fucking cold outside!

Am I a good brother? What all does a man need to be 'good' at? When I die what will my last cogent thought be?

Thoughts flowed randomly with no apparent crystalizing focus until we were unceremoniously rousted from our tents by Freddy at 10 PM. Richard reported to me snoring had emanated from the direction of my tent between 9 and 10 PM. If true, my sleep had been short and absent of dreams. I wasn't feeling rested. Being mustered for the climb I felt I needed to sleep. Indeed, I felt wretched - ready to return to my tent but, instead, I was facing what was- without any doubt- the most arduous physical challenge of my life. What had I done? There's no escaping this. I tried to develop a sentiment of resoluteness.

We were enveloped in Kilimanjaro's inky blackness. I realized I had not experienced the mountain at this time prior and as a result bore witness to the full magnificence of Kilimanjaro's stars for the first time - distended as if a giant magnifying glass had been placed over the entire Kilimanjaro domain proper - perhaps this the result of an atmospheric distortion.

A prominent tangerine-shaded Mars glowed ripe and juicy in the Northeast. Orion, tilted 90 degrees to the angle at which it rests in North America, was rising indolently in the East. Even though I fought the effort I briefly completed the mental gymnastics needed to understand how my location in Tanzania could cause Orion to rotate in this manner.

Several LED flashlights affixed via elastic straps to optimistic foreheads were illuminating our campsite and mess tent with unnatural shafts of stark-white light. Beams darted here and there following each climber's conversations and interests. While most made efforts to cast their lights downward Debbie's periodically danced blindingly across our retinae. Her headlamp was tilted at an upward angle.

Clothing-wise I had over-prepared for the ascent. Dutifully I had followed the guides' advice and dressed excessively. The Canadian ascetic in me should have asserted itself. I knew what cold was like and how to dress for it. At near 0 °C this was not a true cold. For much of my time in Manitoba Canada this would have been considered balmy.

My torso was cloaked in ***<u>seven</u>*** layers: a thermal long-sleeved undershirt followed by a gray T-shirt and a Columbia long-sleeved hiking shirt - a shirt possessing an ostentatious vent in the back. On top of these three layers I had added a hoodie lettered with the name of my son's Phi Delta Theta fraternity, a familiar Patagonia fleece vest (which I'd used in previous expeditions to Nepal, Antarctica and South America), my orange National Geographic-issued parka with its *faux* wolverine fur fringe and my water-permeable GoreTex windbreaker. Even at -40 °C in Canada I had never been so well-insulated.

On the lower one-half of my body I assembled an inner layer of thermal underwear, multi-zippered canvas hiking pants and again a water-permeable GoreTex shell. As much as I have maligned GoreTex to this point it did function well as a windbreaker. On my feet I wore silk liners extending to my knees, thick Danish woolen socks and hiking boots. I wore simple gloves and my comfortable blue Patagonia fleece hat. I filled my pack with three liters of electrolyte-laden water, fig bars, extra water-proof gloves and my 1 kg Nikon camera with both regular and wide angle lenses. I'd estimate my bag weighed 6-8 kg.

Surprisingly there had been no interactions among the hiking groups co-existing in each camp. Perhaps language was the primary barrier. However tonight a nervous energy connected all of the groups to one another. We watched each other. Each camp would be attempting "The Summit" in less than an hour. For each person and for each group there was much to be considered and organized. The same thoughts were in all of our minds: in English, in German, in French and in Italian. And maybe in Swahili.

As our understanding of the seriousness of the challenge registered, the movement of the inflamed stars slowed until they became fixed in the black heavens. There they became even more enlarged. They shone and held us near motionless with their magic. They disclosed the direction of the summit. They informed us no matter the outcome they would radiate their energy again in this same manner the following night. Their wisdom brought each of us some confidence. We could only do our best.

For some this evening represented the culmination of a dream of accomplishing this single mountain. For others this climb allowed climbers to strike-off another continent from the quest of conquering the highest summits on all seven continents: Kilimanjaro, Mont Blanc, Denali, Everest, Vinson, Kosciuszko and Aconcagua. Others like me were opportunists. The opportunity to climb Kilimanjaro unexpectedly presented itself. The climb presented a romantic thought. We retained the belief that we remained capable. And so we engaged.

Chapter Fifteen
The Ascent

By 10:55 PM our team with its three proficient guides had collected alongside the darkened exterior of our quietened mess tent - headlamps shining in anticipation. Even though none of us had been hungry we'd all managed to ingest a very early "breakfast".

The winds had stilled. The weather was chilly - a few degrees below freezing. However, our more than adequate layering rendered that temperature irrelevant. We were done with talking, planning and packing. It was time.

We stood together at the edge of our camp. Our hearts beat cadence together. Eleven PM arrived. No sooner had Freddy broadcast our departure than Debbie proclaimed her need to "go for a wee". Ignoring the truly uncomprehending disbelief displayed upon all of our faces she doffed her backpack and entered the nearby toilet tent three meters distant, zippered herself inside and, with much swaying of the tent and much rattling about, completed her task.

During Debbie's absence the remainder of the group naturally tended to fret. Rich and Richard, like nervous race horses, were most eager to decamp. With Debbie in the toilet tent and with fervently knitted brows they repeatedly enunciated "Let's go!" to no one in particular. Their strong dissatisfaction was noted by everyone but at the same time we each recognized we could not leave Debbie behind. I took the "high road" and retreated to a nearby boulder lying 8 meters away, crossed my arms, observed the entire camp and attempted to display a modicum of equanimity. We wouldn't be the last to depart. We'd be underway soon enough.

Still as we waited the French and the Italians slipped quietly past us toward the embarkation point. They did not talk amongst themselves nor did they look at us. Instead they hiked silently up and over a nearby ridge and ignored the less-accomplished. We paid them no heed. We were at 4,600 meters AMSL and if successful would reach 6,000 meters - the Summit - in 8-9 hours. This needn't be a rush.

By 11:10 PM Debbie had returned and donned her kit. Freddy, fully composed despite the delay, took the lead and beckoned us to follow him along a narrow gravel-strewn path leading to a non-discernable flinty ridge. There our climbing and switching-back began. We followed in single file as there was no alternative - such were the confines of the trail and the light. It was difficult to fathom we would be doing this throughout the night - a time when I'd prefer to be sleeping. I understood there was an aspect of myself that periodically compelled my body to undertake imprudent activities - an aspect of myself I did not fully appreciate.

My head tilted downward to enable my headlamp to illuminate the path and avoid impediments lying ahead. I focused on the rhythmic movements of leather boots belonging to the individual ahead of me and found I tended to stay within one step - whomever it was. Sometimes I got too close and would back off. The titanium tips of my hiking poles scratched incessantly as they sought purchase, arachnoid-like, on the exposed basalt. A rocky outcropping on the summit side of the early portion of the climb asserted itself at shoulder height whereas the rocky ledge on the Base Camp-side subsisted at my knees. Switchbacks occurred every 20-30 meters. If one fell off the trail onto the antecedent path the fall would not have been life-threatening - only 3-4 meters down. Not life-threatening. But no one fell.

We had been instructed earlier in the day to place fresh batteries into our headlamps. Having done so at the beginning of the hike and having used my lamp only sparingly I deferred. I was confident my existing batteries would see me through to the summit. So confident was I in this belief I did not pack my spare batteries-batteries weighing only 25 grams. That would prove to be a bit of a mistake.

There we were - a dozen hopeful souls - animated in the near complete darkness on the flank of Kilimanjaro. Sufficient light from a quarter cheddar-cheese moon and gauzy stars let us sense the immensity of the summit above us - a shadowy and imposingly massive dome. Gazing upward, I could discern headlights of three or four other groups snaking slowly upward - as much as an hour beyond us. Similarly, headlights of the laggards could be appreciated behind us - only beginning to mobilize from Base Camp toward the same trailhead we had undertaken a half hour prior.

During the first hour of the ascent Freddy continued with the lead - maintaining his familiar slow and steady pace. All five women in our group marched in single file directly behind him followed by Rich, Richard, me, the two other guides (Raymond and Obama) and a fourth Tanzanian guide who had mysteriously joined our group. This new addition was familiar with both Raymond and Obama. Oddly he was not accompanying any paying hikers. Later he vanished from our midst as mysteriously as he had appeared. We never did learn the identity of this stranger - from whence he came nor from whence he departed.

The women in our group were pleasantly chatty during this early phase of the ascent - laughing, gabbing and shouting across one another from the head to the rear of their ranks. Rich, Richard and I remained taciturn - limiting our talking to only the essential. We had been in close proximity to one another for the better part of a week. What more of importance needed to or could be said? Especially when we should be sleeping.

Aside from the moderately-challenging switchbacks, the first two hours of the ascent also required us to scramble over and around good-sized ice-covered boulders. These should not have been challenging however the absence of light made them so. At times our aluminum poles were helpful but at other times these needed to be stowed to free our hands for grip. Conveniently our poles were designed to collapse - much like tent poles - and were easily stowed via clips onto our backpacks.

Granular sheets of ice soon began to impregnate themselves aggressively beside us and across our path. But this was not a slippery ice. It had been ground down by previous hikers and was interspersed with coarse Kilimanjaro gravel. Our boots thereby firmly gripped the trail.

Into the second hour of the climb the women were admonished by the guides to "hold your bladders". They would not be permitted to stop frequently tonight. We needed to make good time - to witness the magnificent impressionistic sunrise of East Africa.

The gritty snow hardened and our steps sounded a staccato "crunch". Crunch-crunch, crunch-crunch reverberating among 11 or 12 hikers. Mildly satisfying. Pole pole, crunch-crunch, hakuna matata, pole pole, crunch-crunch, hakuna matata - over and over. Every half hour we were reminded - from ahead of us or from behind- to drink- "sippy sippy!". We didn't stop to drink but instead sucked water from our camel packs as we continued ascending.

The air was thinning. Less and less effort was needed to pull an entire lungful of fiery cold air into my chest and to subsequently exhale. Later calculations revealed this air was nearly 30% less dense than air at sea level. Hence it was not surprising the air felt "thin". My respiration rate was 25 breaths/minute and my heart rate was near 125 beats/minute - still not alarmingly high. I had been working my body for five days and had developed confidence in its cardiovascular capability. This confidence helped. If I were to be told to turn back it would have happened by now.

On other hikes and earlier in this hike I hiked until my heart was beating excessively quickly - possibly 140-150 bpm. Then I would stop for a minute and allow my heart to slow. However, our slow progress tonight - the pole pole method - did not push me beyond what I felt was comfortable. It was clearly an effective technique I could use on other hikes! Slow and steady wins the race! We were all turtles.

It was 12:30 AM. We had been meandering upward for 1.5 hours when we took our first break. This was at a wide aspect of the path and situated amongst a collection of oversized boulders. The women scattered nearby among the massive rocks to tend to their needs while the men remained behind and caught their breaths - urinating in place in the dark. The quarter moon was setting behind Kilimanjaro's Southern flank. This caused the darkened promontory of Kilimanjaro to rise up further. As the moonlight waned the intensity and vastness of the Milky Way penetrated and briefly immobilized us. The rotated figure of Orion still lay to the extreme North- rising. Complete silence. Not even crickets. The cosmic wheels of the universe - of which we were clearly part - were grinding silently. The stars - still inflamed - arched ponderously above. They cast off their moorings and began to labor westward-compliantly trailing the receding quarter moon. One by one without talking we switched-off our headlamps and drank in this unexpected and majestic display. Periodically we were blessed with a brief slice of a fast-moving meteor and all whom had witnessed it shouted excitedly. "There! Did you see that!?" The heavens had never been so accessible nor so kind to us.

This women's bathroom break was not without it's comedy. While each woman had located a unique and "protected" boulder, in the dark it was impossible for each to accurately discern how *protected* each actually *was*. When Natascha's errant head lamp illuminated one of the other ladies *"en flagrante"* laughter and screams erupted above us. "Who's light is shining on me?" someone shouted. It might have been Angie's exclamation. Naturally those words drew all of our eyes upward toward the rocks that otherwise should have been providing cover. We laughed for the next several minutes.

While waiting at this first rest stop we were passed by a solitary hiker accompanied by a single Tanzanian guide - his country of origin a mystery. They seemed to be hiking inordinately quickly and I attributed this to their more impressive physical condition. Only perfunctory greetings - grunts really - were exchanged as the two of them strode stealthily and confidently by us. They were like automatons. They had a mission and it did not include making friends.

We departed again at 12:40 AM and encountered slightly more challenging terrain - steeper, ice-covered with abundant rocks and switch-backs. Pole pole, crunch crunch. Every Step A-Safe Step. One-Two-Three-Four. Over and over again. Conversations had lulled and were tending to whispers. All of us were in our individual present - yesterday gone and tomorrow non-existent. And our present had been reduced to a focus on each of our steps and to wondering about the feasibility of completion. Perhaps my only memorable thought was "Is it really possible to continue with this for seven more fucking hours?" I was not yet experiencing the familiar compression of time that typically developed an hour or two into previous days' hikes. Certainly euphoria escaped me. Hiking in the dark for better or worse required full attention to one's present - to one's footsteps.

I was immediately behind Rich and was studying his boots and the rhythmic movement and grating of his pole tips - one step behind. Our cadence blended. I estimated I placed 5-7 kg of weight onto each pole with each abbreviated step. This approximated the weight of my pack. But more - my poles stabilized me when external visual references - frequent in this blackness - escaped me. More than once my poles spared me a fall. And when they did I felt an increasingly-familiar strain as my underutilized triceps fought to maintain vertical.

To entertain us and to help pass time the guides periodically broke into collective song. One guide would commence with a well-known Tanzanian verse and the others would chime in either via the chorus or for the entire song. When familiar refrains such as "hakuna matata" emerged some of us would join as well. When our guides were not singing we could faintly discern guides from other groups - above or below us - breaking into similar song s- "hakuna matata" reverberating up and down the icy nighttime slope of Kilimanjaro. And so it was in this manner our tiny group of hikers - betrayed only by the lights on their heads, the crunching of their footsteps and their thin voices - wound its way ant-like on Kilimanjaro's darkened flank.

And while this transpired and was registered as significant we understood the Earth also rotated and circumambulated the sun. The moon continued its peregrination Westward and pulled the oceans and its sea life with it. Babies were born and the infirmed died. The war in Afghanistan went into its 12th year. Children in rural parts of developing countries struggled to grow for lack of nutrition, proper sanitation and maternal education. The wealthy became wealthier. Populism tightened its grip on Western democracies. Political prisoners languished in Iran, Saudi Arabia and Guantanamo. The black hole at the center of our galaxy continued to swallow-up vast volumes of interstellar dust - including suns with their planets. And eventually it would swallow the matter constituting our selves. Like insects we could be squashed and no memory of us could then exist. What really mattered except the present? What really mattered besides the night's climb and the attention paid to it by our consciousness?

Because we were hiking fully on ice and coarse snow my toes began to freeze. This despite the two layers of socks and good quality hiking boots. I heard from Debbie she had inserted foot warmers into her boots and I regretted not learning of this innovation prior. There seemed enough room in the toes of my boots for substantial flexion. From thenceforth I scrunched my toes back and forth repeatedly to stimulate circulation, to generate heat via friction and thereby to stave-off frostbite.

I began to incorporate one toe flexion into each step. I was grateful for extra toe space. Prior to this I had not put these boots to this degree of a challenge. And even though I had noted some degradation of the stitching on the inside sole of my right boot I was happy with how they had performed thus far. My thoughts turned again to my daughter Amelia and how she had given these boots to me as gifts for Christmas. "What is she doing now?" "My Dear Amelia".

At 2 AM - three hours into the hike - we stopped for another break. We extracted Mars bars and "biscuits" from our packs and devoured them greedily - the melting chocolate and caramel like liquid energy coursing directly from my mouth to my gut and thence toward my ravenous muscles. We then rehydrated from our camel backs and resolved to continue.

I did a quick assessment of my "condition"- a step-by-step mental process I knew could reveal my weak points and thereby adjust or – possibly - grieve. I was feeling mildly nauseous with a definite "pit" in my stomach. I did not yet have a headache. I was feeling quite short of breath. Excessive effort caused me to gasp for breath and my heart to race upward to 140+ bpm. I was near my cardiovascular limit. I was developing concern about the altitude. But I didn't want to quit.

To bring solace I thought of the good things in my life. My Mom and Dad. My kids. Azizah, my dear, tolerant and patient wife. My sister. All were ok as far as I knew. My red leather couch at home where I have been known to languish. American Dream pizza with its sour dough crust washed down with an amber-colored bitter India Pale Ale - preferably a Tricerahops. A Tricerahops served in a thick frosted 500 ml glass accompanied by a friend who took equal pleasure in both food and drink. Should I not expire, those blessings would return. I resolved to appreciate them more when they did.

We continued trudging upward. And not too distant from us came the distressing sounds of the solitary hiker - the automaton - who had mechanically accelerated past us earlier - the hiker from the unknown country - retching violently and dispiritingly into the still night air. On and on it went - ferocious heaving with some productive vomiting - for nearly five minutes. Was it altitude sickness? Would he and his guide soon pass us again, this time on a downward trek? The hiker had evacuated his stomach and continued upward. And who could blame him? I was told it is a relief to vomit if one has altitude sickness.

We stopped again at 3:30 AM - 4.5 hours into the night's effort. By this time no one had any interest or strength to talk. I rested against a rock in the darkness having doffed my backpack and hiking poles. I was too tired to dig through my pack and locate any sustenance. However, I did follow instructions to hydrate. The air was thin, cold and dry. We were sweating under our layers of clothes. Water was leaving our bodies at rapid non-discernable rates. It, along with essential electrolytes, needed to be replaced.

The air was becoming less dense and the stars gazed down upon us with even greater concern. Never had I seen a display of the heavens so transcendent. It was as if the density of stars exceeded the blackness of the emptiness of space. Indeed, the stars were close enough to touch. Whenever I felt the energy to do so I lifted my arms as I had done earlier on this hike and swirled the stars. And when I dropped my arms I watched as they dutifully reversed direction and spiraled back into their original positions. How did they know from whence they had derived? What tethered them? I didn't have the mental strength to summon an answer.

At each of these rest stops the guides queried us on our health. Anything relating to nausea, vomiting or headaches represented a perilous sign of altitude sickness. The nausea I had felt earlier seemed mostly dissipated however I still harbored a nagging hollow pit in my stomach and was devoid of appetite. The thought of food was mildly-revolting. Thoughts of anything other than one's present condition had deserted us. We were alive. We were in the dark. And we had distance to cover. Elation - should it arrive - could wait.

At this most recent stop we ended-up staying for much longer than anticipated. Debbie had been hiking with hand warmers and the ones she had inserted into her gloves at Base Camp had “run out”. She needed new hand warmers but they were not to be found amongst the well-known - if not appreciated - dozen or so zippered external and internal pockets of her backpack. Using their headlamps our three guides searched her pack for ten minutes before locating unused hand warmers at the bottom of one of the pockets. Unbelievable as it was it all fit. A pattern had emerged and could be relied upon. Again Rich, Richard and I looked into each others’ eyes knowingly during the extended search for Debbie’s hand warmers. It would have taken too much effort to say what we were individually thinking. We each knew. The guides certainly demonstrated infinite patience. They were guiding us not only in hiking but also in forbearance.

We were into our fifth hour. Time began to compress and distort. Whereas the initial 2-3 hours of the night’s hike had taken forever, each hour thereafter slipped by more rapidly. It no longer seemed unusual to be up and out of bed at 4 AM on the side of an East African slope with fellow mountain climbers. Here we were! Eventually this would be finished with. Maybe there would be a good story.

As the night wore on we began to anticipate the first sign of a sunrise - the appearance of a promised thin line on the horizon in the Eastern sky - evidence the cosmic wheels we saw evidence of the evening prior had continued to turn - evidence time had not stopped. Sunrise, when it greeted us, would provide encouragement.

Trudge, trudge, crunch, crunch, squeeze toes, squeeze toes, pole pole, sippy sippy. Every Step A-Safe Step…and on and on following the boots of the person directly in front of me. I continued to work my poles into the ice and rocky edges of the path. Each step only 15 cm in length. Each step audible in the broken ice and gravel - as on a movie sound track. Multiply that 12-fold and add in the scraping and searching of twelve sets of poles with their metallic tips striking iron-laden rock. Those were our sounds. No one talked. The guides had quit singing long ago.

I passed time by counting 100 steps and then looked around to determine whether anything had "changed". Is there any evidence of a sunrise? I was vigilant. I assessed my physical condition as I had on Day One and throughout and found I was still doing remarkably well. Mentally I felt strong and "in the present". On the physical side, my ankles were sore and there was soreness also in my lower back. However, this was nothing compared to Day One. I was scoring at no more than a "10" on my improvised 50-point scale. My quadriceps were feeling strong - the result of five days of conditioning. Instead my greatest worry was the possibility of frostbite in my toes. I feared the moisture my feet were generating via perspiration was sabotaging them. Past days had taught me my socks became moist by the end of each day. It was well below freezing and my socks were certainly wet. I was hiking on ice. If I wasn't careful my toes *could* freeze. I redoubled my efforts to flex my toes back and forth aggressively across the soles of my boots with each step in order to generate as much heat as I could. At this rate - I thought to myself - I may rub holes into my socks.

At 5:15 AM, nearly six hours after departing base camp, a thin lighter contour appeared atop a foamy carpet of leaden clouds on the Eastern horizon. Sunrise was at hand. At first I was uncertain this line truly represented the dawn of the new day - it could be an atmospheric distortion I thought. But slowly color was added to the line - peach, burnt yellow and orange - and the line began to both thicken and widen. It stretched to encompass fully 90 degrees of the horizon and was quickly reaching further North and South. Distant clouds began to take on an uneven appearance - possibly the beginning of cumulus formation. From gray they took on a violet tone then mauve. And, as time passed, the thin line began to accumulate colors approximating citrus - tangerine, lemon and maybe even some lime. Cirrus clouds above became flushed and framed by a cerulean sky. It was glorious to behold.

I was not feeling 100%. Intentional analysis of my condition informed me I was ill - the nausea had returned. I did not have a headache but my gut just felt "off" - I could retch should I will it. Part of the blame may have been my hydration strategy. I had stubbornly supplemented my water with the mismatched combination of hydration salts and together their sickly-sweet tang caused me gag as I hydrated. Hydration aside, altitude and exertion must certainly have contributed to my overall sense of malaise.

I had not appreciated the importance of "Stella Point" as an intermediate destination on this night's last climb. Stella Point rested at the crest of tonight's scramble at 5,756 meters AMSL - *ca.* 600 meters above Mawenzi. As our hike progressed Stella Point came to represent a very important destination because, after one reached Stella Point, I learned the remaining hike to Uhuru Summit became comparatively easy.

The morning's sun was revealing the extent to which we were surrounded by snow, by ice and by collections of creviced aquamarine glaciers. We had departed a graveled and lunar-like Base Camp seven hours ago and found ourselves in a completely-transformed and unfamiliar environment. Blue ice. Pink snow. Thin, searing-cold air barely registered as air in our lungs. The new legs that had managed to carry us up through the night were tiring. To the extent it could, the sun buoyed us.

Stella Point draped over us commandingly as a snow-covered ledge. It then arched upward and southward gracefully toward Uhuru Peak. Well above us an unknown and solitary hiker stood watching down toward us and periodically shouted "Keep going! You're almost here!" I wondered if he was the one who had vomited after he passed us a few hours earlier? Around him I noted others were congregating on what appeared to be the longed-for plateau. The unknown hiker's admonitions injected me with some needed energy. We had only 100-meters yet to climb to reach Stella Point. One hundred meters! But damn! Those 100 meters took another half hour of intense effort - such was the pace we were only capable of at this altitude - perhaps a few cm of altitude gain with each labored step.

The latter two hours of climbing had caused each of us to fully retreat into our minds and to focus on finding the strength to continue. The stretch just below Stella Point was the steepest of the entire night's climb. Because of the required focus none of us had been aware of the others' physical conditions or of whom might be most affected by the combination of effort and altitude. Hence it was not until I had nearly reached Stella Point I became aware Natascha was struggling. She could barely stand and was incoherent. No wonder I had not heard any conversation from her for the past two hours!

By the time I had arrived at Stella Point the batteries in my headlamp had fully expired. The meagre sunlight and the imperfect view of my friends' hiking boots in front of me had buttressed the last hour of my climb. But still, absence of a strong beam was causing me to stumble over rocks I should have seen. It was becoming increasingly difficult to see the footsteps of antecedent hikers. This caused a small level of anxiety to rise in me and I wished for the sun to rise more quickly. And I castigated myself for not following Freddy's request we replace batteries in our headlamps the night prior.

At Stella, as at other significant locations *en* route, a sign stood to commemorate the achievement: Stella Point. 5,756 meters. Rich, Richard and I assembled in front of the sign and maintained brave but exhausted, wind-burned faces for photos. I was glad to have arrived but was cognizant of being in an environment and situation that were unfamiliarly non-physiological: cold, extremely thin air, exhausted, old. Angie was surprisingly emotional with having reached this point - hugging and kissing each of us. Tears ran copiously down her face. Encouraged by Angie's display of emotion I too was emotional and struggled to hold back my own tears. We were all so relieved, exhausted and happy because we knew, barring gargantuan misfortune, we were individually going to succeed in summiting. Now we knew!

Elation grew to the extent it could in our near-defeated bodies and minds.

Richard too was visibly affected by the altitude. He walked with only moderate stability - wonkily swaying from side to side and seemingly not fully appreciative of his accomplishment. He was exceptionally buoyant and remarkably loquacious as he staggered about. It was as if he had just consumed a substantial amount of alcohol. Gillian had a severe headache and reported feeling "wretched". Perhaps both suffered from inadequate respiratory capacity associated with the colds they harbored.

I believe four of our eight hikers were substantially affected by altitude: Natascha, Angie, Richard and Gillian. But of these four only Natascha presented a real concern. The rest of us (Rich, Debbie, Alex and me) and the guides seemed relatively unfazed by the near 6000-meter altitude. Certainly the air was thin but I believed I could still think and function properly.

Stella Point constituted a plateau at the volcanic edge of the Eastern side of Kilimanjaro. It represented a meeting point at which the many other access trails to the summit converged. The plateau lay within the shadow of an overhanging southern ridge sheltering anyone at Stella from the South-east morning sun. From Stella the hike to the summit required another 1 km of hiking with an additional 300 meters gain in altitude. Compared to what we had completed in the last few hours this would be a "cake walk". Uhuru Summit appeared tantalizingly close - requiring only a ramble up and across the volcanic snow-covered ridge. Indeed, a Volkswagen bus would have no difficulty in traversing the remaining distance - such were the abundant width and gentle incline of the path. There was nothing separating any of us from reaching Uhuru.

We collected or backpacks and hiking poles and began our final assault. Richard and I hiked side-by-side and I did so because I was concerned about his demeanor. He was staggering and erratic. Yet he seemed to have no awareness of his moderate, albeit somewhat humorous, disability. I harbored no doubt Richard possessed the wherewithal to complete the ascent to Uhuru unaided. Such was the metal I knew he was constructed of.

We stopped periodically. Just past the arched ridge protecting Stella Point we gained a vista of an immense basilica of blue ice constituting one of Kilimanjaro's mammoth diminishing glaciers - a glacier projected to be "gone" within a half-century.

I was hiking with two lenses - a regular 55 mm and a wide angle zoom (10-22mm) - for my Nikon camera and was finding it onerous to doff my backpack and switch lenses as different photo opportunities presented themselves. Richard filled the gap by volunteering to become, in his words, my "photo bitch". I stopped frequently and allowed him to eagerly plumb the depths of my backpack in search of the alternate lens. It was an endearing endeavor for both of us. "Photo bitch". I liked it. Even at this altitude he retained a modicum of humor.

The glacier was nothing less than stupendous. When my son and I had traveled to Antarctica a year prior our "expedition leader" had remarked, upon coming across an impressive hotel-sized, cavern-laden iceberg - *"if on this planet there is a civilization that worships ice, this must certainly be one of its cathedrals*". Sure, his exclamation was more than a little hyperbolic and I learned later he had been a drama major in college. But without a doubt the massive blue-ice glacier just below me would easily have qualified as one of the great cathedrals worshiped by the same civilization. Standing 100-200 meters off the trail at 50-80 meters in height this multi-spired, aquamarine, blindingly white and sapphire glacier stood with promontories and precipices putting the Gaudi cathedral in Barcelona to shame. Its full attributes proved impossible to capture in a photograph - such was its majesty. Richard did his best in alternating the lenses I hoped would capture the stunning beauty resting convincingly in front of me. Yet I failed. My photos did not provide the glacier the justice it deserved. Nevertheless, it remains indelibly burned into my memory.

Between Stella Point and Uhuru Summit 25-30 hikers labored both upward and downward. Surprisingly there was no sign of the French nor the Italians. Perhaps they had already summited and then descended via one of Kilimanjaro's alternate routes. Those heading downward from the summit uniformly provided encouragement and smiles to those endeavoring upward. All enthusiastic about what they had just accomplished and wished to be part of the success we ascendants were about to achieve. An hour later, our roles would be reversed. We had become "family" of sorts.

I made note of the ages of the summiteers. The median age of those we encountered was mid-30's but there were others who extended into higher age ranges - possibly a few into their 60's. I was among the oldest to be summiting.

Yesterday's squall carrying the spray of ice crystals from Uhuru southward as a glittering diamantine veil was absent. The air was still- nary a trace of wind. Kilimanjaro's sky had taken on the deepest blue I had ever witnessed- decorated by elongated wisps of deep pink cirrus. Below lay a continuous base of frothy linen clouds. Illuminated with an otherworldly pink-orange light the Kibo cinder cone swept abruptly up and away toward the North and Uhuru. I tried to capture this artist's palette of colors in photographs but I failed. The early-morning light was both too capricious and too subtle to apprehend. Photos cannot capture temporal color in the manner of the human mind.

Richard and I continued our meandering progress toward Uhuru. The air, more thin, stung as I took in each breath. I worried it might damage the epithelial layer of my lungs. I tried to distract myself by appreciating Meru - the tiny cousin of Kilimanjaro whose rounded and purple-hued summit was visible above a cloud layer to the South-west - a few thousand meters below us.

Richard, becoming more affected by altitude, staggered but remained steadfast in intent. Periodically I took his left arm in my right arm and directed him upward. Despite his infirmity he remained good natured and resolute. He was going to make it and so was I. I would make sure he reached the summit as I knew he would do for me. This realization was a bit of a shared indulgence for the both of us. We weren't there yet. We had harbored doubts. But nothing would prevent us from individually reaching the summit. Still, I was too exhausted to feel elation or any other positive or significant emotion. I was just glad to be here and to know I had succeeded in this more than improbable mission. I was glad to share this experience with a friend. We had reached the top of Africa together. It was a meaningful effort. Light years from my couch. Indeed, this would be the closest I would ever get to the stars - at least under my own power.

During our final effort our guides paid Richard and I no heed because all three were tending exclusively to Natascha. We caught glimpses of her and noted both Raymond and Obama were supporting her as she staggered erratically toward Uhuru - bent sideways - like a broken doll. Her eyes rolled and she was barely conscious. I was convinced it would be far better to evacuate Natascha immediately rather than convey her further upward into an elevation with less oxygen. However, evacuating Natascha was not my decision. Further, Richard and I had our own infirmities to contend with if we were to summit.

From where I am uncertain but Rich joined-up with Richard and me as we approached Uhuru. The three of us were destined to reach the objective together!

The Summit came into view - identified by the familiar presence of a nondescript 3-meter tall brown painted sign with yellow lettering indicating we had reached Uhuru. This was the one of the "world's tallest volcanos" and constituted the "Wonder of Africa". As we approached the sign loomed large over us - set deep in ice and backlit by the reassuringly deep blue sky. We could not immediately embrace the summit. Instead, a collection of a dozen colorfully-clad and animated climbers milled around the summit sign's base basking in their achievements and in their heightened friendships.

We had reached the summit! Our minds had willed it and our bodies had complied. Nothing could take this achievement from us. What else might we be capable of? We could tell our grand-children about this. In the meantime, we were here. This was why we had undertaken the effort. I knew each of us felt immensely proud. What else could we know?

++

We posed individually and then collectively at the summit for photos. Natascha, Angie and Debbie had been sponsored by a hospice in Portsmouth, UK and had been promised a donation of the equivalent of $200 should they display a hospice banner at the summit - a lot of effort for $200! This they managed despite Natascha's near unconsciousness. Natascha sat beside Angie and Debbie as the photographic evidence was collected.

I had commemorative photos of myself taken at the summit as did others then we coalesced around the summit marker for a group photo. We reveled. Smiles spread from ear to ear. Guides joined us for more group photos. We shouted "Hakuna Mata!" and "Kilimanjaro" as the photos were snapped by strangers using our cameras and iPhones - a favor we subsequently returned to them. Debbie in her lush pink jacket splayed herself endearingly across almost the entire Kilimanjaro Summit sign in a gesture of accomplishment - a broad smile affixed. Indeed, summiting was a joyous communal celebration - mixed with abundant measures of disbelief.

The view from the summit was spectacular. The volcanic summit swept downward into an extinct caldera - dormant for 150,000-200,000 years. In the opposite direction clouds obscured the remote East-African plain - the Rift Valley and the Oldupai Gorge-200 km to the West - from which all of humankind had derived. This was a site where Leaky, only in the late-1950's, only 60 years ago, provided convincing evidence of the origins of man - not from Asia - but from Africa. My ancestors had lived here - 100,000 years and 4,000 generations ago.

Perhaps the ancestors who departed 100,000 years ago still spoke of Kilimanjaro's last eruption. Because of its close proximity my forbearers presumably knew of Kilimanjaro and were closely connected to groups that ultimately formed our primary ethnic groups: black, yellow, red, brown, and white. They probably referred to it as "the great mountain" or "the snow mountain" in whatever languages that then prevailed. They would have venerated it as they passed through their generations not knowing of what it "meant" nor that one of their descendants might visit one-hundred millennia later. In fact, they could not have understood the concept of a "millennia". They would have lived day-to-day on the abundance of life in the adjacent plains - both animal and vegetable. Perhaps some of them had time on their hands and climbed the snow-covered mountain. I'll never know.

Chapter Sixteen
The Descent (Part 1)

I regretted having to leave. We had all worked so hard to reach this elevation that leaving seemed like abandonment. I wanted to stay longer but all within my group were beginning to retreat. Warm sleeping bags, the comforts of tents and the promise of mitigating altitude sickness beckoned.

The first challenge of my descent was to locate my hiking poles. I had mindlessly discarded them near the summit upon arrival but so had everyone else. My poles were not so distinctive that they were easily-identifiable amongst the collection of joyously cast off poles. While searching I missed Raymond's and Freddy's departure with Natascha to Base Camp. Unbeknownst to me the remainder of the team, with Obama remaining as the sole guide, had similarly departed.

I was momentarily distracted by another hiker - a young man named "Henri" who derived from Finland. Henri was impressed with my camera and beseeched me to photograph him at the summit and to later e-mail him the high-resolution images. His enthusiasm contagious I agreed and completed a ten-minute photoshoot as he progressively removed more and more of his clothing and, to the irritation of others, attempted to scale the fragile Kilimanjaro Summit sign. By the end Henri was swaggering about shirtless - scapula-length blond hair cascading down his tattooed back. We had attracted an impatient crowd because Henri's antics were delaying them. Having extracted him from the sign we exchanged e-mail addresses and he promised to host me in Helsinki should I ever visit.

The nausea was gone. The pit in my stomach was gone. It didn't seem to matter I hadn't slept the night prior. Despite having been awake for nearly 24 hours I wasn't tired. I was reasonably alert. Nor did any other physiological need prevail upon me. All I needed to accomplish was to navigate back down the same incline I had scaled the night prior - back to Base Camp.

The prior evening a suggestion had been made by our guides - "once you 'summit', you can just head down the mountain at any speed you want. If you arrive into Base Camp early, you can sleep for a few hours before we depart for Mweka Camp after lunch". I was resolved to descend as quickly as I could - possibly in three hours - and thereby enjoy two to three hours of uninterrupted slumber before departing for the balance of the day's descent. I hoped to be in the vanguard - possibly arriving by 11:00 AM. My plan was to strike-out downward and race ahead of our moderately-capable group. Base Camp seemed almost visible from the summit - just on the other side of what I perceived as an obvious ridge. The trail was unmistakable. Direction and support were no longer needed. Nor was worry.

Feeling abandoned I navigated back to Stella Point - proffering encouragement to ascendant hikers *en* route. Arriving, I located my hiking partners, sans Natascha, Freddy and Raymond, impatiently waiting for me with Obama. My photographic exploits with Henri had delayed our group's descent by 15 minutes and in consequence I felt sheepish. With some hyperbole, I offered a somewhat unrealistic explanation for my tardiness to gain forgiveness by describing the "wild Finn" who had accosted me and requested photos. However, no one showed much interest in my excuse. I had made a mistake. I should have stayed with my hiking group. But I didn't. Perhaps the altitude *was* affecting me. A warming morning sun and increasing threat of altitude sicknesses had beckoned the group downward aggressively - an imperative. I had interrupted the natural order of things. I sensed the recriminations normally directed, but never voiced, at Debbie.

It was 9 AM and quite warm - probably just above freezing. The wind was still. The sun burned aggressively and was reflected back toward us from the ice pack. We paused to apply sunscreen, remove layers of clothing and retrieve our UV-blocking sunglasses from our packs. And then one by one we bid adieu to Stella Point and commenced our downward treks - treks we had not anticipated would be a challenge.

Departing Stella, the view was to the East and Southeast. The vista included Mt. Mawenzi and a broken layer of pink and golden clouds hovering above the Tanzanian plain more than 5 km below us. The sun was still rising and the heat it generated caused us to halt intermittently and to remove more and more of our clothing. Within a half hour I had removed my outer GoreTex shell, my red down vest, the fraternity hoodie my son had given me and my gloves.

The sun was robust and obliterated many of the subtle colors I had waxed effusively about earlier in the day. Rust, peach, taupe and vermillion were diluted into unimaginative and uninspiring yellow- and dung-colored clays.

Within an hour five of our group (Richard, Rich, Debbie, Alex and Gillian) had accelerated downward leaving Angie and me unexpectedly together as a commiserating and trailing duo. This had not been my plan. My plan had been to be the fleetest and thereby catch-up on my missing sleep in Base Camp while awaiting return of the others and the arrival of a substantial lunch. But as others have opined - if wishes were horses, beggars would ride.

Within an hour of departing Stella Point my quadriceps revolted. The challenge was mild at first and centered in the thickest portions of both muscles. From there it radiated outward and inward and within an hour I was experiencing severe discomfort within the entireties of both quads - from my knees upward to my pelvis.

Another feature of the descent was the soreness caused by the accumulating damage to my toes. While they were no longer in danger of frostbite they were being scrunched forward into the toes of my boots and abraded. I'd experienced toe abrasion a few days earlier while descending from Lava Tower into Baranco Camp. Here I was suffering the same challenge - except this time in spades. The night prior I had taken care to carefully wrap each vulnerable toe with moleskin and other bandages and was hoping prophylaxis would prevent serious damage.

Whereas my inadequate quads and chaffed toes were slowing my descent Angie's knees were hindering hers. We thereby coalesced as a supportive couple - ambling gingerly downward together. Obama, newly aware of our limitations, hung well behind the other five hikers and kept a watchful eye over us. I was still carrying my backpack but Obama had tactfully relieved Angie of hers. I'm certain he had seen this degree of infirmity before. Carrying an extra backpack was routine.

Until now I had not come to know Angie well. From my end of the mess tent she presented as a high-spirited, and vivacious woman who bore some outward indication of having had challenges in her life. We all have had those experiences. Her hair was streaked blond and I judged her to be in her mid-40's. I admired her for her demeanor and her determination to accomplish this hike. Her determination was my own.

Angie had quit smoking at the initiation of the hike - a decision certainly making her effort more demanding. Angie had also experienced physical challenges earlier. Those difficulties had occurred during the descent from Lava Tower to Baranco Camp on Day Three. There Angie arrived in Baranco Camp fully one hour behind the rest of our group. Today's effort was another descent far more aggressive than what the descent into Baranco Camp had demanded. It was not surprising Angie would find challenge in today's downward hike as well.

The first two-thirds of the downward trek toward Base Camp followed the precise trail we had adhered to on the way up. It was actually of some interest to be able to marvel at what we had climbed only a few hours earlier. However, at some indecipherable point Obama intentionally deviated and took a more direct route downward - a steeper route devoid of both snow and ice and which continued across the wide sweeping Southeastward flank of the mountain. Base Camp, seemed to be coming in to view. Or, was this an illusion?

I had learned sighting a destination was not a precise indicator of the remaining time nor effort required. If anything sighting a destination made the remaining hike more difficult because the perceived achievable distance collapsed at only a snail's pace - especially given the Tanzanian "pole pole" approach to hiking. This was exacerbated further by Obama's overly optimistic prognostications of the time remaining in the hike. The mind was stronger than the body. The hour we anticipated would be required to reach Base Camp stretched ahead of us - further and further. Our insights and the destination played tricks on us. The destination was not the destination. The path was not the path we should be following. How long could this go on?

Within three hours Angie and I were fully down into the lower one-third of the return to Base Camp. We hung together and provided support and when possible a modicum of conversation to one another. Obama maintained a polite but observant distance from us - 50-100 meters downhill - as if this distance from us might compel us to accelerate toward him. In retrospect this was a reasonable strategy. The remaining five hikers in our group were nowhere in sight. They had passed by, down, over and around the expanse Angie and I still needed to conquer.

We were resolute and continued to agitate downward - this despite the unwelcome isolation from the group. We were both struggling. In my newly-understood infirmity I took a step sideways around an uneven and nondescript rock lying across the vertiginous path and my legs unexpectedly gave way. Unexpectedly I had no remaining side-to-side strength. I collapsed into an unceremonious pile to the side of the unforgiving path. Both Angie and Obama watched me hopefully from their distances. Gingerly and with palpable aspects of chagrin I struggled with my poles to bring myself again to vertical. In doing so I lacerated my elbow either on a sharp rock or on my poles. But the laceration did not register and it was only later when I caught up with Obama that he remarked on the rivulets of crusted blood extending the length of my arm. By then the wound had fully clotted and was of no import. Soon after Angie took a small leap downward maybe 0.3 meters down - to a lower portion of an uneven path and her knees gave way. The irregular ground on which she landed rotated her fully 180 degrees and she fell backward into a large rock: striking the rock with her butt. It could have been a lot worse if she had landed with her head or her spine first. For Angie's fall Obama was close enough to spring into action and help support her as she stood. We were a calamity in action.

And so it went for the remainder of the downward strain- Angie's knees barely supporting her, my quads barely supporting me and Obama periodically expressing his concern via his worried eyes and knotted brow. We needed to reach Barafu Camp in time to depart for Mweka. Throughout, the sun gained altitude and dialed-up the temperature. Pressure to reach camp increased.

Angie and I were not the worst "performers" on Kilimanjaro. During the descent we encountered several others huddled miserably on the sides of the trail - either in full sun or in shade - with their friends and guides hovering worriedly nearby. I believe the stricken hikers were suffering from moderate to severe altitude sickness. Altitude sickness and various forms of physical incapacity. They exhibited combinations of immobility, disorientation, vomiting and incoherence. Some projected a vacant stare as if they were completely unaware of their circumstance. Their ages varied from the mid-20's into the sixties. Indeed, they were fortunate to have caring friends and guides near them. As we passed these sad groups we avoided eye contact and gave privacy. It was the same privacy I extend in hospitals when I walk by the open rooms of ailing strangers. We ambled past, understood their situations were not good and hoped we would not find ourselves in a similar condition further on. Neither Angie nor I were in a position to render aid. It was only later we realized these hikers were members of both the French and Italian teams.

On three occasions immobile, altitude-afflicted hikers were rushed by us on one-wheeled gurneys - contraptions requiring active participation of four porters - one at each corner. These individuals had become so incapacitated at altitude that they had lost virtually all physical and mental capability. Clearly these individuals had been amongst our fellow tour groups but we did not recognize them. Afflicted and wretched, they differed from the robust individuals we had become used to encountering. There was a hospital at the base of Kilimanjaro specializing in the care of high altitude sickness. These people were still several hours and a very rough one-wheeled gurney ride away from competent medical care. The likelihood was they would survive. We knew that. But every year a few on Kilimanjaro don't- succumbing to either cerebral or pulmonary edema.

By noon Angie and I were approaching camp- 1 km away. We rounded a bend in the path and deviated southward and I observed two of our porters flourishing idly in the noon sun- beckoning like old friends from a sun-lit hollow beneath a mustard-colored rocky overhang. These were porters who had not summited with us and were therefore rested and clearly happy to greet us. Here were Focus and another porter whose face I recognized but whose name I had not yet learned - presumably Angie's porter. They carried a jug of orange juice and poured large dollops of their magical orange elixir into plastic mugs - pleased to welcome us back into their fold. Their injection of liquid energy and kindness helped us regain some optimism and energy.

We rested with the porters for ten minutes enjoying their hospitality - some of the misery of the descent fading. I took this opportunity to consume more analgesics. I had exhausted my supply of Aleve so was ingesting a European facsimile – Paracetamol - a gift from Angie. Drug interactions be damned! From thence Focus, Angie's porter, Obama, Angie and I descended *en* masse - a caring tight-knit, albeit soundless, group. The sun hovered overhead - the landscape inflamed into a foamy and hostile reddish-brown. Heat waves shimmered threateningly across the parched landscape. Here there was no evidence of avian nor plant life - nor was I capable of communing with any conscious life form save for my rattled mind.

The downward slope narrowed and we entered a last treacherous and rock-strewn series of switchbacks - these too surrounded by towering volcanic outcroppings. Toward the bottom of this slope we were required to traverse a small drop of less than 1 meter. I could have gently eased myself over this drop with the use of my poles. But instead I overestimated my strength. I jumped down into the drop and when I landed with my knees slightly flexed my legs buckled. My arms, flailing helplessly with their poles, lacked the strength to break my second fall of the day. I collapsed and splayed ignominiously on the dusty yellow path - floundering and pitiful. Obama reached back and helped me regain my footing. "Can you make it?" he queried. "Do you want me to take your pack?" The remainder of the hike was expected to be largely "on the flat" and I vigorously spurned his offer. I had not yet been able to admit my obvious marginal capability to myself even though it was becoming obvious to others. Now "on the flat" I planned to concentrate on the rebuilding of the strength in my legs and on regaining some measure of dignity.

Angie and I re-entered Base Camp near 12:30 PM- 3.5 hours after departing Stella Point. All of our remaining six hikers, sans Natascha, were milling about camp but even though they were welcoming I had no interest in chatting. Instead I immediately recoiled to the closest approximation of a couch available to me - my tent. I had Focus remove my boots and collapsed into a mental rehashing of the previous tortuous fourteen hours. My legs ached tortuously and my feet burned. What had I done? Forgotten and irrelevant were the confidence and the understanding I had summited. Summiting was in the past. We were, I was, for better or worse, embarking on a more ambitious journey - an unexpected journey. A journey never discussed nor presented in pre-climb literature - a journey we were wholly unprepared for.

Blissfully alone in my tent I reflected on the effort. We had been awake for nearly 30 hours during which time we had completed three independent efforts - upward to Base Camp yesterday, then to the summit through the night and back to Base Camp. I was becoming aware of our very unfortunate need to continue today's effort downward to Mweka Camp to minimize the likelihood of altitude sickness. If we stayed at Base Camp we risked serious illness. We *had* to get lower. This was especially an imperative for Natascha who was recuperating from altitude incapacity in her tent. After lunch we were to hike another 10-15 km downward. This without any additional sleep. This on my incapable legs and damaged toes. This without any enthusiasm or, more than likely, without inspiration from the ubiquitous ravens.

Yes, the ravens were absent. A short time after entering camp I noted the ravens that had been with us only yesterday had fully deserted us. Their absence engendered in me a distinct melancholy. I had come to anticipate their presence and was used to their ungainly welcoming antics, their direct quizzical looks and their willingness to let us share their corporeal presence. But for reasons I couldn't know they had departed. To where? Perhaps to guide other hikers on Kilimanjaro? With us they were done.

Chapter Seventeen
An Unexpectedly Arduous Descent (Part 2)

Kandoo personnel had been less than forthcoming in describing the post-summiting aspect of the hike. We understood we would depart for the summit very late one evening and return from the summit the next morning; however, it was not clear from either Kandoo's literature nor from the pre-climb briefing there would be virtually no rest between our return to Base Camp and then a further hike down to Mweka Camp. And not only a "further hike" but a very demanding "further hike".

The need for this second descent following our initial descent from Uhuru made complete sense physiologically. But as noted earlier Kandoo's and our focus had been on summiting - not on getting back down. Only now were those methods and the imperatives underpinning them becoming evident.

Mweka Camp - today's ultimate destination - lay at 3,786 meters AMSL - a drop of 870 meters from Barafu Camp. The distance was estimated at 10-15 km. This was to be completed along a "dry river bed"- a descriptor suggesting a laid-back and promising day. A ramble downward perhaps. River beds are flat I reasoned. However, numbers meant very little. What mattered to us were how our legs felt, how our toes felt, how our knees felt and how our stomachs felt. What were our states of mind? Might there be some interesting wildlife to observe? Might Richard's penchant for nature somehow re-ignite itself and divert our attention from an otherwise difficult downward effort?

What also struck me was how such small distances - on foot - came to represent massive undertakings. Whereas 10-15 km could be completed in an ordinary car in less than ten minutes the effort on foot could require the better part of a day. Would it be that a car was available.

I was especially concerned with my toes. While waiting for lunch I removed my dampened socks and tended to my them - sadly discovering many had been bleeding. I gingerly removed the mangled blood-soaked bandages and moleskin I had wrapped around five or six of my most seriously-afflicted toes the evening prior and re-applied fresh bandages. It appeared I would be losing several of my toenails - the right big toe being the most-threatened. The nail on that toe had been pushed upward 2 mm by inflammation beneath. I took the discovery with more equanimity than was deserved. To minimize infection, I administered Neosporin antibiotic ointment prior to re-wrapping my toes and then donned two pairs of dry socks - the familiar inner silk layer and an outer woolen layer. I was grateful to still be in possession of unused dry socks - a blessing to be sure. My toes - even though inflamed and degraded - felt safe, dry and protected. They could re-initiate a healing process. Or at least I hoped so.

Natascha rested out of our sight - recuperating in her tent. Guides reported she was “eating fruit” - a hopeful sign. While on the mountain I was informed when oxygen saturation falls below 92% one is considered “oxygen-starved” because *that* concentration of oxygen is required to “force oxygen into red blood cells”. I was not certain this made sense biologically but I accepted this information at face value. We were informed upon Natascha’s assisted arrival into Base Camp her oxygen saturation registered at 63% - an extraordinarily low number. If her saturation was 63% at base camp imagine what it was at summit! No wonder Natascha was barely conscious at Stella Point and beyond! It was unclear what Natascha’s oxygen saturation was, now she had been restoring oxygen for two hours. I deliberated - how quickly might one recover from severe oxygen deprivation? Could Natascha continue after lunch? Or might she need a one-wheeled gurney-supported evacuation?

A later consult with a physician friend underlined the immensity of the difficulty Natascha was in. According to my friend, Natascha could easily have expired

The call for lunch arrived. I rose sluggishly - my lower back aching and my legs and toes still burning. I placed my boots under the direct sun so the moisture they had accumulated over the past day might begin to evaporate. I crawled on my hands and knees out of the tent door, cumbersomely hoisted myself vertical and made my way uneasily in stocking feet toward the mess tent - perhaps twenty meters away. En route my toes reminded me of their perilous condition. This sucked.

Lunch was a half-hearted affair - this despite our recent success in summiting. No one was transcendent. Our primary discussion centered on Natascha and on whether she would be able to continue or not. "What options might there be?" Alex was especially concerned - borderline upset. Periodically she left the mess tent to check on her sister and returned with grim reports.

Few of us had any appetite. Yet a full-course meal had been prepared. We did our best to show some interest in the food - feeling badly when the good-humored cook popped his head into the mess tent following our meal only to discover only a small portion of what he and his team had prepared had been consumed. Our collective appetite had been diminishing the higher we got. He must have anticipated this and so I felt no shame. His feelings were the least of my concerns.

To our surprise, toward the end of our lunch Natascha injected herself into the mess tent. She had made it to the tent under her own power and - more importantly - was both coherent and energetic. The "old Natascha" had resurfaced with her smiles and off-beat humor. What a difference those final few thousand feet of altitude had made! She regaled us with how badly she had felt, how she had no recollection of the summit or of the guide-assisted descent. Given all she had endured her lucidity was truly remarkable - testament to the importance of adequate oxygen to a functioning brain. That she had no recollection of the summit was truly phenomenal. In my mind she should have been evacuated sooner than she had been.

A mixture of emotions percolated amongst the group. Certainly we were pleased to have individually summited and we each recounted some of our individual summit highlights. However, we were disappointed we couldn't rest in this camp and recover from the past thirty hours of near-continuous effort. A feeling of shared agitation began to escalate among us. We were uniformly upset and unresponsive to the imperative to continue further downward.

By the time Freddy had visited the mess tent a mini-insurrection had developed. Collectively we insisted we stay for an additional night in Barafu. Our tents were pitched. Based on our most recent meal we had more than adequate food. No one was in a hurry. Yet - no matter how forcefully we pleaded, Freddy would not budge. We would be leaving for Mweka Camp immediately following lunch. Freddy appealed to our logic by insisting "if we didn't get down to Mweka we were risking altitude illness". Natascha in particular was at risk. We may be devoid of this affliction but it could rear its ugly head within hours if we didn't make a move. His insistence was grounded on the "climb high, sleep low" philosophy.

Unenthusiastically and a little angry we returned to our tents and packed what we would need for the subsequent slog down to Mweka Camp.

What is the opposite of the word "enthusiasm"? Wrap that word up with anger.

I endeavored to locate optimism. The reference to a "dry river bed" conjured in me an image in me of a gentle, obstacle-free stroll - one where heavy-duty hiking boots would constitute an impediment. A stroll could potentially afford us opportunity to appreciate the flora and fauna of this gentle shoulder of Kilimanjaro. I had studied on some of the resident birds of Kilimanjaro and was hopeful I might encounter the Scarlet-tufted Malachite Sunbird - Kilimanjaro's most spectacular and most rarely-observed song bird. Perhaps, if we were calm, we would encounter this bird on our gentle stroll toward Mweka.

I donned my light-weight Nike "trainers", tied my heavier hiking boots together via their laces and wrapped my laced boots around the handles of the North Face duffle bag Focus would lug downward to Mweka Camp in short order. Again I felt awkward for adding to Focus' load and gesticulated plaintively to him - I needed him to carry this extra weight. He betrayed no reservation and with his compliant eyes showed he had understood my need. I again made the mental note of needing to tip Focus well - sad the Western mind defers to remuneration as the foundation to justice.

We departed Barafu Camp near 1 PM. Departure was a disorganized affair with the five hikers who entered camp first this morning leaving first - accompanied by a rejuvenated Natascha and accelerating downward. This left Angie and I together to again enjoy each others' company on this afternoon's leg.

To locate the Mweka trailhead we needed to pass the Ranger Station where today's hopeful hikers were arriving from below. Roles reversed I looked into the expectant eyes of these new arrivals but offered no overt indication of what lay ahead of them. Perhaps my tired body and weakened stride betrayed me.

Yet in hindsight there remained a not insignificant element of triumph proximate to Angie's and my demeanor that could not have gone unnoticed. We walked with the temerity of success. We were worn but we were wiser. We were proud. We walked reasonably upright. We were like the departed ravens - wiser but distant. A day ago we had not yet owned this confidence. Now we had earned it. Indeed, we had summited. Together we had attained one of the seven peaks - one of the peaks of our Earth's seven continents. We didn't need adulation from these unproven people.

Despite our accomplishment Angie and I constituted the rear of our group's effort downward. Freddy and Obama held back and tended to both of our needs. Perhaps this was unsurprising since neither Angie nor I had distinguished ourselves as capable internationally-competent mountaineers this morning.

Outside of Base Camp we deviated from the previous day's trail and angled Eastward across a flattened and graveled escarpment. Pendulous steel-gray clouds were threatening- obscuring the sun fully. At more elevated aspects of the trail, clouds met the earth and we periodically found ourselves hiking in a depressing, dense fog. Visibility at times shrank to a few hundred meters.

As we descended scrubby olive-colored plant-life began to reassert itself - forbs and small bushes - no more than a meter feet in height. Aside from the grind of our shoes and the scratching of our poles there was no sound. Instead our thoughts echoed as the primary sounds we listened to.

The more capable group (Rich, Richard, Gillian *et al*) periodically came into view- rising over a small knoll 0.5 km ahead of us and then vanishing downward over the crest. Periodically I timed the distance separating us- ten minutes, then twenty. And then their vanguard vanished into the bowels of the afternoon's hike completely. Until we reached Mweka Camp we never saw them again. My team had shrunk to include only Angie, Obama, Freddy and me - the slowpokes.

Within an hour of departing Base Camp, we were passed by our porters - each less than half my age and each carrying half his body weight in familiar irregularly-balanced gear. They had struck our camp at Barafu quickly following our departure and charged aggressively downhill. These wishbone-limbed young men virtually ran down the hill balancing their asymmetric, black and blue plastic-clad loads, with their poor quality shoes and ragged first world-donated clothes. Despite the concentration their efforts demanded, as their nimble bodies lapped us their smiles remained broad and genuine. "Jambo!" they called to us. "Jambo si jambo!" I responded. Not an ounce of fat nor a frown on any one of them. Their world so different from mine.

Of the guides Obama was my least favorite. There needs to be a least favorite just as there needs to be a favorite. He seemed distant and taciturn. He didn't hike with Angie nor me. Instead he walked well ahead of us and rarely made inquiries on our condition. He displayed frustration with our lack of fitness - perhaps justifiably. Freddy came and went and tended to Angie from time to time - especially when she struggled and drifted further behind. He displayed a more upbeat and tolerant demeanor.

By 2:30 PM we encountered the river bed we were to follow for the remainder of the day's hike. Indeed, it was dry but I was disappointed to discover it was densely littered with boulders - large collections of water-worn boulders - boulders that transformed an easy hike into an arduous one.

Angie and I undertook the entirety of the Barafu-Mweka leg of the hike together. Our conversation ranged but the most touching aspect was Angie's description of her husband's illness. We talked about her work with hospice and of how she had come to know others within our hiking group. She was Rich's full cousin. She worked with Debbie and Natascha in Portsmouth, UK. She had a daughter and was very proud of her. She was living a real life and without this hike we would never have met. I enjoyed her company immensely! She was a real person. I sensed in her a great compassion certainly appreciated in her hospice program. The world is filled with Angies - Angies whom we never meet but who make this world a generally good place. Thank you Angie.

Periodically Angie would drift back stop and rest her aching knees. Both of her knees were failing. I would get ahead of her - perhaps 0.2 km - and would wait for her to catch up. There I would rest against a boulder - savoring the opportunity to rest. Within three hours however our situations had reversed. The continuous need to climb over and around ill-positioned boulders and to clamber down the stony river bed was degrading my quads once again. They were burning as badly as they had earlier this morning on the descent from the summit. I was frankly more than miserable and feeling angry with my circumstance. Further my light shoes were not adequately protecting my feet and ankles from the twists and torsions inflicted by the uneven river bed. The weak points of both ankles - especially where the talus meets the tibia - were revolting in agony. I had not expected so challenging a hike and regretted not wearing my sturdier hiking boots.

Angie, Obama and I re-entered a cloying grey fog. At most we could see 100 meters in any direction. Our compatriots had long vanished and thereby provided an acute reminder of my inadequacy. At the parched river's edge the mud had dried and cracked. A dense stand of semi-desiccated brush prevented any consideration of escape to a flatter more tolerant ground.

Within three hours of departing base camp my energy reserves fully evaporated. I felt like an idiot. Again, each step was becoming a labor of heroic effort. I could barely lift my legs to complete the next step. I gazed longingly at the spiky olivine bushes subsisting in tight thickets adjacent to the river bed and thought I might just 'give up' and sleep under any one of them.

What could Freddy or Obama do? They couldn't physically carry me - not that I cared. I was angry. They'd just have to accept my infirmity and possibly accompany me through the night. The guides had two-way radios with which they communicated with Raymond. They could simply inform him we would arrive the next day. We would eat whatever provisions we had packed earlier - even though food held no import to me whatsoever.

I hesitatingly ground to a halt and Obama came to me. Out of earshot from Angie I admitted to him I couldn't go any further. I was fully defeated. And for the first time he showed genuine concern. He had packed mango juice in 100 ml packs and offered me one and then another. I also ate a few biscuits and Fig Newtons. Without recrimination I rested against my rock for another ten minutes - Angie and Freddy hovering worriedly nearby. My head was cast downward and my legs burned. My feet and ankles ached.

I had never in my 63 years felt more wretched. Indeed, I was not going to be able to finish. I felt old. In fact, I was old. I had never placed myself into so perilous a situation prior. I envisioned an inelegant evacuation.

What types of evacuation were possible? Helicopters? Four strong porters with a one-wheeled gurney? I was willing to accept any solution. I no longer cared. I only wanted this to be over.

Earlier this afternoon we had passed a section of the trail containing a haphazard accumulation of rusted yet functional gurneys. It was not clear why this collection was maintained at lower altitude - where climbers were unlikely to need them and where no medical facilities existed. Perhaps they were near a helicopter landing pad. Their proximity made me consider I be evacuated on one. They were only a half hour up-river. We would need two more guides - in addition to Obama and Freddy - to "man" the four corners of the gurney. So easy to glide down the dry river bed on my back. I could watch the sky. It would be like lying on my couch at home. I might catch sight of the departed ravens and determine whether they retained interest in me. If so I would transport myself up and into one of the ravens' bodies and soar past the remainder of the slope.

Obama asked me both incisive and encouraging questions. Angie tried to be supportive and kind. She was doing better than me. If she rested her knees she found reserves to continue.

My dignity no longer mattered. I consisted solely of an angry mind and an incapable body. This is what death would be like.

My mind was spinning with conflicting thoughts. I was in extreme physical distress. I no longer cared whether I had become a burden or not. I could no longer rely upon my body to extricate myself from what I understood was a difficult situation for everyone. Still - despite being angry with myself I knew I needed to be rational and help my colleagues help me. We had our team. My team would deliver me from this ordeal. That was the implicit bargain.

++

Within thirty minutes of resting against my support boulder a miracle took possession of me. I felt a tingling of energy course through my body. A tingling of confidence too. The awareness struck me again - I need to be eating carbohydrate-rich foods to supply my body with the energy needed to get off this mountain! Indeed, I was a slow learner. My forehead wrinkled with minor self-loathing. I knew this well. I had known this after Day 1 and had learned this on other hikes. Why had I forgotten?

Within ten minutes I felt like a person re-born. A large measure of the aching in my quads and ankles had diminished and my mental attitude had improved. I thanked Obama for his support and told him I was ok. His kind eyes betrayed some relief. He informed me we had "maybe two more hours to go at most" and offered to take my pack. This time I acquiesced. I rationalized - the hike was about getting my body up and down the mountain - not my body *and* my pack. Obama was already carrying his own pack and mine as Freddy was carrying Angie's and his. My pack weighed only 7-8 kg but it's absence was a godsend.

I departed and lumbered awkwardly further.

Soon though it became clear the nourishment I was able to periodically ingest could only partially mitigate the limitations of my body. Nutrition helped but did not fully solve my problems. Whereas Angie had a simpler challenge - her knees were overwhelmed - I was suffering from a combination of challenges- insufficient energy, drastically degraded quadriceps, incapable ankles, damaged toes, advanced age and an intensely disagreeable attitude. I was experiencing many less than productive thoughts - I'm too old for this type of adventure. I'm the weakest of the men on the hike. Obama is impatient with me. Why not just give up and sleep here overnight?

Informed we were within 1.5 hours of Mweka Camp my spirits started to rise. The late-afternoon sun had cut through the fog and had begun to warm us. Because it was getting late in the day colors cast by the sun became warmer. Greens were becoming deeper and richer. The browns of the dry and dusty river bed took on a breadth of colors - hummus, rust and peat.

I stopped and noted Obama was gazing off the trail into the brush. He beckoned me toward him and pointed toward something that had caught his interest. Beside him I could see nothing of great interest. But then there was a slight movement and I moved my eyes .... a Scarlet-tufted Malachite Sunbird - the preposterously-named nectarivorous bird I was fixated upon in Oregon prior to departing for Tanzania.

It was 2 meters away at shoulder height - no more than 15 cm in length. I found it remarkable Obama even knew the bird by the exact long name I had learned! By good fortune late-afternoon sun was reflecting off of its otherwise pitch-colored plumage with a dazzling green- and turquoise-dominated iridescence - close to the iridescence of the White-necked Ravens!

I stopped and my eyes met the Sunbird's eyes for a few seconds before it darted into the dense understory. Restorative energy coursed through me - this time independent of food but more grounded in fortitude - perhaps the fortitude my forbearers had mustered when times were grim. I wished my Dad could have been with me. Perhaps he would carve the Sunbird as he has carved so many other remarkable birds. He would apply a concoction of artist's paints giving this bird a lifelike property of iridescence.

We left the Sunbird's habitat and continued downward. We rounded a bend in the dusty river bed and before us lay a camp! Mweka Camp! My heart skipped and I know my face beamed as my legs strengthened. Optimism surged. What a relief! We had made it! I saw the other campers and their tents. I noted the hikers teetered next to camp fires - engaged in small conversations and observed us. Fragrant smoke from their wood fires drifted languidly amongst us and beckoned us to join.

But no. I was to learn. This was *not* Mweka. This was "Millennium Camp" - a camp I was unaware of. Mweka Camp lay at least another hour further down river.

With the Sunbird prominent in my mind I hobbled through this camp - past the sun-bleached tents. I smelled simmering stews and heard soft conversations. It was a torture to walk into Millennium and then walk out knowing solace was not at hand.

We had been on the move for thirty-four hours without sleep. We had been hiking 4-5 hours since Barafu. It was 5:15 PM and light was continuing to ebb. The burst of motivation I had experienced when I encountered the Sunbird was dissipating. Like an unwound clock the wheels propelling me forward ground to a complete halt and I surrendered to the futility of it all. My energy deserted me completely. I came to rest against another opportune boulder.

Obama, Freddy, Angie and I were devoid of nutritional support. I'd eaten very little at lunch and regretted it. Had I eaten well, those were the calories I could have been burning. We'd consumed all sustenance we carried in our packs. I had no hunger but knew I needed more fuel to continue. Reluctantly I reported to Obama I could not continue. I was beaten.

Obama radioed ahead - in Swahili - he had a problem. The elderly gentleman who so much wanted to succeed on this hike was out of energy and needed some sustenance. I wasn't chagrined. I was in full possession of the knowledge my body was incapable of any more work. There was no shame in it. I could sleep here beside this rock. In fact, sleeping here overnight was my preference. I had warm clothes in my pack to carry me through. I could rejoin the group at Mweka in the next morning.

I waited miserably and without conversation in the diminishing sun. After 20-30 minutes two unfamiliar and youthful guides appeared from below. They had hiked-up from Mweka Camp with nutritional support for me in the form of biscuits, popcorn and fruit drinks. Two of them had come because they believed I might need to be physically carried down the remainder of the day's hike.

The Sunbird reappeared in a bush no further than a meter from me. It flitted side to side - its glittering feathers periodically catching rays of the fast-diminishing sun. We glanced briefly into one another's eyes - his melancholy - mine defeated. I recalled portions of a poem by Khalil Gibran concerning "defeat". Perhaps the Sunbird knew some of those stanzas too.

Defeat

Defeat, my Defeat, my solitude and my aloofness,

You are dearer to me than a thousand triumphs,
And sweeter to my heart that all world-glory.

Defeat, my Defeat, my self-knowledge and my defiance,
Through you I know that I am yet young and swift of foot,
And not to be trapped by withering laurels.
And in you I have found aloneness,
And the joy of being shunned and scorned.

Defeat, my Defeat, my shining sword and shield,
In your eyes I have read
That to be enthroned is to be enslaved,
And to be understood is to be levelled down,
And to be grasped is but to reach one's fullness,
And like a ripe fruit to fall and be consumed.

Defeat, my Defeat, my bold companion,
You shall hear my songs and my cries and my silences,
And none but you shall speak to me of the beating of wings,
And urging of seas,
And of mountains that burn in the night,
And you alone shall climb my steep and rocky soul.

Defeat, my Defeat, my deathless courage,
You and I shall laugh together with the storm,
And together we shall dig graves for all that die in us,
And we shall stand in the sun with a will,
And we shall be dangerous.

Digesting the Sunbird's oblique encouragement and what little I could recall of Gibran's poem brought a measure of satisfaction to me. Indeed, I felt a glimmer of satisfaction in experiencing defeat. That glimmer was all I possessed.

****

Ingestion of the newly-conveyed concoction of nutritional support restored a modicum of energy to my body and after a 15-minute hiatus I soldiered downward - legs still burning and weak. Angie was given the same food pack as me and I believe it helped her as well - although we did not discuss it. I appreciated Angie's sticking with me and not leaving me behind as the others had done. Save for her knees she was still doing better than me. Obama was showing me every kindness he could gather. I knew I had underestimated him.

The six of us drifted downward - two porters, two guides and two visitors - one who believed he was defeated and one near defeat.

Initially the two newly-arrived porters walked in close proximity to me. I was wobbly and I believe there had been communication in Swahili they needed to stay close to me should I collapse. I was determined to prove their caution unnecessary. In fact, their presence emboldened me. I still possessed a tiny sliver of pride. I remained reticent to fully embrace defeat and revel in its sweet empowerment.

Muscle contains reserves for extra effort - both energy reserves as glycogen and structural reserves as functional contractile proteins. Presently my glycogen stories were exhausted and I estimated I retained sufficient structural integrity to stand, to fight gravity when at a standstill and to walk cautiously on a flat surface. I was aware of this and was focused on two imperatives - 1) I needed to reach Mweka Camp without collapsing and 2) should I reach Mweka I needed to eat well to help re-build the structural aspects of my leg muscles and my glycogen reserves during the night. Indeed, I harbored a hope that strength might miraculously recover overnight - as my strength had during the night following Day 1. Perhaps my infirmity could be attributed to another episode of lactic acidosis.

Angie, the porters, the guides and I were becoming concerned about whether we could reach Mweka Camp by dark. Some lacked batteries for our head lamps and we were out of food. Some had no clothing warm enough to carry them through the night. It was nearing 6 PM, the sun was swiftly lowering to our right and the air was cooling noticeably. The loftier trees adjacent to the river bed had quietened and were casting menacing shadows. Avian life had deserted us.

Angie and I hiked in silence generally within 10 meters from one another. Each of my steps was calculated. Each of my steps was excruciating and uncertain. The prospect of having to lift one of my legs over an 20-cm boulder was daunting. With each step I used my hiking poles to eliminate as much weight from my planted leg as possible. Uncertainty prevailed.

We rounded a bend in the river bed near 6:30 PM and a definitive Mweka Camp came into view to our right. The camp was well-sheltered amongst a dense stand of towering trees. We scrambled up the river bank and entered Mweka Camp proper and noted several other groups - as in other camps - had established distinct territories. Our tents were already set-up by the porters - the same porters who had scandalously jogged by us a few hours earlier. The six leading hikers within our group were already settled and chatting amiably amongst themselves but I was stunned to learn they had arrived in camp only 10-15 minutes prior to Angie and me! Debbie in particular had had a tough day.

Indeed, I had managed to convince myself that Angie and I lagged far behind - possibly two hours behind the lead group. The lead group had also struggled - as had we - over the inexhaustible supply of unfortunately-positioned boulders the river bed had spitefully assembled.

We were all feeling horrendous. But - what welcome news to hear we had arrived only a short time following our friends! Everything was relative. For the group what was promised to be a three- to four-hour hike had become a six-hour slog - typical of the excessively-optimistic projections provided by our guides.

Focus was waiting for me. He looked lonely and a little relieved by my arrival. He had likely heard of my difficulties via walkie-talkie communication between porters. Tranquil, he still wore his woolen hat with its two braided strands suspended over his ears - the whites of his sorrowful eyes still stained yellow. He collected my back pack from Obama and ushered me into my tent. There I found my bag reassuringly stowed and my sleeping bag and pad unrolled and expecting me. This time he didn't need to remove my boots. Instead he had carried them down for me from Barafu. He took my poles, collapsed them and stowed them as I pulled off my Nike trainers. I unfurled a $20 bill and gave it to him. His familiar jaundiced eyes met mine for an extra quarter second and before quietly retiring he again placed his right fist over his heart.

I settled into my tent and let my mind wander over the harsh events of the day- the unforgiving events of the last two days! My Lord! What had we done? Thank God I was here! But we weren't done yet. Another day was to follow. More was to be expected of us. All I could do was dispose of discomforting thought and will the rapid repair of my degraded physical capabilities and concomitantly dispose of my sour attitude.

A rest of thirty minutes proved sufficient to restore in me a small measure of strength and a marginally-improved attitude. With those I rose and willed my broken body toward the mess tent - lurching hesitatingly across a spongey camp floor still in my damp stocking-clad feet.

Because this was the last night we would spend with guides and porters our team needed to discuss "tipping". Guidelines on tipping had been provided by Kandoo however there was flexibility.

All of us were enthusiastic concerning the effort our porters had made in supporting us and wanted to give as much as we possibly could without "overdoing it". Gillian took on the task of calculating expected tips and potential tips, of special tips and tips for guides and - after what ended-up engendering a great deal of discussion and consternation - was able to come up with an amount each of us was required to contribute. These funds were then divvied-up into envelopes for the porters collectively, the toilet boy individually (as we felt especially sorry for him) and the three remaining guides collectively.

We all wished to be generous. The Tanzanians guides and porters had provided an outstanding experience and made it possible for every last one of us - except Trish of course - to "summit". Meals had been outstanding and the toilet could always be motivated to flush. Each day our tents and sundry gear were rapidly-ferried past us as we hiked to the next camp and, when we arrived, our tents and gear were always set-up correctly. I believe we all wished we had brought with us more cash so we could have tipped better. Our tips amounted to $250 from each hiker - possibly $2,000 total. Using my 10X "developed-world:developing-world multiplier method" the buying power of these funds in Tanzania should have been near $20,000.

By 8 PM we had returned to our tents - our first opportunity to entertain the prospect of sleep in *thirty-eight hours*. My chest was terribly congested. I wheezed and coughed, to no avail. I was certain I had become afflicted with Gillian's cold - a cold still lingering among other members of our group. I appended "Gillian's cold" to the list of ailments I needed to recover from during the subsequent eight to ten hours of rest.

My tent was adjacent to Debbie's and Natascha's. To entertain them I began to feign snoring - the worst possible snoring I could muster. At first they were apprehensive. "Was this level of obnoxiousness in snoring truly attainable?" It was not long before they giggled - having realized I was only jesting. The giggling only spurred me onward with an ever more ridiculous round of "snoring". My buoyant spirit was returning. I believed the worst to be over.

Chapter Eighteen
The Last Day

A very short ten hours later our team was unceremoniously rousted from its collective deep slumber and beckoned toward the mess tent. This was to be our last day with our Tanzanian friends. They would soon strike camp and sprint downhill toward their month-long vacations. The cold I thought I had acquired from Gillian the night prior had phenomenally vanished. Perhaps last night's worrisome congestion was simply the result of being worn down and inhaling so much dust on the desiccated river bed. I scrutinized the weak points of my body (quadriceps, ankles, toes, lower back, lungs, mind) and was disappointed to discover my quads continued to ache - they were even warm to the touch! This excess warmth was evidence of active repair not of repaired tissue nor of lactic acidosis.

A phenomenon known as rhabdomyolysis occurs when skeletal muscle break-down becomes extensive. Rhabdomyolysis results from release of myoglobin - a protein that captures and stores oxygen within muscle - from damaged muscle fibers. Urine becomes turbid and tea-colored. Kidneys are subsequently challenged to remove and filter this large and intact protein and become subject to failure. Worriedly I relieved myself into a nearby bush and was reassured to find my urine stream remained clear. Indeed, things could have been worse...... at least I wasn't yet literally falling apart. There was some comfort in this.

I was reticent to peel off yesterday's socks and the crusted bandages covering my toes. Blood had been seeping not only through the two layers of my socks but, I was worried, through the leather toes of my hiking boots- staining their exterior. My toe nails were certainly peeling away. Blisters were being worn off. Today's hike was promised to be far less demanding than yesterday's. Hence I left the previous day's bandages in place - too fearful to take a gander at my toes' condition - truth be told.

Having made the mistake yesterday of forgoing hiking boots I donned them today. Once on they empowered my feet and ankles like comfortable well-fitted gloves can do for hands. Both ankles heaved audible sighs of relief when I cinched laces tightly around them.

We congregated in the humid mess tent and ingested an obligatory breakfast - coffee, tea, hot chocolate, eggs, potatoes, sausages and toast. Gillian - engagingly pilot-like - re-visited the group's decisions for the porters' and guides' tips and ensured monies were accurately counted and disbursed into appropriate envelopes. Each of us appreciated her attention to detail.

The camp was abuzz - like a hive. Throughout Mweka Camp hiking teams were preparing for their last effort - packing gear, striking tents and compressing any stray kit into the inelegant bags used to ferry equipment down the remaining shoulder of Kilimanjaro.

The Italians, the French and the solitary hiker who had vomited abundantly two-nights prior - the same people with whom we had hiked throughout - had mysteriously reappeared - in the dead of night following our own arrival the previous evening. Indirect communications with our neighbors informed me one member of each of the French and the Italian teams were amongst those whom we passed on the descent from the Summit. Two had collapsed and needed guide-assisted evacuations. The hike had torn them ragged. I had no longer recognized them on the descent because they no longer presented as uniform teams. Angie and I had ignored their afflictions to bring lesser ignominy upon them. Without doubt both the French and the Italian camps appeared solemn on this morning. Some limped and there was little conversation amongst them. I believe their solemnity related to the missing members of their teams. That our team had reached Mweka relatively unscathed was thus rendered even more remarkable.

Because Kilimanjaro's rainy season was nigh the river bed adjacent to our camp would soon be filled with torrents of water. While hospitable today the lower environs of Kilimanjaro would soon transition into unwelcoming. Time was of the essence. We had to leave.

The end of the climbing season implied, upon reaching the base of Kilimanjaro today porters, the toilet boy and guides would wish each other "safe journeys", convey their best wishes to their friends' families and return to their villages throughout Tanzania. There they would be reunited with wives, children, girlfriends and family - to their familiar more comfortable lives and to languages they were used to speaking - all flush with cash - to *their* metaphorical couches. The next climbing season – an abstraction.

Energy spilled over in our camp where camaraderie and excitement prevailed even amongst the substantially immobilized hikers. Each time I encountered a guide whom I knew we exchanged handshakes, broad white smiles and first pumps. I dug down deep to appear grateful and enthusiastic. I captured photos of those I recognized.

The morning was damp and the ground heavy with dew. A dense canopy of trees hung over us and prevented any of the tawny morning sun from drenching us. A delicious mixture of fragrances permeated and levitated the group. It had rained abundantly during the night and I took care in packing my gear to avoid the mud straining to accumulate. What was already clinging to my boots was more than sufficient. Focus - his familiar and thin frame - stood by patiently - waiting for me to complete my meagre work - he would strike my tent and add my duffle bag to the communal pile of gear he and others needed to haul the remaining distance - his melancholy of last night still palpable.

Our cooks prepared a special cake to commemorate the team's success - chocolate with thick creamy icing. To this- semi-intelligible words - "Congratulation, mt XIU, 5895 mt" had been added using what appeared to be a devastatingly-delicious caloric-rich orange icing. A rudimentary image of Kilimanjaro had also been applied with the same orange icing on the lower portion of the cake. Given our group consisted of nearly forty people (hikers, guides, porters, cooks, toilet boy) the cake needed to be cut into at least 40 small portions so everyone received at least one bite-sized piece. I arrived a little late and little of the cake remained. Still I was able to recover a cube of cake - fortunately a corner piece covered on two sides with the buttery sugar-laden icing. It melted as pure energy in my mouth and coursed directly to my muscles where it was rapidly converted into glycogen. I could have eaten the entire cake.

Following breakfast and cake our entire Kandoo community gathered within an adjacent glade for the formal presentation of the aforementioned tips and for speeches. Richard had been selected from amongst our group to give a "Thankyou speech". Because most of the porters did not understand English his speech was translated by Freddy contemporaneously.

Richard delivered an excellent speech commenting on - among other things - "your excellent teeth", the accomplishment of someone who was of "Neil's age", the excessive and unexpected arduousness of the preceding thirty-six hours (and the need for amending), the porters' good humor and above all our collective sincere appreciation for the effort the Tanzanians had individually and collectively made on our behalf. The swollen tip envelopes were distributed after which porters and guides formed a line and filed by us one-by-one shaking hands and fist-bumping. As Richard had observed gleaming-white Tanzanian smiles were shared generously throughout. "Genuinely Thankful" seems too inadequate a phrase to describe the appreciation that our group was feeling for our support team. Instead it bordered on love.

Following presentation of tips our Tanzanian hosts broke into familiar communal songs - those we had heard both on the second morning of the hike and during the nocturnal ascent of Uhuru. As before, one of the porters or one of the guides would take the lead and intone an obvious Tanzanian lamentation after which the full Tanzanian ensemble would break into a chorus of "hakuna matata". Within two choruses each of us had become sufficiently emboldened by the refrain to sing and dance along. This we accomplished while clapping our hands and swinging in circles - our transient clot of humanity. For a brief period of time - race, national origin, age and economic status vanished - we were overwhelmed with love and respect for each other. We were supremely in the present - perhaps never more so. This needs to be remembered and communicated over time- that we danced together – that we loved each other- that we made each other happy and that we created and shared friendships. Raven's lessons were validated.

There is a meaning to life - and it is simple - to know friendship, to know love and to bring happiness to others.

It had been a remarkable experience. These were the people who had made the impossible possible. Throughout they had shown good nature, contentment, stoicism, patience and kindness. I often forgot to take pause to consider and to appreciate efforts of our support people. Most didn't hike with us nor did they camp directly with us. They had labored somewhat removed. It had not been possible to have conversations with many of them. However, these people had done their best to provide a meaningful and successful adventure and they did it with smiles on their faces and with concern for our success and well-being even though the climb had not been easy for them either. I was pleased Richard truly rose to the occasion and communicated to these gentle souls our appreciation of their livelihood. I hope they retain a memory of us - because we do of them.

The celebration ended and we milled aimlessly about exchanging hugs, handshakes, fist bumps and smiles - all in some astonishment the end was at hand. One by one we drifted back into our campsites to complete our remaining ordinary tasks. More than a little sadness was percolating among us to be certain. I was appreciative the porters' songs had been in a minor key.

The hike this morning to the exit of Kilimanjaro at Mweka Gate was expected to be short - only 4 km- a distance my car could cover – depressingly - in 2.5 minutes. In order to keep the group together Angie and I were assigned to the lead so the remaining hikers would be held back and we would hang together. Richard and Rich took up the rear of our troupe. I was buoyed periodically when I heard Richard's familiar loud laugh - a response perhaps to something humorous Rich had said. The ladies in betwixt reemerged as light-hearted and chatty- commenting on any new flowers we passed - needing to understand the appellations and fragrances of each.

None of the flowers we encountered trailside were flamboyant. Instead Kilimanjaro's flowers were uniformly subtle - drawing little attention except from those who had intrinsic interest in plants. The most frequently encountered was the Kilimanjaro impatiens (*Impatiens kilimanjari*) - a Kilimanjaro-specific flower our female colleagues identified and appreciated immensely. I spent a little time inspecting this species and noted it had developed a strategy to trap small insects deep inside a long and spiral tubular structure located beneath its fuchsia-colored petals. We also encountered a vine-like Morning Glory but my post-hike research could not divine a genus nor a species.

We had re-entered the tropical rainforest of Kilimanjaro's lower environs. Last night's heavy rain had rendered the trail's clay surface into the personification of treacherous - extraordinarily slippery. Trees arched heavenward 20-30 meters and stout twisted vines hung from the canopy they provided to near the ground. The thickness of the canopy still prevented virtually any morning sun from reaching us. Where sun did penetrate it did so in dazzling shafts of yellow. A cacophony of plant life thrived. Plaintive cries of hidden monkeys and sharp calls of birds periodically pierced the otherwise quiet- the pristine. At other times all that was audible were twenty-two boots kneading a muddy path. We were a pensive and amiable group - chattering quietly and stopping frequently to appreciate the luxuriant beauty.

Because I had been placed at the lead of the hike with Angie I felt pressure to maintain a reasonably brisk pace. In short order I discovered I possessed zero reserves in muscle strength whatsoever - so close was I to the edge - the edge of collapse.

My legs were "shot". On this point there was no equivocation. But I was not alone in my discomfort. Angie's knees were "shot" as well.

My misery animated itself and tried to commiserate with Angie's misery so neither of us was individually responsible for slowing the entire descent. I was grateful my team stayed with Angie and me. In fact, early in the day's hike all seemed content and appeared to value the slower pace. Our pace allowed opportunity for others to appreciate subtleties of Kilimanjaro's living attributes.

Midway through the day's hike I made the mistake of springing down into a small drop in the path - a 0.3-meter depression. I collapsed onto the path sideways, landed on one of Angie's aluminum hiking poles and snapped it fully in half. One of our guides quickly surrendered one of his poles for Angie to use for the remainder of the day. At this time, I was still leading the pack and everyone beheld my humiliating flop. The entire right side of my hiking pants and my right arm were smeared with dung-colored Kilimanjaro mud - a reminder to me and others of the precariousness of the path.

Our porters and other groups' porters began passing us within twenty to thirty minutes of our departure from Mweka Camp. Today they were in a greater hurry to escape Kilimanjaro and begin their vacations. They were in an even greater rush than usual. On three or four memorable occasions porters accomplished spectacular falls - their 20-30 kg of gear splaying willy-nilly along the path and into the adjacent forest. Peeved and chagrined they picked themselves up - assisted by their colleagues - wiped as much of the mud from their clothing as possible, reassembled their ungainly loads and continued their downward sprints. It would have been comedic had there not been significant risk of injury - considering their speed, the bulk they were carrying and the presence of sharp-edged rocks and boulders within the path. These rocks, if encountered directly, would cause severe injury.

As the morning progressed the temperature increased, humidity thickened and we stripped to a minimum of clothing. Unexpectedly the heavy canopy condensed and the trail darkened. The incline and slipperiness of the clay worsened. For survival I stopped frequently and planned-out the sequence of footsteps required to circumvent a rock, a drop or a protruding root. This became essential because none of us were willing to fail so near to the end of the hike - so difficult was it to regain one's footing following a fall. We maintained three of our four points always connected to the ground or to a stable collection of rocks for protection.

Richard was cognizant of my struggles and was kind enough to periodically advance and keep me company - a pleasant distraction. We maintained a perfunctory conversation but within a few minutes he understood I was not able to simultaneously maintain conversation and navigate the path - such were my limitations and the focus I required to navigate. When he realized I was incapable of meaningful conversation he gently excused himself and retreated to the rear and re-engaged with Rich - his rearward chortles providing periodic confidence.

Soon the more capable hikers (Gillian, Natasha, Alex, Debbie, Rich and Richard) forged ahead with Raymond. Angie and I were just too cautious and enfeebled for them to continue with us. Indeed, it required more energy and more concentration for them to walk slowly - at a speed below a reasonable pace. Freddy stayed with Angie and Obama stayed with me. There was no shame in this. We needed only for the end to come.

Within an hour Freddy took charge of me and Obama took charge of Angie. The infirmities Angie was laboring with were less debilitating than mine. Slowly Angie and Obama drifted ahead of Freddy and me and the two of us were left to commiserate in the rear. Freddy took my pack as Obama had done the day prior and we hiked side-by-side exchanging pleasantries. I was interested in the politics of Tanzania and in Tanzanian culture. Freddy was only too happy to share with me his views on both. Perhaps as expected Freddy was none too appreciative of the quality of governance in Tanzania. These conversations helped pass the time.

An hour with Freddy passed. Even traversing a flat section of path was more than difficult. While the path was reasonably flat there did remain some sections where careful navigation over and around rocks - or small descents around obstacles - was required. These were more than I could withstand. Freddy's diversionary tactic of commenting on Kilimanjaro's flora and fauna aided a little.

I was reaching the dangerous point where I barely retained strength to stand with my knees locked - let alone flex my knees and walk on a flat surface. My legs wobbled both forward and backward *and* from side to side. The latter disability was a first for me. I struggled to maintain even a modicum of control of my stature. But I was a realist. My mind still functioned. Freddy was not going to be able to carry me out. He promised we had less than two hours remaining and the path would be gentle. I needed to go on. There was no alternative except to collapse onto the path and whine. I remained unwilling to fully collapse. I fought to maintain a positive outlook.

Eight young ladies from France sashayed by us displaying no ill effects of summiting. They prattled amongst themselves amiably as they passed and I did my best to appear robust and unaffected in their presence - to assert my virility. But I was confused - how could anyone project so little infirmity at this stage of the hike? But maybe they had not summited! Maybe they were only hiking the less than challenging shoulder of Kilimanjaro for a day! They didn't have a guide. No...they were out for a stroll. There was a good reason for my disability. I clung to that belief to buoy my strength.

Muscles, tendons and ligaments providing stability to my knees were dog-tired. Pole pole. Wobble wobble. Hakuna matata. Kil-i-man-ja-ro. One Two Three Four. Ev-er-y Step a Safe Step. This-Is-So-Fucked-Up. Over and over in random order - my weary and ineffective incantation. Over and o'er. Focus on the incantation. Forget the hurt. The end is near. People have endured far worse. Death Marches in World War II. In this manner I could pass a minute. And then I would focus on getting through the ensuing minute.

On this last day of hiking Freddy frequently telegraphed his excessively optimistic view of the time required to reach our destination. When in fact the destination would be 90 minutes away he'd estimate "1 hour away". At one hour away he'd say "soon". In this manner we were always "almost there". But when I timed his projections on my watch his Tanzanian version of time was always unrealistic and - like the path - slippery. Time stretched and contracted like a long elastic band - the kind I would treasure and play with when I was a kid. I was left in a form of time warp. How long really? An hour? Six hours? A day? Might we never arrive? Was I condemned to this forever? Was there an end? Would I wake tomorrow morning still on the mountain? Had I died and this was my version of hell? I no longer really knew - nor did I care. I just continued placing one foot in front of the other and hoped the end would come.

We stopped. Freddy had to urinate. We were alone and I was surprised. Presumably out of modesty Freddy walked deep - perhaps five meters into the forest - to obviate any possibility I might view him in this basic human act. Me? I just urinated on the path when the need arose. I was not predisposed to expend any extra energy to walk 5 meters over unpredictable ground for the purpose of modesty.

Sounds of motor vehicles began to register distinctly - signaling a potential and blessed proximity to civilization. Still I'd been subjected to far too many false expectations prior - the appearance of the ersatz "Mweka" camp the previous evening being the best recent example.

I toddled unaided on the port side of a path which had expanded onto an unused road - perhaps eight meters wide. Tread marks and ruts were visible. Freddy traversed the starboard side of the road carrying both his and my backpacks.

I was fully employing my poles but with each step my legs wobbled - even more uncontrollably from front to back and from side-to-side. When I stood upright and fully locked my knees - my legs still wobbled - motions which were becoming more exaggerated. I no longer had the strength to stand motionless. Even standing erect I was near collapse. A moderate wind would have blown me over.

We came to a gentle bend as the path slanted downward and to the right. Freddy had made no prognostication recently upon when we might arrive at the terminus of the hike and, further, I had tired of asking him. I knew I could not place any value on any prediction related to the remaining duration of the hike. I had resigned myself to a never-ending torturous hike - possibly until I fully crumpled. Death would be my only reprieve. In embracing death, I would tumble onto the path, melt into the ground and disappear between the gravel and rock surface - a natural process - a relief. Dispersed along the path and partially consumed at night by forest animals, I would ignore entreaties to continue. There I would completely understand my limitations. There I would comprehend and savor defeat. Defeat was at hand and would be my lover. Her embrace would be as sweet as any I could know. I thought of my admonitions for the meaning of life. Besides knowing friendship, knowing love and bringing happiness to others. Perhaps I needed to add "to know death" to my list.

Thus subsumed - it was with substantial astonishment that a flat expanse accommodating oddly-shaped metal contrivances powered by internal combustion engines came into view 150 meters away and twenty meters below. Those must be cars, I mused. Through the mucus covering my eyes I discerned an eerily-familiar coffee-colored sign with yellow lettering. The sign resembled those with yellow lettering cluttering a previous mortal experience - a distant time spent on a mountain in Tanzania - part of Africa - a time spent with friends. Oddly-shaped stick-like creatures were milling about the base of the sign as they clung to a forgotten world.

The sweet sense of death's close embrace began to release me. Clouds sublimated from my eyes and the comforting dullness lifted from my mind. I returned to a present I had forgotten and was comfortable leaving behind.

This was the end of the hike. Tears welled with joy and my vision blurred. I hesitated. Should I let my tears course fully down my face or should I quell them? I breathed heavily and considered the two options: hold them back or let them course. I wanted to feel the cool traces of the tears as they ran down my cheeks. I wanted to taste their salt in my mouth.

My friends were waiting - each regarding me warily and I imagined both elation and relief on their faces. I didn't wish to burden them further. I needed to appear fully in control of my emotions when I arrived. And so I held my tears back and strode more confidently toward them.

Indeed, my seven friends and two guides had congregated at the arrival sign. I was not certain how long they had been waiting for me - perhaps fifteen minutes? Perhaps an hour? Perhaps several days?

My legs were barely controllable. My upper body swung from one side to the other in partial effort to compensate for my rubbery legs. I was later informed of the "sight" I provided to everyone - my legs visibly wobbling as I navigated downward across the final muddy vastness to reach my friends. Each step was an effort. With each step my knees tried to give way - either sideways or front-to-back - and not in unison. My right leg might bow outward and backward whereas my left leg might bend forward and to the left. All I had to steady myself were my poles coupled with compensatory flexions of my upper body. The supportive elements of my knees had deserted me.

As I approached my friends a minor degree of strength returned - possibly it was the adrenaline. I'd made it. I knew it wasn't pretty. But at 63 years-old I'd made it. Arriving here under my own power was sweeter than arriving at the summit. This was the true goal! Getting down! Completing the journey! Without a doubt I had experienced my true physical and mental limitations - an experience one should not undertake too ofte- maybe only once. Only a fool makes the same mistake twice.

Fifty yards from the destination an individual who had congregated with my team at the commemorative sign departed the group. Oddly the person was walking confidently upward toward me. A woman. Judging by her dress she was not a hiker. In fact, she didn't walk. No- she floated upward toward me - a gentle breeze animating her diaphanous clothing intriguingly. I looked for wings.

It was Trish! The woman I had developed a connection with prior to the hike and on Days 1 and 2 of the hike. Richard's former girlfriend! She had successfully evacuated on the morning of Day 3 and had stayed at the Stella Rose for the past four-five days waiting for us.

Trish advanced toward me - dressed in attractive attire with some make-up on and, when we met, we embraced and, in doing this, she compelled me to fully re-enter the present.

She must have showered daily. I sensed a hint of perfume akin to the nascent memory of *Impatiens*. I was a wretched mess. But I didn't care.

"Congratulations" was all I heard or all I recall. I wrapped my arm around Trish's soft shoulders for support and walked the remaining fifty meters to my friends using her shoulders and her capable body for support. We'd done it! We'd done it as a team! However improbable we'd done it! I'd done it! Nothing more needed to be said. Fully in the present I understood the ordeal was over.

Chapter Nineteen
An Epilogue of Sorts

The hike on Kilimanjaro provided opportunity to witness nature's beauty, to experience another culture and to challenge ourselves both physically and emotionally. But more fundamentally we had opportunity to experience the lessons of Raven- to sense the joys of friendship, of love and of bringing happiness to others- all rolled into an intense experience. And even though it was difficult, it proved to be more than worth the effort. Everyone needs to enrich their lives with challenges - to undertake similar quests - whether more or less extreme.

More extreme exploits belong to those who possess greater physical and mental capabilities than me. Shackleton's heroic exploits of 1914-1916 in Antarctica and South Georgia Island - a voyage my son and I recapitulated on a comfortable cruise 100 years later in 2016. Climbing Everest. Sailing solo around the world across the Southern Indian ocean. There swells are reported to reach 25 meters in height. Rowing a kayak across the Atlantic (three times) - as one dedicated Pole has done. Then there are the Hindu ascetics - the one's who stand on one leg for a decade or who bury themselves neck deep in dirt for years. There are those options.

Less extreme and equally illuminating? An extended late-season weekend near a cottage on a Manitoba lake where the Fall chill has taken hold - where loons call - where waters have become leaden - accompanied by a friend, good whiskey and a fire constructed of fragrant snapping pine.

We need not undertake life-threatening endeavors to derive the physical and mental fruits of a unique and challenging experience.

What *is* important is we periodically challenge ourselves in attainable ways and the challenge be completed in presence of the natural world. That we change it up a bit so every day is not the same as the last day - that we get off of our couches and reach toward the ever-present stars and communicate with nature whether it be constituted by ravens or by other wild life invariably accompanying us when we undertake these efforts. Without those experiences we will become indistinguishable from our couches and become smaller - lesser than the individuals we are capable of becoming. This is our challenge - to get off the couch and learn from the experience. We can't know what we will learn. All we know is what we learn will be worth the effort. In today's lexicon - put yourself out there. Take risks. The greatest risk of all is to take no risks.

Hold on to what you have learned and teach others what you have learned. And while you do - enjoy the friendships, show others that you love them and radiate happiness into their lives. This simple outcome from Kilimanjaro is the distillation of all I learned from taking some risk and pushing myself into this improbable, ill-conceived but important journey.

****

One of the most important aspects of returning to "civilization" was drinking a beer. I gingerly ambulated to a window seat in the mid-section of the bus and was electrified when dear Richard approached my open window with a cold "Kilimanjaro beer"- the first beer I had consumed in a millennium. He had also secured beers for Rich and himself. I easily could have downed the beer in one protracted chug. However, I savored it - taking it down in six to eight individual gulps - the most satisfying beer I have ever possessed.

“If you can’t climb it, drink it” - the slogan of the Kilimanjaro beer brand. Our team, “One Trek Mind” had accomplished both. In my case - marginally.

We returned from the base of Kilimanjaro - again to Innocent and the familiar Stella Rose Hotel - on the same dilapidated bus which ferried us to Machame Gate a very long week prior. There I mourned the loss of most of my toenails - but they eventually grew back. But, even on the night we returned, my infirmity was such that I remained able to navigate the the hotel bar on the third floor. There we drank a liquor prepared from a fermented fruit that elephants periodically consumed and, because of the alcoholic content, caused them to sway from side to side in elephantine drunkenness.

****

On the last two days I had to surrendered my backpack to the guides. If I hadn’t I believe I still would have completed the effort. I would have preferred to have carried it myself. But I was pleased to have made a good decision and cast off extra weight when opportunity presented itself - opportunity in the form of a kind-hearted guide.

I need to make a “shout out” to my dear hiking companions- to Richard, to Rich, to Angie, to Natasha, to Gillian, to Debbie, to Alex and to Trish. Similarly - to our guides- Freddy, Raymond and Obama, Auguste and all of the porters. All of <u>you</u> made this effort possible. The kindnesses, forbearances, humor, entertainment and responsibilities needed were always available within our team. If the entire world was in your collective hands, especially in these troubled days, the Earth would be far better off than it is now. If only it could be so. Collectively you brought the best of the human condition to the fore - courage in face of adversity, humor, empathy, forgiveness, tolerance and appreciation of nature and the diversity of humanity. You were an inspiration and even though you may not feel your lives are as impactful as they might be, the values you hold are the universal values that have allowed humankind to reasonably prosper and the values societies still need. It is an honor to know you all.

++++++++++++++++++++

The chilled beer finished, we motored down the dusty lower slopes of Kilimanjaro toward the Stella Rose Hotel - past lavender-festooned Jacaranda with their flesh-like scent, past yellow-stucco homes with lime green lawns and past handsome Tanzanian schoolchildren in starched cobalt uniforms - returning from school on foot. Not so far from the road lithe and dutiful Masai children clad in regal blood-red traditional dress and beaded necklaces tended their compliant livestock - tended them as they have no doubt tended them for tens of thousands of years. Knowing they continue to farm and care for their livestock encourages me to return to Tanzania - not to climb Kilimanjaro again but to know their culture and our guides' cultures better. They have borne witness to the busloads of interlopers who arrive regularly to challenge themselves and learn from an environment the Eastern African cultures have deep knowledge of - an environment from which all of our ancestors derived - the cauldron in which the firmament of humanity was forged.

Made in the USA
Columbia, SC
08 November 2021

48418919R00164